GUERRILLA ~DISCARD~
HOME RECORDING
SECOND EDITION

HOW TO GET GREAT SOUND FROM ANY STUDIO

(no matter how weird or cheap your gear is)

BY KARL CORYAT

HAL•LEONARD®

Hal Leonard Books
An Imprint of Hal Leonard Corporation
New York

Published in 2008 by Hal Leonard Books
 An Imprint of Hal Leonard Corporation
7777 West Bluemound Road
Milwaukee, WI 53213

Trade Book Division Editorial Offices
19 West 21st Street, New York, NY 10010

Printed in the United States of America

Cover and book design by Stephen Ramirez

Library of Congress Cataloging-in-Publication Data is available upon request.

ISBN 978-1-4234-5446-5

www.halleonard.com

621.3893

Contents

Introduction

This book isn't for every recording musician. Some people may get angry reading what I have to say. Who? Basically, anyone who has spent too much money on expensive recording gear in the quest for a "professional" studio sound. These people don't want to hear that you can make excellent recordings without a $5,000 tube mic or a Massenburg EQ. *Guerrilla Home Recording* is for the rest of us: musicians who just want to create great-sounding recordings and don't have the limitless resources to pursue that goal in a conventional way.

A lot of instructional material on recording steers musicians in the wrong direction. Recording books and articles are usually written by people who know too much for their own good. They forget what it was like to struggle with cheap or weird equipment, to flail away trying to get a decent mix of a song. As audio professionals they've moved way beyond that stage, to the point where only a high-end tube compressor or vintage board is acceptable for their projects. They write about reducing reflections in the control room and building baffles and bass traps, and the subtle differences between mixing to analog and mixing to digital, because this is the level on which they operate professionally, every day. Simply put, they're out of touch with the masses—musicians who still haven't mastered the basics of getting a good sound, who can't afford to upgrade to the best, and who must make do with a bunch of ill-matching gear they've pieced together over the years.

I have good news for you: Contrary to the newer/faster/better culture that permeates the recording-equipment industry, you *can* record a really good-sounding CD with minimal tools. All you need are a few key pieces of gear, and more important, knowledge of a handful of important concepts—along with some experience learning to hear what does and doesn't sound good. Yes, there is a limit to what you can do with obsolete studio equipment, and yes, once you've reached those limits, you can improve your recording potential by upgrading. But in my 14 years as a music-magazine editor in charge of checking out readers' self-produced recordings, I learned that the vast majority of musicians haven't come close to this point. Instead, many of them have bought into the idea that maybe with one more gadget, with just a few more thousands of dollars spent, they'll finally achieve the polished sound that professionals get—because hey, pros use only the best gear in only the best acoustical spaces money can buy. But it's all a lie, fabricated to get you to spend your money. Look at it this way: The best-stocked kitchen with the most professional pots and pans won't magically turn you into a brilliant chef. You need to learn the basics of the craft first. Doesn't it make sense that if you were a professional chef, you could whip up one hell of a soufflé with 20 bucks' worth of thrift-store pots and pans and run-of-the-mill ingredients from the supermarket?

That's exactly what *Guerrilla Home Recording* is about: getting you to the point where you can record great-sounding songs using more or less the gear you already have. This book takes a different approach to home recording: it focuses on *sound* first, with gear taking second place. You'll see very few mentions of specific equipment models or software programs in this book. I even treat the recording medium as a generic "black box" with inputs and outputs, because let's face it, whether you record on an old analog 4-track, ADAT, or Pro Tools, the sounds going in—and the sounds you want to come out—are more or less the same, regardless.

Guerrilla Home Recording assumes you either have a studio that's already set up and working, or you have resources that can assist you—perhaps a book written specifically for your type of system, or at least some well-written manuals. I don't go into the mechanics of setting up your gear and getting devices to work with each other properly, because there are dozens of books and websites that cover this material really

 If You Record On Tape . . .

In the original edition of *Guerrilla Home Recording* I gave more or less equal time to digital and analog recording techniques. But things have changed since then. Without question, these days digital recording on a computer is the way for a Guerrilla recordist to go. Desktop digital recording has become so affordable as well as powerful, analog systems—from the Guerrilla's perspective—just can't compete. So, most of this edition assumes you're recording digitally.

If you don't record on a computer (yet), don't feel that you've wasted your money on this book. For one thing, in keeping with the "no matter how weird or cheap" promise on the cover (and because plenty of analog and ADAT-type systems are still floating around), I've condensed the information on working with tape in Appendix A. Throughout the book, wherever there's related information for analog or ADAT recordists, you'll see a reel of tape pointing to the Appendix. But with the exception of the digital-specific techniques in Chapter 9, almost all of the information in this book can be applied to linear (tape) recording as well as nonlinear digital. That's because the physics of sound is similar whether you record using a top-of-the-line digital audio workstation, a '90s-era ADAT, a reel-to-reel 8-track, or even cassette tapes. And when you do switch over to desktop digital, the book will be here to help you make the transition, and many of the concepts you picked up in the meantime will apply to the new medium.

well, and the specifics change from year to year. Instead, *Guerrilla Home Recording* focuses simply on helping you make superior recordings.

If you have some recording experience and you've done some reading, you may want to forget about everything you've read and follow along as we go back to basics. You might be surprised by what you discover. For instance, you may not have thought of recorded sound in terms of three simple "dimensions"—dynamics, frequency content, and pan position. But if you can properly manage these three properties for each sound you record, and you mix with all of these properties in mind, you will make recordings that will impress all but the most critical listeners. And you won't have to spend a fortune on gear or a ton of time reconstructing your space to do it.

The idea behind *Guerrilla Home Recording* is perhaps best summarized by one reader's online review of the first edition: "After reading the first couple of chapters, I thought, 'Maybe this book is too basic.' After reading further, however, I discovered that I may have overestimated my understanding of the basics of recording. *Guerrilla Home Recording* has made me realize that I have much more powerful equipment than I thought I had. I just have to learn how to use it."

CHAPTER 1

What Is Guerrilla Home Recording?

Guerrilla Home Recording is the pursuit of professional sound in ways that don't require you to spend a lot of money. The American Heritage Dictionary defines a guerrilla as "a member of an irregular military force operating usually in small, independent groups capable of great speed and mobility." As unsigned musicians, we may not be military, but we are irregular, we're independent (for now), and if we know what we're doing, we're capable of recording music at great speed. Guerrilla warfare subverts a traditional military force in a low-budget, underhanded way: making the greatest impact with the fewest resources. As history has proved, guerrilla warfare can be highly effective under certain conditions. Similarly, Guerrilla Home Recording musicians can deliver a big impact on the music world, by self-producing a lot of great-sounding music without relying on the industry's traditional, slow-to-react infrastructure. That's what this book is about. A revolution is afoot—musicians of the world, unite!

To help explain what Guerrilla Home Recording is, I'll relate a story about how the term came about. (If you're new to recording, don't be put off by some of the terminology in this chapter; it will all make sense once you've read the whole book.) Many years ago I was having dinner with Richard Leeds, then the art director of *Keyboard* magazine. Rich, a home recordist himself, was interested in knowing how I got a certain drum sound on one of my songs without using live drums or even a sampling keyboard; I had one cheap drum machine, a Tascam 38 analog ½" 8-track, and a Yamaha SPX90 multieffect. I explained that I put together the drum pattern on the drum machine, used the same machine to record a sync tone onto the tape, and then individually laid down one track per drum sound—each of which I had sampled (from vinyl records) into the SPX90's one-half-second of memory. I'd make one tape pass per drum sound, getting the drum machine to trigger each sample at the appropriate times. Once I had laid down the kick, snare, hi-hat, and maybe a tom or two, I mixed the tracks—each one EQed properly, along with cymbals and other sounds coming out of the drum machine in real time, and perhaps a gated reverb on the snare, again courtesy of the SPX90—and recorded the stereo blend onto two of the Tascam 38's open tracks. The result was a stereo submix of custom-sampled drums plus reverb, with six tracks now available for other instruments. I didn't think this process was particularly innovative or special; I was just making do with the limited gear I had, using a few creative ideas to get the best possible sound. But Rich was impressed. He suggested that I write an article on "guerrilla recording techniques" for _Keyboard_. I never did pitch the idea to his magazine (a few years later I did write a recording column for _Bass Player_)—but the term "Guerrilla Home Recording" has stuck with me ever since. It's what I do, and it's what I think every home recordist working on the cheap should do.

Get Over Yourself

Another tale: A few years later, I found myself in someone else's modest project studio recording a demo for my band, Pillars of Jeleaux. I was about to lay down a bass track when I noticed that I was going straight to tape, with no compression or any other processing on my sound. I asked the engineer why. "We'll compress you in the mix," he smirked in a somewhat condescending manner. "That's the way the pros do it!" The demo ended up sounding pretty bad (we never used it), and "that's the way the pros do it!" became an inside joke among my bandmates.

This engineer embodied a problem that's very common among home- and project-studio owners: although he wasn't a professional, with years of training and experience in a top studio, he wanted to be _like_ one. He was a classic wannabe: He was intent on using traditional recording techniques in a facility that was limited by his personal budget. But the approach backfired: the result was much less than a professional sound.

Although it's often said that there are no rules in recording, the first rule of Guerrilla Home Recording is: _Get over yourself._ You may have already read too many interviews, trade-magazine articles, or recording books for your own good. And if you've spent time in a really good pro studio, the place's glamour may have rubbed off on you, turning you into a wannabe as well. You have to get over this. Until you can afford to sink one or two million dollars into your facility, build acoustically treated performance and control rooms, and have a mic collection, console, and racks of outboard gear to match, you're like me: a musician who records with less-than-ideal tools. That's not to say your goal should be anything less than a record that sounds 100 percent professional. It just means: don't delude yourself along the way.

Consider the history of the recording studio. When the Beatles made _Please Please Me_ in 1962, the folks working at Abbey Road Studios looked more like NASA engineers than Butch Vig or Timbaland. They wore white lab coats. They analyzed. They calibrated. To them, recording was a precise electrical- and acoustical-engineering process that required a serious background in math and physics. And even though most engineers today no longer look like Ed Harris in _Apollo 13_, the engineering culture still exists. (They are called engineers, after all.) This is great in a pro studio—

when you're in charge of running a priceless vintage mixing console, you should know what a capacitor is. But elements of this engineering culture have trickled down to project-studio wannabes as well as the authors of recording books and articles, and in my opinion, that's not a good thing.

It's easy to take something you've read in a recording article as gospel, especially if it was written by someone with impressive credentials. But realize that many of these people live in a different world than we do. They can do things the conventional, "serious" way, because they have the resources. We home recordists, though, might have to perform a few tricks and pull a few strings to get great sounds. It might mean using a stompbox as a signal splitter, or using that curly-cue Radio Shack "guitar cable" for an effect send because you're out of good cables. The engineering establishment would scoff at such practices—that's _not_ the way the pros do it! Of course, they want you to think the only way to get a good sound is to use their skills and a facility that charges $150 per hour. But attitudes are changing—even among top musicians, many of whom are recording their own "pro" tracks at home, without having gone to engineering school.

Bottom line: believe in yourself. Trust that with experience, ear training, forethought, and most important, an approach that acknowledges your studio's limitations, you _can_ make music that for all intents and purposes sounds every bit as good as a professional studio recording. And you don't have to pretend you're a pro to do it.

The Digital Advantage

There's an awful lot you can do with an analog system and a heap of cagey creativity. (See Appendix A.) But nothing will supercharge your recording power more than going digital. Sure, there are naysayers who insist analog sounds better and always will. That may or may not be true—but forget about them. The level of sonic distinction between a "warm" analog recording and a "sterile" digital one is so fine, it's not even worth talking about here. Suffice it to say that unless you're recording on some ancient 8-bit medium or overloading your system with ugly digital clipping, as far as you're concerned, _no one will know_ what medium you're using. It won't make the difference between getting signed or not getting signed, or getting a gig at the local 1,000-seat club. The benefits far outweigh the possible downsides, period.

A few of the plusses of recording on a digital audio workstation (DAW):

Editing capability. In my analog days I used to have fun splicing together sections of tape and "flying in" parts off a DAT machine when I decided to rearrange a song late in the game. But I'm really glad those days are gone. When you're recording digitally, it can take mere seconds to double the length of a verse or tack the intro back onto the end of a song. These are things most analog recordists probably wouldn't even consider as options. Recording digitally gives you options—tons of them.

Cost. A reel of tape for an analog 8-track can cost $50. The same amount of audio, recorded digitally, can easily fit onto two DVD-R discs, at a cost of under a buck. And a $200 hard drive can store the audio equivalent of about 180 reels of tape, for a savings of $8,800. Case closed.

No erasing required. Since digital storage is so cheap, you almost never have to erase a digital track. That guitar solo might have been *almost* perfect—but do you really want to record over it in the hope that you'll nail the next take? These are the kinds of decisions you have to make with analog gear. On a DAW system, you can just mute the near-perfect take and try again—and keep on trying until you *do* nail it.

Track flexibility. On a DAW, the number of tracks you can record is limited by your computer's processor, its memory (RAM), and your hard drive's speed—the system doesn't have a fixed number of tracks like an analog machine. Perhaps even more important, even if you don't plan on having a lot of tracks playing back at once, the *total* number of tracks a song can have on a digital system is virtually limitless. You can have eight tracks going during a verse, and if you want entirely different sounds for the chorus, eight different tracks can start playing when the chorus begins (see Fig. 1). On an analog machine, trying to get that same verse-chorus transition could make for a very tricky mix—you might have to mix the song in sections and edit together the parts later. But if you're recording digitally, the transition can be both seamless and easy to accomplish.

Fig. 1 A digitally recorded song can have many tracks, even if only some of them are playing at a given moment. Here, eight vocal tracks in a verse give way to eight different tracks in the chorus.

Digital doesn't degrade. I love listening to songs in progress over and over while I try to come up with ideas. But I used to hate the idea that with every pass of analog tape, a tiny amount of oxide sloughed off and the tape demagnetized just a bit, making the sound incrementally worse with each listen—not enough to hear, but enough to make me paranoid. With digital recording, you always know that the one-thousandth playback sounds *exactly* the same as the first playback. (Just remember to back up your work; otherwise the current playback could be the last—forever.)

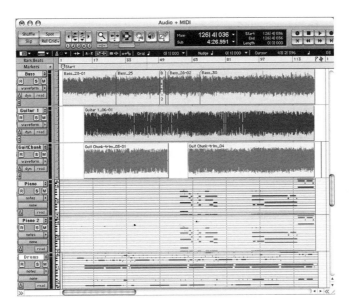

Fig. 2 Audio tracks (top) sitting alongside MIDI tracks (bottom) in a digital recording program.

Seamless integration of audio and MIDI. With an audio/MIDI digital recording program, your audio tracks lie side-by-side with your MIDI tracks (see Fig. 2), making it much easier to build up massive arrangements of MIDI tracks, which you can then move around along with the audio tracks to your heart's desire. When you're slaving a MIDI recording program or drum machine to analog tape (see Appendix A), sometimes it seems that the planets need to be aligned in order for everything to work together. This is rarely the case with an integrated digital program; usually, either it works or it doesn't.

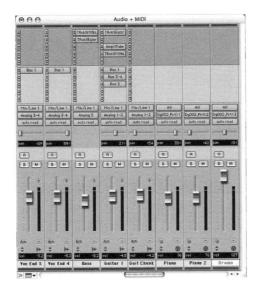

Fig. 3 A virtual console, with audio channels (left) and MIDI channels (right).

Automation, anyone? Many pro recording studios have consoles that memorize every move that was made during mixdown, allowing the producer and engineer to get very fine with their mixing moves, with the board automatically reproducing them time and time again. Even some of today's semi-pro boards have a certain amount of automation built in. But with a good digital recording program, full automation is part of the package. Incorporating "virtual console" windows that look like mixing boards (see Fig. 3), the programs let you click a button, run the song, and move a fader up and down. The next time you play the song, check it out—the onscreen fader moves all by itself. Many programs also allow you to automate EQ, effect-level, and plug-in setting changes. This capability works perfectly with the next concept, "mix as you go."

Mix As You Go

see pages 219, 220

In professional recording, it's standard practice to lay down all of the tracks, and then at a later date, "wipe" (reset) the mixing board and start mixing the song from scratch. That's fine if the board has endless channels as well as tons of sends and returns, the studio has a truckload of outboard gear, and the mixing engineer's ears are so golden he can throw together a sweet-sounding mix in 90 seconds flat. But we need to take a different approach. Part of Guerrilla Home Recording involves mixing as you go—making sure the instruments that are already down are balanced and sound right before adding the next instrument, and constantly tweaking levels and EQs as you listen to playbacks. In the perfect scenario, a Guerrilla recordist could start running a mixdown immediately after putting down the last track and have a mix five minutes later. In reality that rarely happens, but it's something to shoot for.

Why is mixing-as-you-go better than starting a mix from scratch with fresh ears? The main reason is that with our limited resources, we Guerrilla recordists have to make calculated compromises during the recording process. Say, for example, you wanted to add a bit of reverb to the kick and snare drum—but you have only one hardware reverb unit and don't like your reverb plug-ins. At some point you read that it isn't wise to paint yourself into a corner by "printing effects" (recording them along with the track), so you record the drums "dry" (unprocessed), with the intent that during mixdown you'll apply the same reverb on the drums that you're using on the vocals. The problem with this approach is it results in a flatter sound. In the final mix, the vocals and drums don't live in their own unique reverb spaces; they're kind of mashed together. Plus, since both the drums and vocals are feeding into the reverb together, the resulting reverb sound is muddier than if the vocals went through the reverb's complex signal-processing by themselves. The Guerrilla approach would be to record the drum sounds along with their own specially tailored reverb—ideally on separate tracks, or at least in a way so you could easily re-record the drums later if you end up putting too much (or too little) reverb on them. Side benefits: When you're adding subsequent instruments, that tasty drum reverb—which, after all, is part of your vision of the recording—may inspire you to come up with ideas or sounds you wouldn't have otherwise. You'll certainly have a more informed perspective on how the new instruments will work in the final mix, drum reverb and all.

To use another example, consider the project-studio story I related earlier. I was expecting to send my bass through a compressor before hitting tape, because that's what I did at home—but the engineer wanted to compress later. If my bass line went in compressed, from that point on it would be easier to get guitar, keyboard, and vocal sounds that fit well with my bass sound, because it would be more representative of my sound in the final mixdown. If the engineer did have "golden ears" and therefore knew exactly what my bass would sound like post-compression, no problem. If I were a better bassist who could supply more consistent dynamics with my fingers, that would have helped as well. And if the engineer had the resources to go all the way with the big-studio approach, he might have recorded several separate bass tracks (say, one clean direct, one clean miked-amp, and one distorted miked-amp track), allowing for a lot more flexibility at mixdown. But he wasn't; his ears were just okay, and he was recording one raw, boomy direct track with levels that were fluctuating all over the place—which didn't exactly inspire brilliant playing on my part, I might add.

These are only a couple of examples. The point is, you will maximize your sound if you plan things so that the final mixdown is as simple as possible, with minimal added effects, EQ tweaks, and level changes. When you lay down a track and then listen back, what you hear should sound as close as possible to an excellent final mix, minus the tracks you have yet to record. Sure, you give up a little flexibility this way (if you "print" the reverb with the drums, you may not be able to reduce the reverb later without re-recording them), and it requires you to make some guesses and/or use some extra tracks. But these are the kinds of compromises you need to make in Guerrilla Home Recording.

It Helps To Be Hybrid

More and more home recordists are going all-digital—aside from mics and instruments, everything having to do with recording is done inside the computer, including adding effects and mixing. While this offers convenience, there's a lot to be said for combining DAW recording with the old-school signal routing of hardware gear. For one thing, the more that people record using the same plug-ins, amp simulators, and software instruments, the more everyone's music will _sound_ the same. You and the music inside you are unique. Don't you want it to sound unique as well? The most successful artists and producers—at least in certain genres—use a hybrid "new/old" approach to recording, combining the power and convenience of digital with the heart and humanity of gear with real knobs and switches. I think there's a reason for that.

That's why in this book I talk a lot about mixing boards, outboard effects, and hardware MIDI instruments; many people still use them, and I personally think those who do have a recording advantage over those who don't. But even if you don't intend to ever use such devices (they're *so* last century!), at least spend some time understanding how they work. Virtual consoles, plug-ins, and software instruments are designed to operate just like their hardware counterparts, and you won't get the most out of your DAW if you don't understand the older technology it's based on.

Use Drum Samples

Home recordists can record live drums, and plenty do—Chapter 7 explains how to do it. Some do a really good job recording drums at home. But in terms of sound, the drums are a song's most critical element—the part most likely to scream "amateur recording!" to the casual listener. Also, recording live drums introduces a slew of variables into the process. It's just very hard to do well. Therefore, I recommend using sampled, rather than acoustic, drums. This can mean anything from using sounds straight out of a well-programmed drum machine, to employing a sampling keyboard and an extensive library of custom-built drum sounds, to playing an electronic drum kit, to sampling a drum loop from an old vinyl record. If you're a non-drummer or don't have a drummer friend, this is a good thing: with this method it's very possible to fool people into thinking you *do* play the drums. If you are a drummer, don't feel threatened. I'm not advocating just setting up a two-bar pattern and having your drum machine churn out an endless "boom-chuck" sound (although, of course, that can work well in certain musical styles). I do advocate *playing* drum parts, recording your performance via MIDI rather than audio. In Chapter 8 I'll discuss in detail how to do that.

With today's technology, from a purely sonic point of view, it's much easier for a non-professional recordist to get impressive results by creating drum tracks electronically than by miking a drum kit. And if you do your drums well, most people will have no idea that you never put sticks to skins, in real time, while creating your music.

Don't Sweat Acoustics

Most recording books include entire chapters on how to improve your studio's acoustics. But in the Guerrilla studio, the room is irrelevant—you should be able to move your gear into the garage or a VW bus and still get just about the same sound. Our approach involves avoiding the problems acoustics can create. In addition to using sampled drums, this includes close-miking or digitally simulating amps (with most ambience supplied electronically), and using headphones and near-field monitors at low volume levels to listen to your mixes. (More on how to do these things later.) Unless your space is *really* bad—I mean, like a locker room or a steel shipping container—you should be fine. As a musician you probably don't have the time, money, or interest to bother with building homemade diffusers and bass traps. That's okay—it'll be our secret.

Gear That Really, Really Helps

As you may have figured out, this book is *not* about trying to get you to upgrade to the latest, greatest gear. You can make an outstanding recording using gear that's inexpensive or outdated; your ears and your approach are your most important tools. That said, though, there are a few pieces of hardware that I think are important in creating a good recording:

At least two mics. You should have one decent dynamic mic and one decent condenser mic (see Chapter 3). By "decent," I just mean one that's designed for music, not dictation or some such thing. If it doesn't have a detachable cord, or if it has a built-in desk-stand or a little "mini" ⅛" plug, it's not worth using. Spend a hundred bucks on eBay for something a little better.

Some kind of mic preamp or mixing board. You'll need some way to get your mic signals up to a level that's appropriate for your digital audio interface. Most of these interfaces have mic jacks and preamps built in; if yours does, you're all set. The built-in preamps might not be of great quality, but they'll get the job done. But if you already have a mixing board with good built-in mic preamps, consider using that instead. Even though most recording programs offer a "virtual console" onscreen, incorporating a real mixing board into your digital studio allows you more options to route audio here and there, particularly to outboard signal processors. More about this in Chapter 3.

Direct box. This allows you to record an electric guitar or bass without using an amplifier, when you want a very clean sound. If you plug an instrument directly into a mixer's ¼" input jack, you'll get a sound, but not a good one. You need a direct box to record directly; that's all there is to it. Direct boxes are discussed in Chapter 3.

Compressor. This will give you much more control over levels. If you currently don't use a compressor, your recordings will improve markedly once

you get one and learn to use it. Avoid the "easy to use" kind with just one or two knobs; these don't give you enough control. Look for one that at least allows you to set the threshold, ratio, and output levels—and be sure it has an LED or something that tells you when the compression is working. Units without "compressor active" LEDs or meters are harder to use. Compressors are discussed in Chapters 3 and 4.

Expander. Often built into compressors (they're called compressor/expanders), an expander will greatly clean up your recording by eliminating hum and other noise when no signal is present. An expander is the Guerrilla recordist's secret weapon; people will be amazed by how quiet the spaces are between those huge power chords you recorded. Expanders are discussed in Chapters 3 and 4. A "noise gate," by the way, is a heavy-handed type of expander; they aren't as flexible as true expanders, so I don't recommend them for recording.

One good reverb. Since the room is irrelevant in the Guerrilla studio, you need a good reverb to create your room sounds. Digital reverbs vary from awful to great—and this isn't always proportionate to price. For instance, throughout this book I don't mention many specific pieces of gear, but I will say that the Yamaha SPX90 is a terrific old reverb that's still used in some pro studios. Introduced in the mid '80s, it can also perform other effects such as auto-pan, pitch change, and modulation effects. More about reverbs and how to choose them in Chapter 6.

One good pair of headphones. Since the Guerrilla studio room may be far from acoustically neutral and uncolored, you may want to do a lot of your work through headphones. Some models being manufactured today for studio use are excellent—and in addition to being a necessary recording tool, good headphones are a great way to rediscover your favorite CDs. So invest a little money in a good pair.

Headphones Are Your Microscope

In some recording circles, headphones have a bad reputation; they're useful for studio musicians to hear the music they're recording to, but not a lot else. Me, I love a good pair of headphones. I know I'm hearing a perfect stereo image with no coloration from the room I'm in. Using the same pair of phones, a mix sounds identical whether I'm in my studio, the living room, outside—whatever. Even more important, good headphones allow you to hear subtleties and details of a mix that might be audible only with the best studio monitors, a well-tuned room, and a position at the "sweet spot" between the speakers. They're perfect for studying the craft of your favorite producers—how sounds move around the stereo field, how reverbs are brought up and back, how vocals are layered, and so on. On headphones, it's easy to hear if a sound is breaking up the wrong way, if there's a little unwanted click bleeding through on a track, or anything else that requires a really close listen. With practice, you can also get good at subtle sound-shaping on a pair of headphones you know well. You shouldn't rely *only* on headphones; when you want to hear the "big picture" or get an accurate idea of the lows in your mix, real speakers are better. But to zoom in close, grab the headphones. You'll be glad you did.

Bouncing

see pages 220, 221, 223

Bouncing (British engineers call it reducing) is the process of making a preliminary mix of some or all of the existing tracks in order to free up new tracks. (When I described my old technique of recording a different drum sound on each track and then mixing the drums to stereo on two tracks, that was an example of bouncing.) Most people associate bouncing with analog recording, because the main reason to bounce is to free up tracks—and in the digital world, the number of tracks isn't a direct issue. Instead, the most common limitation of digital systems is insufficient CPU power. Bouncing can still help with this annoying problem.

Say you have a dense arrangement involving four or five guitar tracks, each track using two plug-ins to process the sound. During playback, your recording program repeatedly stalls and gives you the error message, RUNNING OUT OF CPU POWER . . . MUTE TRACKS OR DELETE PLUG-INS TO CONTINUE. Well, you could do that, but you don't want to. One solution: Temporarily mute all of the other tracks and bounce the guitars down to one stereo track, with the plug-ins doing their thing. When you're done, *then* you can mute the individual guitar tracks. Not only will this relieve the computer from having to play back so many tracks (which conserves processing power), those plug-ins—which typically eat up more processing power than having extra tracks—are now idle. You have more CPU power to work with, and the program will be less likely to balk.

Of course, bouncing has a downside: You need to get a good mix of the bounced instruments, because once they're bounced, those sounds are no longer individually adjustable. On analog systems this is a serious challenge, because after you do a bounce, you erase the source tracks to make those tracks available again (that is, unless you have an extra multitrack machine and can bounce to a different reel of tape). With the original tracks gone, there's no way to go back and adjust the mix later. But even on a basic digital system, that problem is no more: All you need to do is mute the source tracks. You don't need to erase them. This makes it easy to re-bounce the tracks later if you want to tweak the individual tracks' levels or EQ.

There are times when bouncing is useful even when you aren't going from a large number of tracks to a small one. I've been in situations where there were many rapid-fire edits in a track—too many for my hard drive to handle while it was dealing with all of the other audio. This caused the program to stop each time it got to that section of the song. So I soloed the troublesome track and simply bounced it to another track. Whereas the audio previously consisted of many tiny audio clips edited together (the hard drive had only a few hundredths of a second to find each of them), the bounced audio consisted of a single, continuous audio file—same sound, but much easier for the drive to handle. End of lock-ups.

Non-Real-Time Processing

For effects like EQ and delay, most digital recordists use plug-ins in real-time mode, meaning the plug-ins do their thing while the track is playing. This is a very flexible way of working, as you're always able to tweak the plug-ins' settings, even while you're mixing down a song. But as I mentioned, plug-ins quickly eat up a computer's processing power. One workaround—if your plug-in format allows it—is to process each track individually with its plug-ins while the recording program is stopped. This creates a new digital file on your hard drive for each track, with the plug-in already applied to the sound, so all you need to do is play the track and the effect will be there. This allows you to play dozens of tracks at once, each with its own plug-in (or several plug-ins), even though doing so requires exactly the same CPU power as the same number of tracks *without* those plug-ins applied. It's essentially the same principle as "printing effects," which I mentioned earlier—except that as with bouncing, since you can save the source tracks, you can always go back and re-process a track later as needed. More on this technique in Chapter 9.

Recording MIDI

Digital recording programs allow you to record MIDI information from keyboards, drum machines, etc., as well as audio. This is great news for unskilled keyboard players like myself. As with drums, recording a MIDI version of a keyboard performance, rather than the actual audio, allows greater flexibility; you can move around and adjust individual notes (or entire sections of a song) after you've played them, and you can even change the sound altogether. That harpsichord part isn't quite mellow enough?

see pages 223, 224

How would electric piano sound instead? A couple of clicks later, you're hearing the same exact harpsichord performance on electric piano. As a bonus, a MIDI track eats up very little CPU power as compared to an audio track.

MIDI Instruments: To Record Or Not?

Regarding incorporating MIDI instruments (including MIDI drums) into your recordings, there are two schools of thought. One school says that MIDI parts should remain that way until mixdown—that is, each time you run your recording program, your studio's MIDI devices are actively producing sound, which you record only when it's time to mix the song. The other school says that you should record or "print" the audio of all your MIDI instruments alongside your vocals and acoustic instruments.

A big advantage of the first method is that you can tweak the notes and performance aspects up until the last minute; if something sounds rhythmically loose or you want to change the register of a keyboard part, you can do it very easily. You can also change the sound completely, of course, right until mixdown. It's also a way to preserve the sound and avoid the generational loss that can result from recording a sound during tracking and again during mixdown (although this isn't a major issue in a digital studio).

The primary advantage to printing your MIDI instruments is that the audio will be right there alongside your other audio, and that's where it'll stay. If you don't print your MIDI instruments and you come back to a song a year later, you may have lost or forgotten the exact keyboard patch or drum bank you had used. Mixing-board or effect settings may have changed. Maybe you don't even have the keyboard or electronic drum kit anymore—then you'll need to recreate the sounds somehow. The main downside of this approach is that it uses up audio tracks, and it also takes a little more effort.

Ideally, you'd keep (and use) your MIDI tracks and also print them to muted audio tracks as a backup. Or, you could use only MIDI tracks until you're done with the mixdown, and then print all of the MIDI as part of the process of archiving the song. It's an extra step, but if you open your song years later (or bring it to someone else's studio), you'll be glad you did it.

CHAPTER 2

Principles Guerrilla Recordists Need To Know

Just about every recording book has a chapter like this—the one where you see diagrams of sine waves and graphs of frequencies, and so on. I'm going to take a slightly different approach; rather than paraphrasing stuff from a physics textbook, I'll try to relate everything to the music you hear and the music you make, or want to make, and I'll try not to make your eyes glaze over.

I hope you won't skip over this chapter. It's important to get a firm grounding in the principles behind sound and capturing sound. Otherwise, you might find yourself flailing away aimlessly in your studio, fingers crossed as you hope to create the sounds you hear in your head. Understanding the important principles will also help you create recording tricks of your own. After all, anyone can follow a set of directions, but understanding the principles *behind* those directions can make following them—and perhaps even more important, deviating from them—easier and more effective. Look at it this way: You can do a decent job of brushing your teeth by just doing it the way you've seen everyone else brush. But if you really want to keep your teeth clean, you'll pay attention to the dental hygienist's little lectures. You'll understand that plaque and tartar build up at the gum line, and holding your brush at a certain angle and brushing in a certain way for a certain amount of time will maximize the removal of that stuff. If you should switch to an electric rotary toothbrush, you'll be able to apply your knowledge to this new tool with maximum benefits. Lame analogy? Perhaps, but at least I hope I convinced you to keep reading. (Don't forget to floss.)

Basics Of Sound

All music consists of sound, and all sound consists of sound waves. These waves can be (1) traveling through the air, as in the case of live acoustic music, (2) passing through a wire in the form of alternating current, also known as AC—for example, what happens when you sing into a microphone, or (3) fixed in a medium that stores approximations of these waves, as in a CD. Our job is to move between these worlds: translating sound waves that are traveling through the air into electrical signals, and then fixing those onto a hard drive or reel of tape. That's all recording is.

Sound easy? Well, here's where it starts to get a bit more complicated. The human ear and brain are so unbelievably good at making another translation—turning sound waves in the air into a conscious perception of that sound—that they put to shame every man-made invention dealing with sound. You probably know what it's like to sit in a concert hall and listen to a live orchestra. In a world with perfect technology, we'd be able to set up two microphones (one representing each ear) in the concert hall and record the sound, and when we played it back, the result would be a perfect recreation of what it's like to listen to the orchestra from that same position. But in reality, this isn't possible. Even the best microphones are inadequate at replacing the human ear in this fashion, and even the best recording media, amplifiers, and loudspeakers have weaknesses that further diminish a two-mic approximation of the concert-hall listening experience.

The art and science of recording, by sheer necessity, is a process of compromising and compensating for the inadequacies of technology. In the concert-hall example, this might mean carefully placing five, ten, or more mics closer to the orchestra, and blending the signals just right, perhaps shaping each mic's sound a bit and giving it the proper place in the stereo field. Even though two $10,000 mics out in the middle of the hall might create a great-sounding recording, using ten of these mics—along with some skill—could create a recording that sounds *more* like what you'd hear if you were actually sitting there in the middle of the hall. Strange, isn't it? That's the world of recording!

Okay, enough about concert halls and $10,000 mics. I'm just giving an example. Using cheap mics and blending "real" sounds with electronic sounds, not to mention tricky instruments like electric bass, makes things even tougher for the Guerrilla recordist. But before tackling these challenges, you need to know what you're up against.

Dynamic Range

You've probably heard of decibels (dB) used to describe degrees of loudness. You may have learned in high-school biology that 0dB (zero decibels) is defined as the threshold of human hearing, or the point where sound *just* begins to get audible. As sounds get louder, the dB number used to describe them goes up. I remember my biology teacher, Mr. Forbes, writing on the board what the other end of human hearing was: 120dB . . . THE WHO. From complete silence to concert-level rock & roll—these are the extremes between which live music exists. Degrees of loudness are referred to as *dynamics*, and the territory between the quietest and loudest extremes is called the *dynamic range*. Dynamic range expresses the difference between the extremes. Pain typically begins to set in at around 120dB, but ears are said to have a dynamic range that is greater than 120dB.

Unfortunately, conventional recording/playback technology cannot capture and reproduce sounds with such a broad dynamic range like that found in nature, or even at a Who show. That's because recording requires the use of electronics, and electronics inherently have some degree of background *noise*, a blanket of hiss caused largely by electrons moving at random. Think of the hiss that you hear when you turn up a stereo when nothing is playing. (Sometimes this is called the *noise floor*; like the floor of a room, you can't go any lower, try as you might.) This noise establishes the lower limit of the dynamic range. For recorded music, it's always less than 120dB; on a CD, the dynamic range is around 90dB. This means that the loudest sounds that can be stored on a CD are about 90dB louder than the hiss you get when you record absolute silence onto a CD. (A 90dB dynamic range is really good, especially when you consider that old vinyl records topped out around 50dB; sometimes, that figure was much lower.)

Because of the technological limitations, when music is recorded, its dynamic range must be *squeezed* between the lower and upper dynamic limits of whatever medium is being recorded onto (see Fig. 1). Otherwise, the music might get either too loud to be recorded without distortion, or too quiet to be heard under the noise floor. Squeezing the dynamic range in this way is called *compression*; we'll discuss it in detail in Chapter 4.

There's another factor working against us: If you record a song that makes dramatic use of the entire dynamic range—the proverbial whisper to a scream—the song won't be able to compete in the rock & roll world. That's because for many years in popular music, there's been a sort of arms race, an incessant pressure, to make every song sound louder than the next guy's songs. Loudness, particularly in rock & roll, tends to sound good and creates a strong visceral impact. Also, the human ear is less sensitive to bass and treble frequencies than it is to midrange frequencies, so the exciting highs and lows seem to disappear as music gets quieter. For these reasons, people have generally

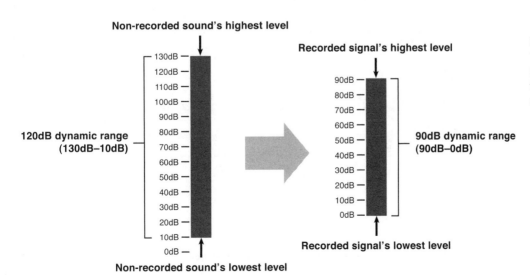

Fig. 1 A sound with a 120dB dynamic range must be "squeezed" to fit into a compact disc's dynamic range.

tried to make their recordings consistently loud, and they generally avoid letting the dynamics vary greatly from one moment to the next.

Let's look at an example: Say the loudest moment of a song you've recorded is 20dB louder than the rest of the song. Meanwhile, your arch-rival has recorded a song in which the loudest moment is only 5dB louder than the rest. When played back, most of your arch-rival's song will sound 15dB louder than yours (see Fig. 2). Result: Your arch-rival's song is big and rocking and thumping, while your song sounds little and tinny, with no definition.

Don't get discouraged. Your arch-rival may not know how to use things like limiter plug-ins, level automation, and mastering to optimize his music's place in that restricted window of dynamic range. But enhanced with these powerful techniques (discussed in later chapters), your next song just might blow his out of the water.

Fig. 2 Even though both songs have the same dynamic range, song B will sound louder overall—and therefore generally better—than song A.

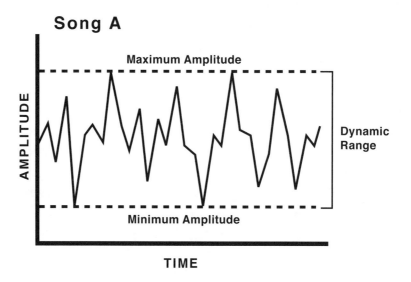

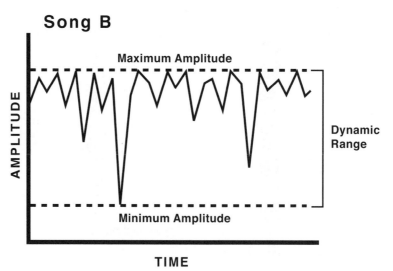

What's the Frequency, Kenneth?

Our ears aren't perfect. We can't hear all sounds—like the sound of a dog whistle, or certain kinds of communication between elephants. The dog whistle is called *ultrasound*; it's too high for us to hear. The elephant rumblings are called *infrasound*; they're too low. Music, and anything else that's audible, consists of sounds with frequencies in between these ranges. People use terms like a "high voice" or "speaking low" all the time, though these phrases can be misleading. Highness and lowness can refer to either loudness or frequency, and it's an important distinction. Right now we're talking about frequency, or what many people call pitch (although that can be a little fuzzy as well).

With regard to sound waves, frequency refers to how many waves are reaching your ears per second. When a car with a subwoofer goes by, you hear a booming sound; those are low frequencies, meaning the waves emanating from the car are long and widely spaced—maybe only 30 of them pass by per second. In this example, we say the sound has a frequency of 30 Hertz (Hz), "Hertz" being the unit that's used to describe frequency. But imagine that the same car's driver suddenly slams on the brakes to avoid something, causing the tires to screech. That's a high-frequency sound, at something like 4,000Hz, or 4kHz (kilohertz). A lot more waves of this sound will be produced and heard per second than from the subwoofer.

You might notice, though, that even while the tires are screeching, you can still hear the subwoofer. (It's one loud subwoofer.) How can high-frequency and low-frequency sounds travel through your walls, and be heard by your ears, at the same time? Because a sound wave can carry many different frequencies at once. Think of it in terms of water: If you go to the ocean, you'll see waves crashing at a certain rate; this rate is the frequency of those waves. But throw a rock into one of those big waves, and you'll see a lot of smaller, closer-together waves propagating outward from where the rock hit the surface. The other waves are still going, only with smaller waves on top of them. This is exactly what happens with sound, too (see Figures 3a–3c).

In fact, almost all sound waves *do* consist of more than one frequency; the only sound that doesn't is a simple sine wave generated by a synthesizer. To get an idea of what a sine wave sounds like, pucker up and blow—whistling is about as close to a sine wave as you can humanly produce. Dull, muted sounds like these are said to have fewer *harmonics* or *overtones* than bright, complex sounds like brass instruments and cymbals. Harmonics or overtones are frequencies that are blended in with the sound's lowest frequency, which is called the *fundamental*. The fundamental frequency is the pitch that the ear tends to hear, while the harmonics or overtones contribute to the sound's quality. (In other words, take away the harmonics and you'd still hear the same pitch, but that pitch would sound different. It might go from sounding like a trumpet to more like a flute, for example.) The ratio of the harmonic content to the fundamental, as well as the frequency ratios between the fundamental and the harmonics, are largely responsible for determining what an instrument, a voice, etc., sounds like.

Fig. 3a A low-frequency sound (about 33Hz).

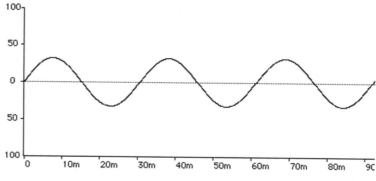

Fig. 3b A higher-frequency sound (about 250Hz).

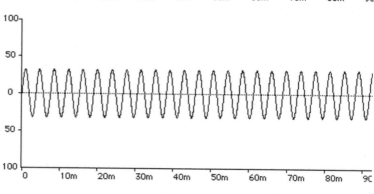

Fig. 3c A sound wave carrying both frequencies—what you'd get if you added Figures 3a and 3b together.

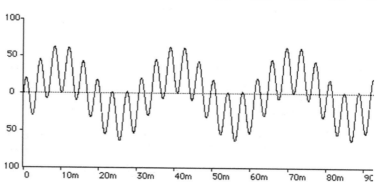

Often the frequencies of harmonics exist in whole-number multiples of the fundamental frequency; for instance, a sound might have a fundamental at 100Hz, with harmonics at 200Hz, 300Hz, and so on. These sounds tend to be tonal or pitched, like that of a woodwind or brass instrument. In some sounds, however, the harmonics are more randomly related to the fundamental. These tend to be more "clangy," like a bell or ride cymbal; in extreme cases the sounds are noisy, like a cymbal crash or woodblock. (Hear a cymbal crash and I bet it won't inspire you to think of any pitch in particular.) The noisiest sound of all, not surprisingly, is called just that: *noise*. "White noise," for example, is by definition a sound containing all frequencies combined in equal proportions. (The term makes an analogy with white light, which comprises all of the visible-light spectrum's colors in equal proportions.) White noise is a random wave; there's no repeating pattern, because a repeating pattern would suggest that it has a fundamental frequency, which it doesn't. But if you added in, say, a 50Hz sine wave, the resulting wave would have elements of both the repeating 50Hz pattern and the random noise pattern. And if you listened to that sound wave, you'd hear a wash of noise with a 50Hz hum blended in.

The Frequency Spectrum

So far we haven't talked a lot about music, but here's where it starts getting a little more useful. The range of audible audio frequencies is analogous to the spectrum of visible light, a.k.a. the colors of the rainbow. (With light, low frequencies appear red and high frequencies look blue.) The most common numbers given for the ends of the audible frequency spectrum are 20Hz on the low end (anything lower is considered infrasound) and 20kHz on the upper end (anything higher is considered ultrasound). The majority of recorded sounds exist between these endpoints, from 20Hz to 20kHz, and the roles that different sounds play in this frequency spectrum—as well as the frequency *components* of individual sounds—is one of the most important concepts for a recording musician to grasp. The better a handle you have on it, the better equipped you'll be to make wise decisions when making recorded music.

It helps to look at the frequency spectrum not as a whole but in terms of frequency *bands*. Many people are familiar with the terms "bass" and "treble" from the controls on their stereo, but this is much too vague and broad for our purposes. We're better off thinking in terms of at least five bands: lows, low mids, mids, upper mids, and highs (see Fig. 4). Engineers break this down further into as many as 31 bands, but this is fine for now. Here's the significance of each of these bands, and their approximate boundaries, with reference to a rock & roll recording:

Lows (roughly 20Hz–150Hz) are the domain of the beefy part of the kick-drum sound and the bass guitar's fundamental. A lot of lows tend to make a recording sound powerful, even if they appear only now and then. The downside of lows is that they

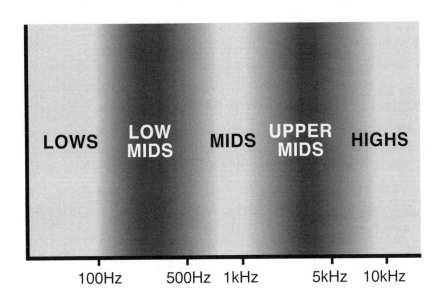

Fig. 4 The audible frequency spectrum is easier to understand if we break it into frequency bands.

can get in the way of other sounds if not managed properly, because the lower in frequency a sound is, the more efficiently it "masks" (covers up) other frequencies. Lows also carry the most energy of all frequency bands.

Low mids (150Hz–600Hz) are often where you'll find the frequencies that give the bass guitar its note definition, as well as the *oomph* of a snare drum or distorted electric guitar, and the "body" of an organ, electric piano, or acoustic guitar sound. Low mids give a recording a certain fullness. They're like the meaty or fibrous portion of a meal—without them, you're left feeling a little hungry. However, if overdone, low mids can muddy up a mix. Frequencies in the low and low-mid ranges (and within these ranges) don't get along very well with each other and are tough to keep in check, so too much energy down in this area can make a mix sound like a gooey, muddy mess.

Mids (600Hz–1.5kHz) are the frequencies that the ear is most sensitive to; they're the frequency spectrum's heartland. If you listen to music coming out of a small transistor-radio speaker, or through a telephone, you're hearing mostly mids, because these systems aren't good at reproducing low and high frequencies. Hold a paper-towel tube (or a seashell) up to your ear and you'll hear what it sounds like when mid frequencies are emphasized. Because our hearing is naturally tuned to this band, these frequencies tend to catch our ear; the fundamentals of many melodic instruments tend to be found here. (Not surprisingly, the parts of the human voice most important in speech are heavy on the mids—it's why you can often hear what someone is saying through even a lousy phone connection.) Lay the mids on too heavy, though, and your music will tend to "honk" or just sound strangely off. The trick is keeping these frequencies in balance and proportion with the other bands.

Upper mids (1.5kHz–6kHz) affect what is commonly called "presence:" If these frequencies are muted, a sound will seem to recede into the distance, whereas if the same sound has a lot of high mids, it will seem more in-your-face. But pour on the upper mids too much and your song will be fatiguing to the ear, even irritating. Up in this range, we're hearing almost entirely harmonics, with few if any fundamentals. Overly hyped upper mids are common in amateur recordings; an inexperienced producer might want each sound to pop out, so he enhances the upper mids everywhere. The result is just an ear-numbing wash of harshness, with no instrument particularly "present" in the mix. Upper mids, like all the frequency bands, need to be managed with discretion and taste.

Highs (6kHz–20kHz) create a "bright" sound; they tend to be the first frequencies to go away in a low-fidelity recording. But as with upper mids, trying to compensate for lost highs can have bad-sounding results. It's best to get a recording that faithfully captures highs in the first place. Perhaps more so than any of the other bands, highs can be divided into several other sub-bands that are useful to think about. The lower end of this band is responsible for run-of-the-mill brightness, like most of the frequencies from a cymbal crash. Higher highs (say, in the 10kHz range) are responsible for crispness in a sound, like the "zing" of new acoustic-guitar strings. The highest highs (above 12kHz) are perhaps the hardest to describe; many people use the word "air" to describe these frequencies. When they're there, a sound can have a certain lightness, openness, or clarity; when they're missing, a sound might seem lifeless or empty. If you record a sound without capturing the highest highs (for example if you use a poor microphone), you won't be able to create them after the fact. Attempts to boost this sub-band can make a recording sound brittle. This is particularly true in digital recordings, because where analog media might tame and sweeten those uppermost highs, digital systems tend to capture them as is, which might end up being too much of a good thing.

So, what does it all mean? Basically, every band has its good features and bad features: too much of any one of them, and not enough of any one of them, will usually make a recording sound not as good as when they're all balanced with each other. So, what's balanced? Isn't that subjective? It is but today's recorded popular music has certain standards that have evolved over the years. You probably won't turn on the radio and hear a song that's a relentless blast of highs with a thin bottom end, because such a sound would probably be too extreme for contemporary pop-music sensibilities. So, your best bet in learning about how your own recordings stack up to those of the pros is to put them up against professional recordings. It's a sobering thing to create a setup where you can "A/B" your music against a recording that you admire, but it's a great way to listen closely and try to hear weaknesses in your recordings. For instance, even after 20 years of making music, I sometimes notice that the low mids in my music are deficient. When this happens, I might turn up the organ, electric piano, or rhythm guitar slightly in the mix (particularly if the part is played in a low register). This often provides a fullness that fixes the problem. I'll delve further into this idea in Chapters 5 and 10.

Equalization

You've heard of equalization, or EQ, before—hey, I mentioned it a few times in Chapter 1. It refers to the electronic alteration of a sound in order to adjust the balance of certain frequencies relative to the others. There are EQ plug-ins for digital recording programs, EQ circuits are built into almost all mixing boards, and there are also outboard rackmount EQs. Good mic preamps also often have EQ circuits built in. Equalization is one of the Guerrilla recordist's best friends, along with compression and expansion (see Chapter 4). EQ comes in handy because rarely in the home studio do we capture a sound with just the right frequency proportions for the recording we're making. At some point, those proportions will likely need to be adjusted, the way you might add salt to a soup you're cooking as the other ingredients go in. A highly skilled engineer might be able to get a sound just right at the outset by, say, using a certain microphone and placing it a certain way. In the Guerrilla studio, though, things aren't quite that easy. So EQ helps you make corrections as the recording takes shape, especially if you keep in mind the "mix as you go" idea mentioned in Chapter 1.

Watch That Boost

Be careful when you're boosting a frequency band to bring out a particular aspect of a sound. If you're trying to find the frequency where the "snap" of a kick-drum sound lives, for example, your ears can kind of fall in love with the sound of that "snap" once you find it. Your intent was only to accentuate it a little, but without realizing it, you may have gone too far. A good rule of thumb is that after you find the sound's key frequency, turn down the EQ boost until the sound seems appropriate in context, and then turn it down some more—maybe halfway between its original position and the position it was just in. Then re-check the boost later, after you've forgotten what that overly boosted "snap" sounds like. If necessary, adjust accordingly.

Overall, it's better not to have to use EQ. Depending on the quality of the EQ circuit you're using, it can lend a plasticky, non-musical artificiality to the frequency region it's affecting. But even if you don't have the greatest EQ, you can get away with using a little (for any particular frequency band, for any particular sound), with basically no harm done. However, if you find yourself turning a knob or sliding a slider halfway or more past the center point, it might be time to consider re-recording that part or using a different sound altogether. Finally, it's usually better to cut frequencies rather than boost them, whenever this is an option. Cutting often results in a more natural sound (and it sounds less like, um, an EQ boost)—plus, cutting doesn't boost your mix's overall levels, which can lead to other problems down the line, as we'll see.

Shelving EQs (see the EQ Types sidebar) are useful for adjusting highs and lows, but you'll get more mileage out of a *sweepable mid* EQ. "Mid" means that the circuit lets you boost or cut a range of frequencies somewhere in the middle of the spectrum, and "sweepable" means you can select the center frequency of that range. This is useful because it allows you to target a specific aspect of a sound that might need emphasis or taming. Say you have a kick-drum sound that's nice and beefy, but you can't hear the "snap" of the beater hitting the drum head very well. Boosting the lows will just make the kick beefier—maybe too beefy. What you want to do in this case is crank up that mid control to a much higher level than you'd probably want to use, and slowly sweep the frequency control across the mids and upper mids while the kick-drum sound is going through the EQ. If the EQ is fully parametric, meaning it has a bandwidth (Q) control as well, set the bandwidth to be moderately narrow. At some point as you sweep, you'll hear the "snap" of the kick-drum being dialed in. Once you've found the key frequency for that attack, back off on the boost and tweak the bandwidth parameter until it sounds more appropriate in context.

By the way, toying around with a sweepable-mid EQ on all sorts of sounds is one of the best ways to train your ears about the effects of boosting and cutting certain frequencies. And training your ears is a very good thing. I'll talk in more detail about how to use EQ in Chapter 5.

EQ Types

An equalizer circuit can be as simple as a single knob—a guitar's tone knob is a type of EQ—or it can have several dozen controls. EQs are classified by the manner in which they shape a sound's frequency content; the same terms are used regardless of whether it's a standalone rackmount EQ unit, an EQ circuit on a mixing board, or a software EQ plug-in. Here are some types of EQs you're likely to encounter:

Shelving EQ. You've known this one since you were a kid: The bass and treble controls on a home stereo are shelving EQs. These affect all frequencies above or below a certain frequency. For example, a bass control, when turned down from its mid point, might cut all frequencies below 100Hz; when turned up, it will boost the same frequencies. Shelving EQs are most useful when a sound just has too much highs or lows and these frequencies need to be tamed. Of course, shelving EQs can also enhance highs or lows, but use them judiciously—particularly when boosting lows, because of the way low frequencies carry so much energy.

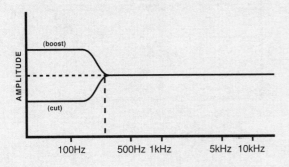

Highpass/lowpass filter EQ. These are kind of like cut-only shelving EQs—they cannot boost frequencies. A highpass filter cuts low frequencies (allowing the highs to pass through), while a low-pass filter cuts highs. Unlike shelving EQs, though, these filters are said to "roll off" all frequencies above or below a certain point—meaning the further a frequency is from that point, the more

the filter affects it. For example, if you're cutting lows with a highpass filter that operates at 100Hz, energy at 60Hz will be cut somewhat, but energy at 40Hz will be cut even more. (With a shelving EQ, both frequencies might be cut the same.) The sharpness with which the filter rolls off frequencies is expressed as a "slope" in units of decibels per octave (dB/oct). The higher the figure, the more potentially extreme the EQ. Some of these filters have set parameters; others, particularly in the form of EQ plug-ins, allow you to set the frequency cut-off point and/or the slope.

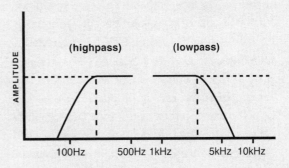

Bandpass EQ. Also sometimes just called "mid EQ," a bandpass EQ affects midrange frequencies but leaves highs and lows more or less alone. A mid EQ is most useful when it's either parametric or semi-parametric (see below). You might also run across the term *notch filter*; this is a kind of band-pass EQ that only cuts a specific frequency range. This kind of EQ is especially useful in live sound systems, as it can help eliminate feedback squeals at the precise frequencies where feedback occurs.

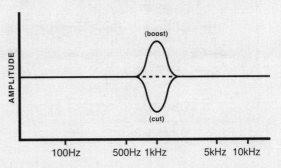

Graphic EQ. You've seen this on home stereos or instrument amplifiers: It's a number of sliders arranged together, any one of which can cut or boost a band of frequencies. Each slider controls a bandpass EQ circuit, except for the highest and lowest ones, which control shelving circuits. Graphic EQs are named because the pattern formed by all of the sliders represents, more or less, a graph of the EQ's effect on the sound, with frequency on the horizontal axis and degree of boost or cut on the vertical axis. A graphic EQ is often useful for subtle, overall shaping of a sound; for instance, with some practice you might learn that your singing voice benefits from being boosted a little here, cut a little here, boosted a little there, etc. Graphic EQs sound best when you build a smooth, curvy contour on the sliders, but some cool effects can be produced by boosting or cutting only certain sliders by a large degree. (Always listen for distortion anytime you're radically boosting frequencies.) There are wonderful graphic EQs out there as well as horrible ones. But all else being equal, more sliders is better, because they allow more precise tone shaping, and because each slider affects a more narrow range of frequencies. The 31-band graphic EQ, which has three sliders for each octave (an octave represents a doubling of the frequency), is a fairly standard piece of studio gear. You'll hear this type of EQ called a *one-third-octave* graphic EQ.

Parametric EQ. This is the kind we Guerrilla recordists (as well as most pro engineers) like the most. A parametric EQ is so named because each frequency band allows three parameters to be set: amount of boost or cut, the center frequency, and the bandwidth (also called "Q"), which is how wide a chunk of the frequency spectrum, on either side of the center frequency, is affected. With a parametric EQ you can make a broad contour on a sound by specifying a wide bandwidth, or target a specific frequency range. If a snare-drum sound has an annoying ring, for instance, you can locate where in the frequency spectrum that ring is occurring, and soften it. A pro studio might have one or more dedicated outboard parametric EQs in a rack, but most home recordists encounter parametric EQ in the form of plug-in parameters, or on their mixing board, in the form of "sweepable mid" EQ knobs. This is a valuable tool for the Guerrilla recordist to have; it's especially useful for enhancing instrument separation (see Chapter 5).

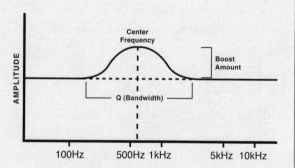

A **semi-parametric EQ** is just like a parametric EQ, except it has a fixed (non-adjustable) bandwidth. Budget mixing boards' mid-EQ controls commonly use these less expensive circuits, but that's okay; being able to sweep the frequencies is more important than being able to set the bandwidth.

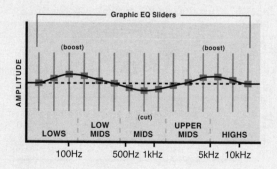

Mono, Stereo & Panning

When you play a CD, you're actually hearing not one recording but two: one for the left speaker, and one for the right. These two recordings can be called *channels* when spoken of individually, or together as a *stereo pair*. They're locked together in time on a CD, but they're otherwise independent; if you wanted to, you could make a CD that plays a different song out of each speaker at the same time. In the early years of recording, music consisted of only one channel, because home playback systems had only one speaker. This is called *monophonic*, or "mono," sound. In the 1950s, music started being commercially released in the two-channel *stereophonic* (stereo) sound that we know today. Stereo provides a more interesting, realistic listening experience, because it allows sounds to appear to exist in different places in space and to move around. It also helps us Guerrilla recordists, because being able to place sounds in different parts of the stereo field—that imaginary listening space encompassing both the left and right channels—makes it easier for us to separate the sounds. And separation, as we'll see in Chapter 5, is an important feature of a well-made recording.

You can record a sound in stereo that plays back as a mono sound, simply by making the left and right channels identical. When the same exact sound is playing out of both speakers, the sound appears to come from between them, or to come from both of them as a whole. But if the sound is louder in one speaker than in the other, it will appear to be coming more from that speaker. If another sound is playing at the same time but it's coming more from the other speaker, the two sounds will be separated somewhat in the stereo field: one will be kind of on the left, the other kind of on the right. And if a sound begins to decrease in volume in one speaker while it gets louder in the other, the sound will appear to move across the stereo field. This placement in the stereo field is called *panning*—a sound can be "panned" to the left, or it can "pan" from one side to the other. (The word is short for "panorama" and is derived from the terminology of cinema.) Along with dynamics and frequency content, panning is one of the three most important factors determining a particular sound's place and function in a recording. Panning also creates opportunities for artistic expression, as the

---

The Three "Dimensions" Of Recorded Sound

Throughout this book, you'll see three terms being used over and over to describe sound: dynamics, frequency content, and pan position. If you think of every recorded sound in terms of these three "dimensions," it becomes easier to understand how that sound fits into a mix with all of the other sounds. For example, if you want an instrument to be a focal point, you'd probably record and mix it so that it's loud, bright, and panned to the center. When we discuss the principle of instrument separation in Chapter 5, you'll see how this approach to sound management can give each sound its own unique place in a mix, which—when applied to all sounds—generally makes a recording sound better and more professional.

way you pan a sound, and the way its panning position changes over time, is a choice you make during the recording's creation—one that has a distinct effect on the way the finished recording sounds.

Tracking vs. Mixing

Recording consists of two phases: *tracking* and *mixing*. When you're tracking, you're recording individual sounds (or perhaps several sounds at once, or in the case of live recording, a whole band) in a form that is not yet a finished stereo (two-channel) recording. Usually, this means that for any particular sound, you're taking one mono channel or two channels (if you're recording that sound in stereo) and recording the sound to one or two tracks of a computer's recording program, or to a multitrack recorder. After all of the tracks are recorded, they are all played back at the same time and "mixed," or "mixed down," to two channels in stereo (or more in the case of surround sound) and recorded somewhere else. During mixdown, the level, EQ, and pan position of each sound determine its role in the final mix. For example, you could make two versions of a song by doing two mixdowns: one in which the rhythm guitar is playing softly and off to one side, and another in which the rhythm guitar is panned to the center, extra-bright, and loud. Obviously, these song versions would be quite different, which is why mixing decisions are important, both technically and artistically.

Digital vs. Analog

Sound can exist in either *analog* or *digital* form. Even if you're recording digitally and never intend to touch an analog recorder, it's important to know what the terms mean. All sound, no matter how it is recorded, is analog when it reaches your ear, and sound is often in the analog realm at various stages of the recording process. So it helps to know what's going on when sound makes the transition between these two worlds.

Analog recording has been around for well over a century. Thomas Edison famously developed a way to record sound onto foil, and later, wax cylinders. If you were to take a microscope and look at the grooves Edison's machines made in the wax, they would look like sound-wave diagrams, with repeating patterns that represent the frequency components of the sound that was recorded. Whether we're talking about wax, vinyl LPs, or magnetic tape (which captures sound in magnetic form, not in a way you can see with a microscope), we say that the waves that are recorded are *analogous* to the original sound waves that traveled through the air (see Fig. 5). By this we mean the recorded waves are identical (well, almost) to the original sound, with peaks and valleys and smaller wavelets in all the same places. Similarly, when a cable is carrying an analog sound, the electrons in the cable are moving back and forth in a way that's analogous to the sound wave being represented. It's similar to the alternating current (AC) that comes out of a wall outlet, except that kind of signal is a sine wave with a single frequency (60Hz in the U.S.) and amplitude (110 or 220 volts, much stronger than in cables carrying sound) rather than being a complex wave that's constantly changing.

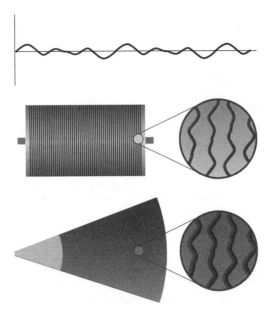

Fig. 5 If a sound wave (top) were recorded onto an old-fashioned wax cylinder (center) or pressed onto a vinyl LP (bottom), you could see the wave's shape in the grooves under a microscope. For this reason, the grooves are said to be an analog representation of the sound wave.

Digital recording is very different. A digital recorder converts an analog electrical signal into a set of numbers that can be written onto a hard drive or some similar medium. It does this by analyzing, or *sampling*, the position of the wave many thousands of times per second, and assigning a number to the wave's position at each sample point. This isn't a perfect process, though, because a real sound wave (and its electrical analog) is continuous, comprising an infinite number of points. The digital version is limited by how many samples were taken per second (called the *sampling rate*), as well as the *resolution* of each sample. Resolution refers to how many numbers are used in each sample to define the position of the wave at that point. Resolution is expressed in *bits*, a digital measurement unit. If more bits per sample are used in a digital recording, and if the sampling rate is higher, the recording will be more accurate, allowing for more detailed high frequencies (see Fig. 6). Early digital recording systems used eight bits per sample; slightly better systems used 12 bits. Commercial CDs use 16 bits, which today is considered the minimum bit resolution for digital recording. Today's superior systems use 24-bit resolution, which results in quieter, smoother-sounding recordings. CDs contain data that was sampled 44,100 times per second, which is referred to as a 44.1kHz sampling rate. This, too, is considered the minimum for high-fidelity music; some recording and playback systems can operate at 48kHz, 96kHz, and even 192kHz.

There's an endless debate about the sound quality of digital vs. analog recordings. Analog systems are prized for their "warm" sound and gentle, natural-sounding compression of volume peaks, while digital tends to "color" (alter) the sound less; analog freaks often say digital systems sound "cold" or "clinical," perhaps because they record *too* faithfully. Even digital enthusiasts argue about how valuable higher bit resolutions and sampling rates are with regard to the resulting sound. For Guerrilla

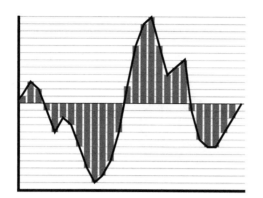 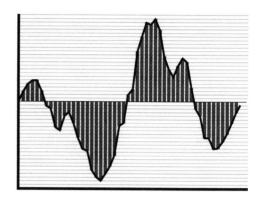

Fig. 6 These diagrams represent two ways of expressing a wave shape digitally via individual samples (gray bars); the horizontal lines represent bit resolution. A digital system with a higher sampling rate and bit resolution (right) will create a better approximation of a sound wave's shape (black curve) than one with a lower sampling rate and bit resolution (left).

Home Recording, digital sounds just fine. And yes, you can make a slightly better recording by employing a higher bit resolution and sampling rate—but for our purposes, 16 bits and 44.1kHz sampling is plenty. You can record using better specs if you want, but doing so will require more hard-drive space as well as more CPU power from your computer.

There is one critical thing to understand when you're recording digitally. Analog systems are somewhat forgiving at the maximum end of the dynamic range; as I mentioned, analog tape is known to gently tame a recording's loudest moments. Digital, though, is not. Since it uses a range of numbers to describe a sound at any given moment, once it hits the top of the range, there's nowhere to go. A digital system can't magically create new numbers to describe the sound. As a result, if you go over the top of the range, the sound will distort in a really ugly way. Unlike analog distortion (a distorted electric-guitar amp is a type of analog distortion), digital distortion is horrible, unmusical, and useless. So while you can get some cool effects by "baking the tape" on an analog machine, you must stay under that upper limit on a digital system. All digital systems help you to do this, for instance lighting an LED that stays lit if you reach the "over" point. (If that happens, you'd better go back and redo the part.) You don't want to be *too* safe with your levels, because digital systems don't perform as well with quiet sounds as they do with loud ones. You want to reach a happy medium, or perhaps "a happy moderately loud" would be a better way to put it. More about maintaining good levels in Chapter 3.

Signal Levels

Recording would be a lot easier if there were only one type of cable, all plugs and jacks fit together, and all equipment operated at the same signal level. But things are more complicated than that, and it's essential to get a handle on all of the differences and what they mean in the Guerrilla studio. The explanations that follow are a bit simplified and loosey-goosey. Technical audio geeks don't like to leave out details, which is why some recording books include lots of dazzling formulas and rigorous explanations. I'll spare you the technical details and just tell you what you need to know to make a good recording.

An analog audio signal requires at least two wires (conductors) to be carried by a cable: one conductor, called "hot," carries the actual signal, and the other, called "ground," completes the circuit and provides a place for the electricity to return. Keep in mind that since the current is an alternating one, the electrons aren't actually going anywhere other than back and forth—but the signal is being fed into the cable at one end and being detected at the other, so the signal *is* traveling, in the form of waves. That's why you'll read about "signal flow," or hear that "the signal goes from point A to point B." Anyway, a signal can travel down a cable at different intensities, depending on where it's coming from and where it's going. That's where volts come into play: we describe the signal's maximum strength as a voltage. It's a reference number to help us understand how pieces of audio gear fit together; it isn't necessarily a direct measurement of the signal.

The signal coming from a microphone is the weakest kind of audio signal. A microphone picking up a loud sound generates only a few dozen millivolts (thousandths of a volt)—very small. This is called a *mic level* signal, and a signal that small is fairly useless for most audio gear unless it is first amplified. Amplification refers to increasing the voltage while maintaining the integrity of the sound being represented. Some amplifier circuits are better than others at doing this; good ones are clean and quiet, while bad ones introduce noise and/or distortion, which is an alteration of the sound waves' shapes. If the circuit changes the wave shapes, the sound will change—sometimes in a good way, but often, in an unwanted way.

Amplifiers designed to accept mic-level signals are called *microphone preamps*, often called "mic pre's" for short. A mic pre boosts a mic-level signal to *line level*, which is the signal level that operates inside digital audio interfaces, mixing boards, and rackmount effects. In a line-level signal, the maximum voltage reached is somewhere in the order of one volt. Most mixing boards have built-in mic pre's, and some of them are pretty good. There are also standalone mic pre's, which can range in price from affordable to incredibly expensive.

A third kind of signal level, called *instrument level*, is generated by electric guitars and basses. Instrument level is usually weaker than line level but stronger than mic level. I say "usually" because instrument level varies quite a bit; some guitar pickups are much more powerful than others, and some instruments contain onboard preamps that boost the signal even before it leaves the output jack. Guitars and basses are either plugged into amplifiers designed to accept instrument levels, or they're recorded *direct*, meaning the signal remains electronic all the way through the signal chain to the recording. But first, a direct-recorded guitar or bass must go through a direct box, which I mentioned in Chapter 1. Many direct boxes don't actually amplify the instrument signal up to line level, so you still need a preamp to do this; a mixing board's mic preamps are often fine for the job.

Synthesizers and drum machines create yet another kind of signal level; often it's lower than line level but much higher than instrument level. Generally, you can treat this kind of signal like a line-level signal, although it may need to be boosted a bit to bring it up to true line level.

I've spoken of signal level in terms of voltage so far, but actually, recording engineers rarely use voltage to describe signal levels. More often, they use the decibel—the same unit to describe sound intensity. But in this context, decibels aren't absolute as with sound (where an 80dB sound corresponds to a specific loudness that's more or less universally agreed upon). Regarding electrical signal levels, decibels are relative, meaning they describe a level as it compares to some other constant or standard level. For instance, in a digital recording program, everything is based on the maximum signal level allowable; a signal that reaches exactly that maximum can be described as 0dB—zero decibels—with lower levels described in negative numbers, such as –3dB or –10dB. (And you thought 0dB was *quiet!*) To complicate matters, engineers have invented different kinds of decibels, specifying them with a letter at the end of the abbreviation, such as dBV or dBu. I'll mention those again a little later, but don't worry too much about the distinctions between them.

Signal-To-Noise Ratios

Line level is the recording studio's "home base" type of signal level, so you generally want to bring mic- and instrument-level signals up to line level as early as possible in the signal chain. The weaker a signal is, the more susceptible it is to being corrupted by noise. If you intentionally added the same amount of noise to two signals—one weak and one strong—the strong one would be less affected by the noise, because when the weak signal (plus the added noise) is eventually amplified to match the stronger signal's level, the noise will be amplified, too. The *signal-to-noise ratio* is important in understanding this and anything having to do with noise. It's another decibel measurement, again of the relative kind: it expresses the *difference* in strength between the signal, meaning the good stuff, and the noise—the bad stuff. The higher the number (in decibels), the greater the difference between the signal and the noise—in other words, the less significant the noise is compared to what you want on your recording. We say a recording with a high signal-to-noise ratio is a *quiet* recording; one with a low ratio is a *noisy* recording. In studio contexts, "quiet" and "noisy" normally refer only to the noise, not the signal.

Naturally, in the studio, we like high signal-to-noise ratios, because unless your goal is actually to record noise (and sometimes it is), quieter is always better. For example, 90dB is a very good ratio, about what you get from a digital audio workstation. (If the 90dB figure sounds familiar, it's because I mentioned it earlier in the discussion of dynamic range. Dynamic range expresses how quiet a signal *can* be on a particular medium; signal-to-noise expresses how close you actually got to that ideal. If you did everything perfectly, both figures would be the same.) In making a good recording it's important to maximize the signal-to-noise ratio every step of the way, as we'll see.

Cable Types

Naturally, line-level signals need to be able to go from one place to another, such as from a mixing board to the digital interface that connects to your computer. But weak mic-level and instrument-level signals need to go from one place to another as well, because often a microphone or instrument doesn't contain a preamp. So, there are different kinds of cables to carry different kinds of signals—and they're all designed to prevent noise from being added to them.

The simplest type of cable is the kind that connects a table lamp to the wall outlet: two conductors—"hot" and "ground"—running right alongside each other. But a cable like this is useless for carrying audio. Why? Because, particularly around electronic equipment and fluorescent lights, there's energy constantly buzzing through the air at the same frequency as the alternating wall current (60Hz), often blended with harmonics or multiples of that frequency (120Hz, 180Hz, etc.). This energy tends to creep into wires, so it shouldn't surprise you that if this stuff gets into one of your studio cables, you'll hear an added 60Hz hum or buzz when the signal is turned back into sound. The longer the cable, the more likely this is to happen. This can destroy your precious signal-to-noise ratio, so it needs to be prevented.

Shielded cable is an effective way to do this. In this kind of cable, the ground conductor is in the form of a tube-like sheath that surrounds the hot conductor for the cable's entire length. When a cable is shielded, the ground conductor intercepts the 60-cycle-per-second hum so it never makes it to the hot conductor, and the signal remains pure and quiet. (Incidentally, the only type of audio cable that doesn't require shielding is the one that connects a power amplifier to a loudspeaker. Since it's in the last link of the signal chain, this signal will not be further amplified, so any noise picked up will not be audible.)

Shielded cable is fine for line-level signals and even not-too-long cables carrying instrument signals—but what about mic-level signals? These weak signals are extremely susceptible to being corrupted by noise, so even shielded cables won't cut it. The solution is a third conductor in what's known as a *balanced line*. A balanced line carries two copies of the signal: one on the hot conductor, and a mirror-image version of that signal on what's called the "cold" conductor. The third conductor is a shielded ground. If any 60Hz noise makes it past the ground (and a little bit always does), it goes into both the hot and cold conductors equally. At the end of the cable, the cold conductor's mirror image of the signal is flipped again and combined with the hot signal—and like magic, the noise on both lines cancels itself out (see Fig. 7). The balanced line is a brilliant invention! Guitarists will recognize this noise-fighting approach; it's similar to the way humbucking pickups work.

Most mic signals are carried along balanced lines, but not all; some cheaper mics use regular shielded cables. Try not to use mics like these; they're just too noisy—and anything that cheap will probably sound bad, anyway.

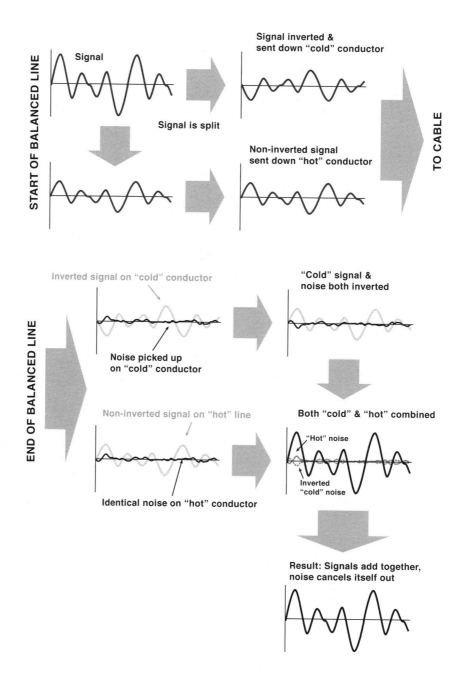

Fig. 7 At the start of a balanced line, the signal is split, and one of the two conductors is phase-inverted (top). At the other end of the cable (bottom), the inverted side is reversed again. When the two sides are then re-combined, noise picked up along the cable's run cancels itself out.

Plugs & Jacks

As there are different types of cables in the studio, there are different types of plugs (the "male" ends of cables) and jacks (the "female" sockets that accept plugs). Collectively, plugs and jacks are known as connectors (see Fig. 8).

1/4" connectors. The bread-and-butter of home-studio connector schemes, the ¼" plug and jack are also archaically called "phone" connectors, because they were originally developed for telephone operators. The inputs and outputs of most semi-pro (and some pro) studio gear use ¼" connectors. They're easy to use, and shielded cables with ¼" connectors are widely available as guitar cables or higher-quality studio cables. You should always have plenty of these available, of different lengths—they'll always come in handy.

1/4" TRS connectors. TRS stands for "tip-ring-sleeve," describing the parts of the plug itself. These connectors can accommodate three conductors. You see them on headphone cables—that's one hot conductor for the left channel, one hot conductor for the right, and a single ground conductor for both sides. If you ever need to split the signal coming from one stereo jack into the two separate channels (and this is the kind of thing that can happen in the Guerrilla studio), you'll need a "Y" adapter. These often have two standard ¼" jacks along with the one ¼" TRS plug. Radio Shack sells them, but the ones sold in music stores tend to be more reliable. Over the years I've gone through many Radio Shack "Y" adapters that eventually crapped out.

Another common place you'll find TRS connectors is on a mixing board's insert section (see Chapter 3). A TRS jack can send *and* receive two different signals at the same time: it sends a signal on one hot conductor and receives another signal on a second hot conductor, with the third serving as a ground for both. Again, to use one of these jacks, you'll need a "Y" adapter, although there are also "Y" cables made just for this purpose. In either case, one end of the fork goes to a jack that spits out a signal, and the other goes to a jack that takes in a signal.

Since they have three conductors, ¼" TRS connectors can also form the end of balanced-line cables. Some balanced cables have a ¼" TRS plug on one side and an XLR (see below) male or female plug on the other. These allow you to send signals, for example, from a DI or preamp to a digital recording device's balanced ¼" analog input.

1/8" connectors. Also called "mini" or "mini-phone" plugs and jacks, these are the kind found on an iPod or Sony Walkman. As with ¼" connectors, if they're dealing with a stereo signal, they'll be of the TRS variety. You'll want to stock up on adapters

Fig. 8 Left to right: A standard ¼" plug, ¼" TRS plug, ⅛" plug, RCA plug, and XLR plug.

that go from ¼" to ⅛" and back, both TRS (they do exist) and regular. For instance, if you wanted to split an iPod's stereo signal into left and right, you could plug a ⅛"-TRS-male-to-¼"-TRS-female adapter into it, and then plug a ¼" TRS "Y" cable into the adapter. Some headphones have built-in ¼"-to-⅛" adapters that snap or screw on, enabling you to use them on different kinds of equipment, large and small. Of course, as a Guerrilla recordist you can use one of these as an adapter for other functions—just don't lose it!

RCA connectors. Also occasionally called *phono* or *coaxial* connectors, these are widely used on consumer stereo and video equipment, as well as on some older semi-pro studio gear. An RCA plug consists of a small rod surrounded by a sleeve. Even if you have no RCA connectors in your studio, they can still serve a function: Shielded consumer cables with RCA plugs on both ends are a lot cheaper than cables with ¼" plugs, and if you find yourself short a cable or two, they're as near as the local Radio Shack or Circuit City. They conveniently come in lengths of three feet, six feet, and longer. And since they're usually stereo, they're two cables in one—just stick on four RCA-female-to-¼"-male adapters, and you've got a handy double-cable for about ten bucks. Tripled cables (for audio + video), and even quadrupled cables, are available as well, and you can chain them together with RCA-female-to-RCA-female connectors. Those always come in handy, so buy a bunch. You can never have too many adapters in the Guerrilla studio.

XLR connectors. This is the standard plug and jack for microphones and mic cables. Unlike most cables, those with XLR connectors usually have one male end and one female end, so they can be easily daisy-chained. Balanced XLR connections are also preferred on pro gear, even for line-level signals. Some mixing boards offer XLR balanced master outputs, but unless you're feeding a power amplifier or powered speakers with built-in balanced XLR or ¼" connectors, stick with the unbalanced ¼" outs.

There are also such things as XLR-to-unbalanced-¼" adapters, but these incorporate extra components (transformers) that change the signal's electrical properties. This may or may not audibly affect the signal, depending on the situation.

 Speaker Cables

Just because a cable looks like a shielded cable, it might not be one. Except when you're connecting a power amplifier to a speaker, never use a cable with SPEAKER CABLE printed on it. These are heavy-duty cables that aren't shielded, so they're very susceptible to noise. Conversely, never use an instrument cable to connect a power amp to a speaker; it's not built to take strong current and could overheat and melt.

Nominal Operating Levels

In a couple of places I've mentioned the terms "semi-pro gear" and "pro gear." I'm not making arbitrary value judgments here; these are actually two established divisions of audio equipment. Whether a piece of gear is considered "pro" or "semi-pro" (the latter is also sometimes lumped in with stereo-store "consumer" gear) depends on something called its *nominal operating level*. This refers to the maximum voltage at which its circuitry is designed to operate. Think of it as the difference between a professional race car and a regular sports car: Pro-level gear is designed to run at "hotter" internal signal levels than semi-pro gear, so the potential signal-to-noise ratio is greater on pro gear than on semi-pro. The specification used to describe pro gear's nominal operating level is +4dBu (often informally referred to simply as "+4"), and the spec for semi-pro is –10dBV (or just –10). (The letters *u* and *V* after dB specify exactly what kind of decibel it is.) I mention the numbers only so you'll recognize them in ads and user manuals. Suffice it to say that pro gear runs "hotter" than semi-pro gear—electrically speaking, that is, not necessarily temperature-wise.

Some gear allows you to specify whether you want it to operate at +4 or –10. My mixing board, for instance, has a switch on the back for this purpose. I leave it set to -10, because pretty much everything else in my studio operates at –10. With the switch set here, the board sends its stereo output through its unbalanced ¼" master-out jacks. However, there was a time when I needed to mix down to a professional-level DAT recorder, so I changed the switch to +4; this caused the board to send its stereo output through its balanced XLR master-out jacks instead. That worked out well, because the pro DAT deck had only XLR balanced inputs, which were designed to accept the hotter +4 levels.

Grounding & Loops

Everyone knows that some electrical wall outlets have two slots and some have the two slots plus a hole, and that the latter variety is said to be *grounded*. This is a little confusing, because earlier I said that "ground" is one of the two conductors in an audio-signal cable, but bear with me. Electrical power in the form of 110-volt alternating current comes out of one of the outlet slots, called "hot" (as in an audio-signal cable). The other slot, in the context of a home's electrical power, is called "neutral"; it serves the same function as the ground conductor in an audio-signal cable: it completes the circuit and provides a place for the hot conductor's electricity to return. The third conductor on a grounded outlet, called "ground" in this capacity, is normally not used—it provides an *alternate* path for electricity to travel in the event that something goes wrong with the circuit. This makes the outlet safer, because if there isn't a direct alternate path to ground (which, in many homes, leads to a long copper stake driven into the earth near the electric meter), a wayward electric current might have to go through you instead. Ouch.

So grounding is good, right? In terms of safety, definitely—but grounding can also cause annoyances in the studio. Most studio gear needs to be grounded (which is why the power cords' plugs have three prongs), but if you set up your studio in certain ways, this can cause pieces of gear to add that 60-cycle hum to the audio going through it. This hum can easily become unacceptably loud, and the uninformed recordist can go crazy trying to figure out how to get rid of it.

The cause of this mysterious hum is called a *ground loop*. Ground loops happen when there are two or more different paths to ground among all of your studio gear. For example, if you have a mixing board, computer, and effects rack all plugged into different outlets—and all of this stuff is connected together via audio cables—you're asking for ground loops to occur. This is particularly true if the outlets are connected to different electrical circuits in the building.

The key to preventing ground loops is to provide every piece of gear the same path to ground—for instance, by plugging everything into the same power strip. This technique is called "star grounding"—think of the electricity's source as the center of the star, with all of the power cables coming out of that one source. You may have learned that it isn't safe to plug so many things into one outlet. Except for power amplifiers and powered monitors, studio gear doesn't suck up that much power—not as much as, say, a toaster, a coffee maker, and a microwave oven all plugged in together. As long as your home's electrical system is reasonably up to date, it shouldn't be a problem. (I have never blown a fuse or tripped a breaker with my studio gear.)

Even if you practice star grounding, you can still have problems with hum. If you want to take an audio feed from a DVR, for example, you'll want to disconnect the cable-TV signal going into it. The cable's shielding provides a path to ground that's entirely independent from your home's grounding, so the audio from the DVR will hum like crazy if it stays connected. But sometimes you just cannot figure out why a piece of gear is humming. In that case, sometimes it's necessary to defeat the ground on that piece of gear by using a three-prong-to-two-slot grounding adapter. This should be a last resort, though, because it is potentially dangerous. When the ground is defeated this way, *you* become the only path to ground in the event that a problem develops with the neutral conductor—and that can be deadly.

Some pieces of gear (for instance, bass amplifiers with direct-out jacks) have "ground lift" switches on them. If you're having a problem with hum or even radio sounds coming from such a piece of gear, try flipping this switch. The noise may disappear like magic.

MIDI Basics

MIDI, which stands for Musical Instrument Digital Interface, is a protocol by which electronic instruments can "talk" to one another. MIDI's first attraction was that it allowed you to play multiple synthesizers with just one controller keyboard, and it was such a success, it immediately became an industry standard. MIDI allowed for the proliferation of the digital sequencer, a piece of hardware that recorded and played back MIDI data.

The robotic, perfectly timed rhythms of sequencers—which could be synchronized with drum machines, also then a fairly new invention—created a sound that's now forever identified with '80s music. Music has changed a lot since then (although some styles still retain that robotic feel), but MIDI is still a vital part of the recording studio.

A MIDI signal does not carry any audio data; rather, it specifies details about note-related events, for example: "note 71 on" (the keyboardist played a *B* above middle *C*), "velocity 125" (the note was played very hard), and "note 71 off" (the player released the key). This is cool, because unlike audio, which eats up a lot of hard-drive space, all of the MIDI for one song can fit into a very small computer file—maybe just 100 kilobytes or so. MIDI also allows you to record a performance and then completely change the instrument's sound afterward. Turning a piano solo into an organ solo can be as simple as changing the program on your synth—in terms of MIDI, the notes are the same regardless. It also allows you to change the performance after it's recorded, for instance changing the key, adding fills, etc., all without compromising the initial performance's quality. This allows for tons of after-the-fact flexibility—and flexibility is a very good thing in the Guerrilla studio.

Most home recordists record MIDI data using their regular audio-recording program. This typically means that during playback, the program is sending the data either to another program that generates audio (such as a software synth), or out of the computer to some kind of MIDI interface, which sends and receives data both

MIDI jacks, which allow pieces of electronic gear to communicate with each other, on (top to bottom) a keyboard, MIDI interface, multi-effect, and drum controller.

from the computer and from external pieces of gear (synths, drum machines, etc.). The manner in which you set up MIDI in your studio is beyond the scope of this book; it varies widely and can get quite complicated if you're coordinating numerous pieces of external hardware with several software programs. There are plenty of resources out there to help you choose and configure your MIDI gear. In Chapter 8 I'll explain how you can harness MIDI's flexibility not only to make your recordings sound more "real," but also to make you sound like a better musician than you really are.

CHAPTER 3

A Guided Tour Of The Signal Chain

In order to wrap your brain around the principles of recording, it helps to think in terms of the *signal chain*. This term describes the path that an audio signal (or electrical sound waves, if you prefer) takes in your studio as it goes from its originating source to a version that's fixed on a recording medium (such as a compact disc). A common and useful way to visualize this path is to imagine the signal as water flowing through a series of pipes. Of course, this is just a visualization aid; as we saw in Chapter 2, electrons in an alternating-current audio signal don't actually flow like water, but in effect, a signal does flow from one place to another in the form of waves. We say the signal travels *down* the signal chain (the way water flows downhill), and we may speak of an effect box *downstream* (later in the signal chain) or a mic preamp *upstream* (earlier in the chain).

Gain Staging

Recall from Chapter 2 that unless you're intentionally recording noise, you always want signal-to-noise ratios to be as high as possible: more signal, less noise. This means that at any particular point in the signal chain, you'll get the best results if you make the signal as "hot" (high in level) as possible without causing distortion at that point (see Fig. 1). But equally important, you also have to make sure your hot level isn't creating distortion at any point downstream in the chain. Complicating this is the fact that a signal chain is made up of *stages*, with signal amplification or attenuation occurring at each stage. A signal's level can go up several times in different stages of your chain, and it can also go down at certain stages, and perhaps up again later still. As a recording engineer, your job is to properly manage the signal-to-noise ratio at every stage of the signal chain—making sure the signal is hot enough to keep noise at bay, but not so hot as to create distortion in that stage or in any stage downstream. This management process is called *gain staging*, "gain" referring to the amplification (or attenuation, which is negative gain) that occurs at each stage.

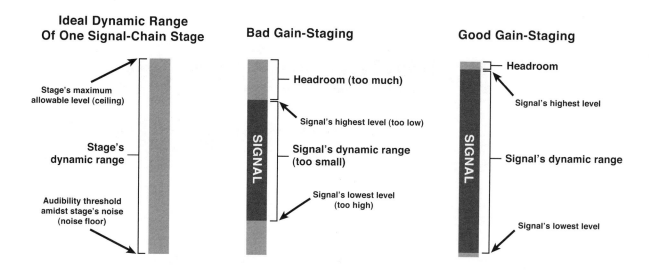

Fig. 1 Good gain-staging means making the most of each stage's ideal dynamic range (left). At center, a signal's dynamic range is much too small for the stage it's passing through. The signal is both too weak and too noisy—too much headroom remains at the top, and the signal's noise level is well above the noise floor. Result: A noisy recording with little dynamic impact. At right, the signal's dynamic range is much larger—almost, but not quite, as large as the stage's. Result: A clean recording with maximum impact.

If gain-staging is new to you, it might sound like a lot of work—but it quickly becomes second nature, something you do automatically whenever you set up a signal chain or change an existing one.

Let's follow the path a signal might take in a Guerrilla studio—first in a tracking session, and then in a mixing session.

Microphones

Sound waves in the air need to be converted to electrical waves in order for us to do anything with them. The microphone is our tool to do this. Microphones come in several varieties. A *dynamic* microphone is the oldest design: basically, it consists of a wire coil suspended in a magnetic field. When sound waves strike the coil, the coil moves along with the sound waves, like a cork in the ocean. You may remember from high-school physics that when a wire coil moves in a magnetic field, a current is induced in the coil. If the coil moves one way, electrons in the coil flow in one direction; when the coil moves back, the electrons reverse direction. Because of this effect, the flow of electrons in the coil matches the coil's physical movement, generating a small AC current in the coil—one that's analogous to the sound waves in the air. So the sound has been converted to an analog electrical audio signal.

Dynamic mics are durable and can handle high SPLs (sound-pressure levels)—meaning they're great for loud sounds—but one problem is that the coil has a certain size and mass, which makes it not terribly sensitive to the tiniest sound waves: high frequencies. Since the highest frequencies are responsible for "air" or "transparency" in certain sounds, dynamic mics aren't the best at capturing these qualities in sounds that are rich in the highest harmonics. For that task, we turn to another class of mics: *condenser* mics. In a condenser mic, a tiny plate is given an electrical charge, and any physical changes in the plate (as a result of encountering sound waves) create a tiny current—an electrical audio signal. Unlike a dynamic mic, a condenser mic requires electricity, a power source, to operate. This is necessary to create the charge in the audio-sensing plate, and also to amplify the signal coming from the plate. (It's considerably weaker than a dynamic mic's signal and needs to be brought up in level just so it can be sent through a mic cable.) This power source can be an internal battery or *phantom power*, which is a steady direct current—usually 9 to 48 volts—sent to a microphone over its own cable. (Because phantom power is a fixed, direct current, rather than a current that's alternating at a specific frequency, it doesn't interfere with the audio signal coming from the mic.) Many mixing boards and mic preamps provide phantom power: You plug in a mic cable and flip a switch, and phantom power is sent up the cable to the mic. If you don't have a device that offers phantom power, and battery power isn't an option, you can purchase a standalone unit to power your mic. Some microphones—particularly expensive tube mics—come with their own power supply that takes care of this.

Choosing A Mic

So when do you use a dynamic mic, and when do you use a condenser? It depends on the sound you're recording. When choosing, think about each type's characteristics versus the sound you're capturing. Is the sound loud? How bright is it? In your song, are the subtleties of the sound critical, or should it convey force and power? For instance, vocals are almost always recorded with condenser mics; they're a major focal point in a song, so you want to capture every detail, and the "air" at the top of a vocal's frequency range adds to its intimacy and emotional impact. A crunching guitar amplifier, though, is best captured with a dynamic mic, which provides more low-end punch and is less likely to distort under loud conditions. Even if you lose a bit of the highs, that's okay—other instruments have plenty of highs, so listeners may never know what they're missing.

In addition to dynamic vs. condenser, mics are classified by another factor, their *directional pattern* (see Fig. 2). A mic can be *omnidirectional*, or "omni," meaning it's equally sensitive to sounds coming physically from the front (straight into the mic) as from the sides and rear. *Directional* or *cardioid* mics, which are more common in studios, are most sensitive to sounds coming from the front ("on-axis" sounds), less sensitive to sounds coming from the sides, and least sensitive to sounds coming from the rear (the latter two called "off-axis" sounds). Cardioid mics are a good choice, because we Guerrilla recordists care only about the source of the sound—not the room's sound. Another pattern is called *hypercardioid*, which is similar to cardioid but even more directional. Some mics (such as the perennially popular) allow you to

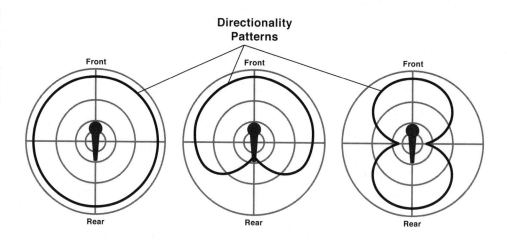

Directionality Patterns

Fig. 2 Omnidirectional (left), cardioid (center), and figure-8 (right) directional mic patterns. Notice that the cardioid mic doesn't pick up sounds that are directly behind it.

switch patterns. The 414 includes a less-common figure-8 pattern, which is equally sensitive from the front and back but rejects sound coming from the sides. This is a good choice if you're recording vocals with another person: one of you stands in front of the mic and the other stands behind.

So, let's say you've hooked up a microphone to a balanced-line cable by way of its XLR connectors. You could plug the other end into a dedicated mic preamp, but let's assume you're like most Guerrilla recordists and don't have an external mic preamp. In that case you'd probably plug into a mixing board and use one of the board's mic preamps to bring the signal up to line level. (If you're recording straight into your computer by way of a digital audio interface and no board, sit tight—I'll discuss that scenario later. But don't skip over the stuff about hardware mixing boards. You'll be much better able to understand a virtual console if you know how a real board works.)

LOOK ■ OUT!

USB Microphones

Some microphones are designed to be plugged directly into a computer via the USB interface. This kind of mic may be tempting, as it allows you to record digitally without the need for a mic preamp, digital audio interface, or mixer. But there's a problem with USB mics: In order to plug directly into a computer, it first needs to convert the analog sound into digital data. Analog-to-digital conversion is a delicate process, one best left to a device actually manufactured for this purpose (as opposed to built into a $100 microphone). Perhaps more important, it's critical to be able to set the levels of the stage immediately before the A-to-D conversion, to reduce noise and prevent digital distortion. Unless the USB mic has a level control and a level meter, this is impossible. You don't know where in the mic's dynamic range your levels are, or how close you are to distortion, until the distortion happens—so it's like you're flying blind. Guesswork like this makes gain-staging nearly impossible and drives amateur recordists crazy. My advice is to avoid using a USB mic unless it's all you've got.

Mixer Channel Inputs

Here's where we begin a close look at the mixing board (a.k.a. the console or "desk"), the studio's equivalent of Grand Central Station. It's certainly possible to record on a computer without a mixing board, but as I alluded to in Chapter 1, having one allows you to use hardware effects. Plus, sometimes it's nice to get your hands on a physical knob or fader rather than tweaking an onscreen one with a mouse. With the takeover of digital recording in home studios, some people now consider mixing boards obsolete and are getting rid of them for cheap—so if you see a great deal on one, jump on it.

I love the way people react when they see my 24-channel board, with its hundreds of seemingly identical knobs. They think I must be a genius—or at least a mad scientist—to know how to operate it. But a mixing board is easy to understand if you break it down into its components. A board has a number of vertically oriented *input channels*, each of which is divided into a number of sections with separate functions (see Fig. 3). The board processes these channels separately, and then it blends them to two (or more) output channels. Mixing boards are designed to make sense: A signal starts at the top (meaning the part farthest away as you stand in front) and "flows" toward you, section by section, so that's how we'll look at an input channel's various components.

The journey of a signal within the board, naturally, begins with the inputs. Input jacks vary from board to board, but most boards have at least one ¼" input jack, and usually an XLR jack, at the top of each channel. Older models may have RCA jacks in addition to, or instead of, the ¼" jacks. In most cases the ¼" jack represents the channel's input for line-level sources (i.e., its line input), but since the output of units like synthesizers and drum machines are close to line level (and usually have ¼" output jacks), this is where these signals normally enter the board. The channel's XLR jack is for an incoming microphone signal or a signal from a direct box—more on that in a moment. Ordinarily, a switch determines which jack is active; if you're plugging in a microphone, the appropriate setting might be labeled mic in.

Powering Up Phantom Power

Get into the habit of switching on the board's phantom power *after* the board is switched on and the mic is connected. Due to possible electrical surges, it may be bad for the mic if you power up your board with a mic already connected and the phantom power on, or to plug the mic into a powered-up mixer with the phantom power already flowing. The safest power-up order to follow is: (1) Turn on the mixer with the mic disconnected, (2) make sure the phantom power is off, (3) plug in the mic, and (4) switch on the phantom power. When you're done with the session, turn off the phantom power first; then it's safe to disconnect the mic and/or shut down the board.

Many boards have an additional tape input jack on each input channel, along with a switch that selects between mic/line and tape (or something similar). This allows the channel to have different roles during the tracking and mixing phases of recording. During tracking, you might set this switch to mic/line and use the mic or line input jacks as appropriate. Then, during mixing, you might set these switches to tape and feed your digital audio interface's (or multitrack's) outputs into the tape input jacks. This is convenient, because you can leave the interface's outputs permanently plugged into the tape inputs and use them only when you need to. If you have enough board channels, you can dedicate certain channels to the interface's outputs and use the others for tracking. If you don't have this luxury, though, you'll be doing a lot less plugging and unplugging by taking advantage of the board's tape inputs and switches.

Maximize Your Levels At The Source

Anytime you're recording an electronic sound-producing device (synth, drum machine, etc.), make sure its volume control is turned all the way up. If it isn't, you'll need to bring up the level later in the signal chain—and that means any noise picked up along the way, such as in the cable or at the input stage itself, will be boosted along with the signal. Assuming the manufacturer hasn't made a product that can accidentally self-distort (which would be pretty lame), there's no risk in turning it up full blast. In the unlikely case that the unit does self-distort (i.e., if you can hear the distortion even when you plug your headphones directly into the unit) just use trial and error, getting the most undistorted sound out of the unit that you can.

Break The Rules!

Many years ago, I got a great "bass" sound by detuning a guitar's bottom strings and overloading the hell out of the mixer's input. That board didn't have XLR mic inputs—just ¼" ins with a switch for mic-level signals. That's the position I chose, with the pad knob cranked all the way up. I picked the "bass" line hard, the overload LED lit up bright, and I got a great, wacky fuzz tone that was very useful after a little EQing.

Even though the "rules" are here to help you get a clean sound for most audio applications, sometimes you can get amazing sounds by just throwing the rules to the wind and simply abusing your equipment. Use common sense—don't plug a guitar amp's speaker output into a mixer's mic input—but know that on most occasions, your gear can handle it. Remember that you won't know what an unusual, unorthodox recording technique sounds like unless you give it a try. In many cases it will sound like crap, but on the occasion that it works artistically, the result can be magic.

Gain-Staging At The Inputs

Setting up the input stage is critical—it's the board's "first impression" of a signal, and if the signal gets screwed up there, it will remain screwed up for the rest of its journey, all the way to CD. To help you, most if not all boards have a knob, switch, or both for setting the input's sensitivity to the incoming signal. Here's your first chance to practice gain-staging: no matter what the signal is, you want to bring it up to line level right there. The input-sensitivity knob is called the *trim pot*. ("Pot" is short for potentiometer, the electronic component that the knob is physically connected to.) If there's a switch, it's called the *pad*. If a signal is too strong for the input, you need to *pad down* or *trim* (attenuate) the signal. How do you know if it's too strong? Well, if it is overloading the input and distorting, it's too strong. Most boards have an LED on each channel to indicate input overload; it might be labeled OL or PEAK, and it might be located at the top of the board (in the input section) or farther down. On my board, in addition to the red OL LED, there's a green LED labeled –20DB, which lights up when a signal entering that channel is 20dB below the overload point. When that green LED just barely lights, I know I have 20dB to spare before I run into problems with overloading the input. If your board doesn't have these input indication LEDs, you'll just have to use your ears. Headphones are a useful tool for listening closely to hear whether distortion is setting in—but usually if a mixer input is overloading, it's immediately obvious.

Let's say you are using the channel as a mic input. Plug the microphone cable into an XLR input, assuming your board has them; if not, you'll need to use a transformer adapter. If the mic is phantom-powered, turn on the board's phantom power. If the board lacks phantom power, you'll have to use an external phantom-power device, or switch to a mic that uses battery power or comes with its own power supply. Or, you can use a dynamic mic.

Once you're sure the mic is active—here's where a green –20dB LED comes in handy—shout "check!" into the mic a little louder than you think you'll get in the performance you're about to record. If you're recording something else, like a guitar amp, play a little louder than you will during the recording. Now, as you do this, watch the overload LED. If it lights already, turn down the trim pot a little and try again. If the trim pot is down all the way and the input is still overloading, you'd better hope there's a switch that will add another level of pad; if not, you won't be able to record that source with that mic unless you put something in between the mic and board to cut the signal. Fortunately, unless you have a *really* crappy mixing board, this is unlikely to ever happen.

If, however, your mic signal is not overloading the input on your first mic check, grab that trim control and turn it up a little. Keep going and see if you can get the input to overload. If it does, back off the knob about one-twelfth of a turn—that's one "hour" if you think of the knob's position as a clock's hour hand. (If you hear someone say something like "turn the knob to 3 o'clock," this is what they mean.) In the case

Fig. 3 A typical mixing-board input channel. A signal starts at the top and "flows" downward toward the fader.

What Is Distortion?

The term "distortion" appears all the time in relation to recording. Distortion refers to the alteration of a sound wave's shape as it passes through a circuit: Something goes in, and something different comes out. Usually, distortion refers specifically to a flattening-out of the peaks in a waveform; this is sometimes called "clipping," because it's as if the tops and bottoms of the wave shape are being clipped off. In this diagram, a sine wave (a) is boosted just beyond the point of clipping (b), and then it's boosted some more (c). Even if the signal is subsequently brought back down to its original level, the waveform's shape has changed drastically (d).

There are two types of distortion in recording: good and bad. Good distortion is a controlled effect that guitar and bass players get by overdriving an amplifier, or by putting their signal through an amp-modeling device. (More about this type of distortion in Chapter 6.) Bad distortion is unwanted distortion, usually caused by the misuse of electronics in the signal chain. When a circuit encounters a signal whose strength exceeds the circuit's capabilities, the circuit is unable to pass the signal through faithfully. It tends to clip off the extremes of the wave shape, which changes the sound, usually for the worse. Part of gain staging is making sure this never happens, so that your signal remains clean and true—and is distorted only where you want it to be.

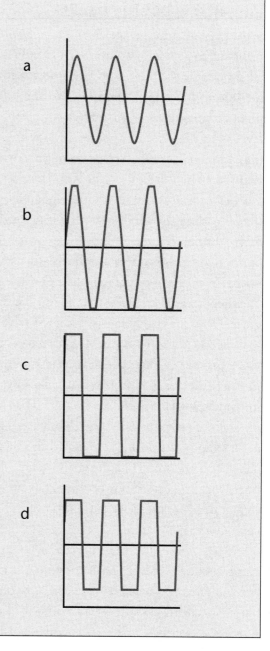

of input overload, safe is definitely better than sorry. You don't want to be singing the vocal performance of a lifetime, only to have it ruined by a blat of distortion at your peak moment. Similar to what I said in Chapter 2 regarding digital recording levels, shoot for sending a *moderately hot* signal to the mixer's next stage. You definitely don't want the input to distort, but you don't want it to be 20dB below distortion, either. If you're –20dB here, you're losing 20dB of your signal-to-noise ratio right off the bat. Why? Because eventually you *will* need to bring that signal up by 20dB to line level, and in doing so, you'll boost the noise floor 20dB higher than it needs to be. And in the recording world, 20dB of noise is a lot—especially when it could have been prevented with a quick, simple pre-recording procedure.

If you're recording a synth, drum machine, or some other near-line-level device, use the ¼" input and the exact same procedure. The levels of electronic sources are more predictable than miked-up acoustic sources, so you can afford to get a slightly hotter signal from them without worrying about mixer-input overload. Still, make sure the biggest, loudest keyboard chord or drum fill in your song doesn't distort the input.

Before we go on to the mixer channel's next section, let's step back a bit and consider another source: the direct input.

Direct-Input Instruments

In the mid 1960s, engineers discovered something interesting: Electric guitars and basses could be recorded "direct," meaning straight out of the instrument, without an amplifier. Up to that point, all instruments—including instruments that had to be plugged into amplifiers—had been recorded with microphones only. It was revolutionary to eliminate the middleman: Instead of plugging a bass into an amplifier, and then miking up that amp to get the sound back into the electrical realm, you could plug the bass straight into the mixing board, resulting in a very clean, predictable sound. This technique required the invention of the direct box, one of the pieces of gear mentioned in Chapter 1. Without getting too technical, a direct box—also called a *DI*, short for either direct input or direct injection (depending on whom you ask)—makes the translation between the guitar's electronics and the mixer input's electronics. To hear what it sounds like to record direct without a direct box, try plugging a guitar or bass straight into the mixer input's ¼" jack, and listen through headphones. Pretty crappy sound, right? All the highs get rolled off when you do this, and you usually

| | **INSTRUMENT TYPE** | |
	Passive	**Active**
DIRECT BOX TYPE — Passive	Neither instrument nor DI can self-distort	Instrument can self-distort and can also distort DI
DIRECT BOX TYPE — Active	Instrument cannot self-distort and cannot distort DI, but DI can self-distort	Instrument can self-distort, and can also distort DI; DI can self-distort as well

Fig. 4 With an electric instrument and a direct box, the possibilities for unwanted distortion depend on whether each is active (battery-powered) or passive.

don't want to start off with a sound that's been compromised so much. A direct box allows all of the instrument's frequencies to pass through to the next stage, the same way a guitar amp's own input is designed to work.

A typical direct box has a ¼" input jack to accommodate a guitar cable, and a balanced XLR output jack for a mic cable. Treat the signal coming out of a direct box the same way you would treat a mic signal: plug the cable into either a mic input on the board or an outboard mic preamp if you have one. The signal will likely be stronger than a mic's, so you may need to turn down the channel's trim pot to prevent overload. And speaking of overload, it's possible to overload the direct box *itself* if your guitar or bass has a built-in preamp, or if the direct box contains its own preamp. Electronics such as those in a guitar or direct box can be classified as either active or passive. Active electronics require a power source to operate (usually a battery) and include some kind of amplification circuit; passive electronics require no power. The difference shouldn't be terribly important to you, except that if you know a circuit is active, the circuit is capable of overloading itself. So an active direct box, even when fed by an instrument with passive electronics (e.g., an electric guitar with standard pickups and no internal preamp), can self-distort. But a passive direct box, when fed by a passive instrument, will never be overloaded, no matter how hard you play. (See Fig. 4.)

We say that a circuit incapable of self-distorting has unlimited *headroom*—headroom is the word that describes the loud end of the dynamic range. (Not surprisingly, headroom is kind of the opposite of the noise floor.) But as soon as an active circuit enters the picture, the headroom has a definite limit, and you need to keep your signal under this threshold. How do you know where this threshold lies? In the case of a direct box that has no kind of overload indicator, you have to use your ears. It's as simple as that. If you're playing guitar, slam an open *E* chord and listen for distortion on headphones. If you're playing bass, pound the open *E* with your thumb or pop the *G* string. The resulting sound should be clean and full, not gritty or grainy. If you do hear distortion, turn down the instrument's master volume knob and try again; if the direct box itself has knobs, try tweaking those instead. Find a setting where you're certain you won't overload the circuit while you're fully rocking out, but not so much that you'll have to amplify your signal—and the noise—greatly in the next stage.

Mixer Inserts

Most decent mixing boards provide an *insert* jack, usually a ¼" TRS jack, somewhere near each channel's inputs. The idea behind inserts is that plugging something into the jack breaks the signal chain at that point, in effect "siphoning" or "shunting" the signal away. Insert jacks are incredibly convenient; I don't know how I could record without them. Inserts are kind of like the effect-loop send and return jacks on guitar amplifiers: they allow you to grab the line-level signal, run it through external processing gear, and then return it to the main circuit to continue on. This external processing gear can be anything you need for a particular task (see Fig. 5).

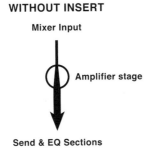

WITHOUT INSERT

Mixer Input

Amplifier stage

Send & EQ Sections

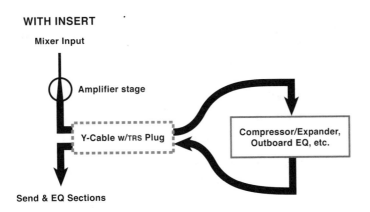

WITH INSERT

Mixer Input

Amplifier stage

Y-Cable w/TRS Plug

Compressor/Expander, Outboard EQ, etc.

Send & EQ Sections

Fig. 5 An insert point breaks into the signal chain with a single ¼" TRS plug, allowing you to shunt the signal out of the board for external processing. A "Y" adapter, along with the TRS plug, provides both outgoing and returning paths for the insert.

Why are inserts necessary at all? Couldn't you just process the signal before it even gets to the mixing board? Maybe—but for best results, you should always bring all incoming signals to line level as early in the chain as possible. If you don't, you'll have to feed the external processing gear a weaker signal, resulting in the potential for additional problems (if it's even possible; few outboard processors accept mic-level signals with XLR jacks). The mixing board's input section is the best tool for the job of collecting a variety of inputs and bringing them all up to line level. That's what it's for—use it!

When I'm tracking, I use the insert on practically every signal that goes into my board. After trying numerous approaches, I've settled on using the insert to run the signal through a compressor/expander (see Chapter 4) followed by a 31-band graphic EQ, which is normally set to bypass mode. This way the graphic EQ is essentially out of the circuit, but it's instantly available should the need arise. So, I have one TRS "Y" adapter, which is connected to my compressor/expander/EQ sub-chain, hanging around the back of the board ready to be stuck into an insert jack. During tracking I usually use only one or two board channels as inputs, so this "Y" adapter usually remains in place in one of the insert jacks. If I need to take the insert sub-chain out of the main signal chain, or if I need to use the sub-chain on a different channel, or if I'm mixing a song and I need to run one of the channels through the sub-chain again, I can just yank the adapter out of its "home" and plug it into a different insert jack.

As you can see, the insert is a convenient option anytime you need to stick an external electronic circuit somewhere into the middle of the signal chain.

One last point about inserts: An insert is a proper signal-chain stage and should be treated as such. Amplification may very well be going on somewhere in the insert sub-chain, so watch your gain-staging to avoid unwanted distortion or undue noise. If you're close to running out of headroom at the input stage, it's certainly possible to overload the main signal chain's next stage with just a slight boost in the insert sub-chain. Most external effect devices have a master-out level control as well as a bypass switch, so a good way to gain-stage in the sub-chain is to bypass the effect(s), watch the board's meters, and compare the resulting signal with the non-bypassed version. If you find that a sub-chain device is boosting the signal level, turn down its master-output control until it more closely matches the bypassed version. If there is more than one device in the insert sub-chain, perform this procedure for each, in the order that the signal flows. The good news is that this is pretty much a "set it and forget it" situation; I haven't had to tweak the output levels in my insert sub-chains for years. But be aware that there's always potential for trouble in the sub-chain. For example, to prevent distortion from happening after the signal gets a radical EQ boost, try to cut some frequencies to balance the ones you're boosting—that way, the overall level won't be very different. (Remember that low frequencies carry more energy than high ones.)

Effect Sends

On most boards, after the inputs and/or inserts you'll find the effect send (sometimes called aux send) section. An effect send is kind of like a partial insert. Instead of interrupting the signal chain and shunting away the signal entirely, an effect send takes only a portion of the signal to be used for some purpose, usually to send to an external effect whose sound will be mixed back in at some later point in the chain. Actually, though, "takes" isn't an accurate word here, because an effect send doesn't remove any of the main signal; the signal remains unchanged as it passes through the effect-send section. (See Fig. 6.) Imagine if a water engineer could build a dam that diverted some of a river's water into a pipe without reducing the river's flow downstream—that's exactly what an effect send is like.

Fig. 6 In an effect send, the channel's signal gets duplicated for some purpose at a specific level, as determined by the knob. The main signal passes through the circuit unchanged.

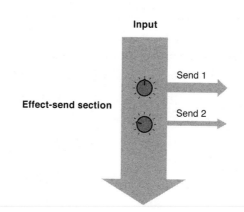

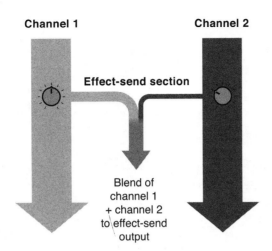

Channel 1

Channel 2

Effect-send section

Blend of
channel 1
+ channel 2
to effect-send
output

Fig. 7 When the same effect sends on two different channels are turned up, they both contribute to a blend at that send's output jack.

Most mixing boards have at least one row of effect-send knobs (one send per channel), and they usually have a master effect-send knob off to the right of all the input channels, as well as an effect-send output jack on the board's back. If your board has two, three, or more rows of send knobs, each row probably has its own master send knob and output jack. More rows of effect sends means more flexibility—but for simplicity's sake, let's assume for now that your board has just one row. If a signal is coming down channel 1 and that channel's effect-send knob is turned all the way down, there will be no signal at the effect-send jack. But turn it up a little, and a low-level version of the channel's signal will begin to come out of the jack. As you turn up the effect-send knob, the signal at the effect-send jack will get louder. Now imagine that a different signal starts coming through channel 2 as well: if you turn up channel 2's effect-send knob, the effect-send jack will have a blend of the signals coming through channels 1 and 2. (See Fig. 7.) The proportion of the signals in this blend depends on where the effect-send knobs are set; if you want more channel 1, turn the channel 1 knob higher than channel 2's. Typically, you send this blend to an external effect—reverb, for instance—and since you rarely want reverb added equally to all instruments, you use the effect-send knobs to determine which channels get a lot of reverb, which get only a little, and which get none at all. The master effect-send knob sets the overall level so you can get the right amount of signal going into your effect device—not enough to overload it, but enough to keep its signal-to-noise ratio high. (Does this sound familiar?) You *could* set this level by turning all of the individual effect-send knobs up or down by the same amount, but if a lot of channels are involved, this quickly becomes a headache. The master knob just makes life a little easier.

As I mentioned, most boards have more than one row of effect sends. (You might read that a board has "four effect sends"; that means four sends per channel, not four knobs overall.) If you have only one external effect, more sends won't really help you. But you can create some very nice spatial sounds by having two different reverbs

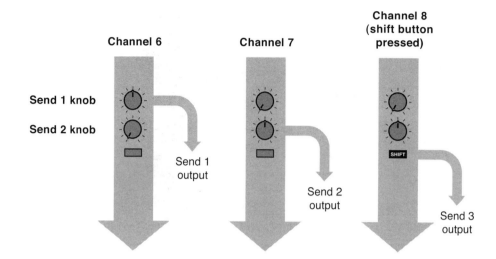

Fig. 8 A shift button next to a send causes that send's signal to go to a different output, effectively creating three independent send mixes from only two rows of knobs.

going at once during a mixdown, which pretty much requires two sends to accomplish (although you could get around it with some creative rigging). Still, you can make an excellent mix with just one good reverb and careful use of those individual effect-send knobs. More on how to use reverb in Chapter 6.

One clever feature employed on some boards' effect-send sections is a "shift" button on each channel. This allows you to split, say, two rows of effect sends into three: Depressing the shift button causes one of the two effect sends to pass a signal to a third master send knob and output. (See Fig. 8.) By shifting the sends on only some of the board's channels, you can create three entirely independent effect-send blends with only two rows of effect-send knobs. (Of course, each channel can contribute to only two of these blends—one for each send knob.) If a board has four sends, a shift button may split them into six.

If you send a signal to an external effect, at some point it has to return to the main signal chain, right? That's where *effect returns* come in. But effect returns are usually located at the end of the board's signal chain, so we'll get to those a little later.

Pre/Post Switches

I mentioned that in a mixing board, a channel's components are generally laid out in the order that the signal flows. While that's true for the most part, a switch labeled "pre/post" (or just "pre") can change the order of the components in the chain. This switch, typically found in the send section, lets you choose *where* in the signal chain the send happens. If it's on the default setting, called post-fader, the send signal is actually taken at the end of the channel's signal chain, after the last component, the fader (discussed below). If you set an effect send to pre-fader, though, the send is taken before the signal is turned up or down by the fader at the end (see Fig. 9). In pre-fader mode, changing the signal's level at the fader won't change the level going to your effect. For example, if you have a vocal coming through the channel and the

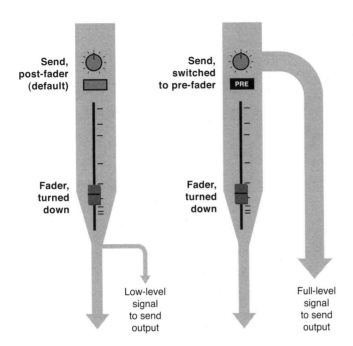

effect send is feeding a reverb, pushing the "pre" button lets you fade out the vocal until nothing is left but pure reverb. But if you want the reverb level to follow the signal's overall level (which is preferable in most cases), set the effect send to post-fader. That way, bringing down the fader will also bring down the level going to your reverb—instant reverb fade, perfectly matched to your vocal fade.

EQ Section

We don't need to pause here for long, because we discussed EQ in Chapter 2. You'll usually find the board's EQ section after the effect sends. The simplest (and least useful) board EQs have two knobs: high shelving and low shelving. If there's a third knob it's for mids, and if there's a fourth knob, it's probably for specifying the mid knob's center frequency. Some semi-pro mixing boards have as many as seven EQ knobs: high, low, high-mid, high-mid frequency, high-mid Q (bandwidth), low-mid, and low-mid frequency. If you paid attention to the previous chapter, you'd know that this means the highs and lows are the typical shelving types, the high-mids are fully parametric, and the low-mids are semi-parametric. This setup is highly flexible and rivals the EQ capabilities on pro boards—but I'm not going to tell you that you need to upgrade to a board with so many EQ knobs, because you don't. Having only shelving high and low EQs, plus a single semi-parametric (sweepable) mid, can work fine.

With a modern digital audio workstation and EQ plug-ins, though, you almost don't need any hardware EQ in your studio. But it's great to have available both software EQ and hardware EQ (either from an outboard device or from a mixing board), and hardware EQ won't sap any of your computer's CPU power to do its thing.

As with the insert sub-chain, you should regard a mixing board's EQ section as a proper gain stage as well: boosts here can create unwanted distortion in the next stage. Don't boost too much, try to cut frequencies as well where possible, listen closely (good headphones are always useful for detecting the first signs of signal breakup), and if you run into trouble, trim the signal a bit at the board's input stage. The price of a clean, quiet signal is eternal gain-staging vigilance!

Monitor Section

Not all boards have this section, which may be called something else (my board calls it "mix B"). A monitor section is similar to the effect-send section: it allows you to create at least one independent mix of the signals going through the board's input channels. However, unlike mono effect sends, the monitor section often lets you create a *stereo* mix that's separate from any other mix that the board might be creating. This is useful during tracking, especially if two musicians are playing at the same time: a bass player may want to hear more drums, while a singer may want to hear more guitar. Being able to set up two entirely different mixes allows you to give each musician what he or she wants. If you're recording a whole band live, you'll probably be using the board primarily to create a line-level signal of each instrument so they all can be recorded independently. But the musicians won't want to hear all the instruments up full in their headphones while they're playing, so the monitor section lets you set up a musician-friendly monitor mix without affecting the levels going to tape or disk. There are other ways to use the monitor section as well, even if you're recording by yourself; I'll get to them a bit later in this chapter.

Pan Pot & Fader

We've come almost to the bottom of the board as the signal travels down the channel; it will eventually have to go somewhere. Along with the assign switches (see below), the *pan pot* and *fader* determine where the signal goes, and how much will go. Mixing boards are generally manufactured to mix sound in stereo (two output channels, left and right), so we need to be able to tell the board how to distribute all of its various input channels between the left and right output channels. That's what a pan pot does: It specifies where in a two-channel stereo output—or any pair of channels, really—the individual signal should be placed. For instance, if you turn the pan pot all the way to the left, the signal will go only to the first of the two channels. If it's a stereo signal, we say the sound is "panned hard left." In this case, it will come out of the left speaker only.

The fader, right at the bottom of the board, is that all-important control that sets the signal's level as it leaves the channel. Think of it as an output valve: the higher it's set, the hotter the signal will be going to wherever it's going. Some faders are labeled arbitrarily, for example 0 through 10; others use decibel markings, with

0dB up around the three-quarter mark, positive numbers above 0dB, and negative numbers below. On these boards, you'll find $-\infty$dB at the very bottom, representing "signal completely off." The 0dB point represents what is called *unity gain*—it means the signal at this stage is neither boosted nor cut. It's merely passed through at the same level that it entered the fader.

The faders are a mixing board's sexiest feature, and some faders are definitely nicer than others. Expensive boards have faders with a smooth, syrupy feel that's conducive to flawless fade-ins and fade-outs; cheaper boards have faders that feel lightweight, rough, or otherwise just cheap. Some boards are advertised as having "long-throw" faders, meaning they have a longer travel from one end of their range to the other, which allows for more precise and subtle level settings. Sweet faders are a nice luxury, but they're by no means necessary to create a good recording. In fact, after I converted to a digital system and started doing most of my mixing within the computer, I cut back on my fader usage by probably 95 percent. Digital recordists could get by with a board that has no faders at all—although faders always come in handy, even if it's just to give a mix last-minute adjustments that you don't want to make in the virtual console.

Busses & Assigns

Up to now, all of the input channels have remained more or less separate, but here is where the mixing board combines things. The simplest boards have just two output channels—the left and right sides, each with its own output fader and output jack. If a board has eight input channels and two output channels, we describe it as being an 8×2 board: eight ins, two outs. In that case, each input channel is assigning its signal to the two output channels; the pan pot's position determines how that signal is balanced between them. Pretty simple.

More flexible mixing boards offer *busses*, which are additional output channels (plus their associated faders and jacks). On a board with busses, usually there's also a master stereo output, which is like the two output channels in the simple 8×2 board described above. An input channel's destinations are determined by *assign switches*, which are usually located near the channel's fader. Each assign switch represents a pair of busses (busses 1 and 2, busses 3 and 4, etc.), and there's also a switch for the master stereo output (labeled simply L/R or mix). These switches allow you to route an input channel's signal to the master stereo output channels, to any pair of busses, or any combination thereof, for maximum flexibility (see Fig. 10). The input channel's pan pot determines how the signal is balanced between each pair of channels. For example, say you assigned input channel 8 to send its signal to busses 1 and 2 plus busses 3 and 4, as well as to the master stereo output channels. In this case, turning channel 8's pan pot all the way to the right would send the signal to bus 2, bus 4, and the stereo output's right channel, with nothing going to busses 1 or 3 or to the left channel (see Fig. 11). Got it?

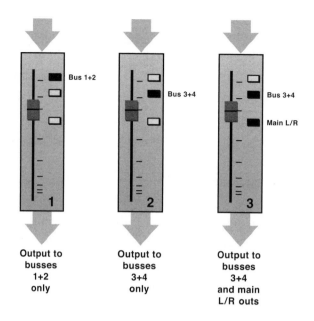

Fig. 10 The assign switches determine where the channel's signal gets routed: to one or more pairs of busses, the main outputs, or all of the above.

When you're tracking, you typically set up your busses to send signals to your digital audio interface or multitrack, completely independently of the master stereo output channels. A mixing board with four busses is ideal for recording four tracks at once; one with eight is ideal for recording eight. In this arrangement, you'd use a cable to connect each bus's output jack to the corresponding input on the interface. This way, if you had a mic plugged into input channel 8 and you wanted to record it on the interface's input 1, you'd press the bus 1/2 assign button and turn up the bus 1 fader. (If you wanted to make sure no signal was going to bus 2, you could also crank channel 8's pan pot hard-left, or make sure the bus 2 fader was all the way down, but this would be necessary only if you were also recording a different instrument

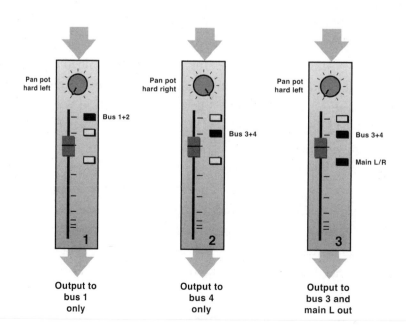

Fig. 11 The pan pot determines where the signal gets routed between a pair of busses, or between the left and right sides of the main output.

onto input 2 of the interface.) So here's what's happening: You sing, and the mic's signal enters input channel 8, goes through the effect-send and EQ sections, and goes through the pan pot/fader/assign switches, which send the signal to bus 1. Bus 1, in turn, sends the signal to the interface's input 1, causing a signal to appear in that input's meters in your recording program. Fig. 12 is a diagram of this signal chain.

That's great—but how do you hear yourself to make sure you're singing with the tracks that have already been recorded? One way would be to assign the mic's input channel to the master stereo output as well as bus pair 1 and 2; when you plug your headphones into the board, you should hear yourself. It's more flexible and convenient, though, to create a monitor mix using the monitor section, if your board has one. If so, there will be a way to get the monitor mix to your headphones—check the board's manual. It's usually just a matter of hitting a button near the headphone jack.

Each bus may also have its own switch for assigning the signal to the master stereo outputs. If you activate it, you'll hear the signal from the bus blended into the stereo output signal (without affecting the signal going to the bus's output jack). This is another way to monitor yourself while tracking.

By the way, if you hear a mixing board described with three numbers, the middle number refers to how many busses it has. For example, "8×4×2" means the board has eight input channels, four busses, and the usual master stereo output.

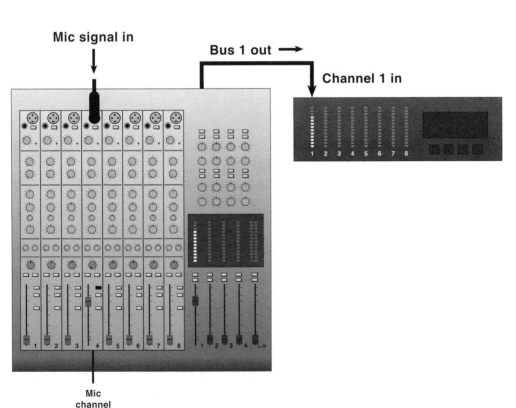

Fig. 12 In this signal chain, a mic feeds an input channel on the board; the board is configured to send the signal out of bus 1 to input 1 on the digital audio interface or multitrack recorder.

Mic signal in

Bus 1 out ➡

Channel 1 in

Mic channel

Mute, Solo, Lo-Cut & Phase Switches

Most boards offer a mute switch near each input-channel fader; this simply turns off that channel, as if you pulled the fader all the way down. These buttons are handy for quieting unused channels on the board, or removing a group of sounds (such as all of the vocals) for a quick check during a mixing session.

A solo switch is kind of the opposite of mute: it mutes every channel *other* than the one you're soloing. Soloing a track is usually done more as a diagnostic procedure than as a part of actual tracking or mixing; for example, if you're hearing some gritty distortion in a mix but you're unsure of what track it's on, soloing tracks one by one usually reveals the culprit—and it's a lot easier than trying to do the same thing with the mute buttons.

Some boards have a "lo-cut" switch on each channel. This is essentially a shelving EQ with a sharp rolloff of the lowest lows. It's most useful when you're recording vocals or other mic sources, where there may be rumbling sounds picked up through the mic stand, or "P-pops" or other breath noises, that you don't want on the track. Just remember to disengage this switch before you record a bass or kick-drum track—otherwise those critical frequencies will be filtered out, and the track will be ruined.

Pro boards and a few semi-pro boards also incorporate a phase switch on each input channel. This may not seem to do anything when you try it, but actually it flips over the audio signal so it becomes a "mirror image" of itself. If a sound starts with its wave shape going up, and then you hit the phase switch and play the exact same sound again, it will start with its wave shape going down (see Fig. 13). This button is most useful when you're recording with more than one microphone. For instance, if you have two mics on a guitar amp and you're blending them together into one output channel, you'll want to make sure the waveforms from each mic are reinforcing each

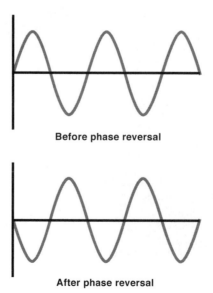

Fig. 13 A board's phase button inverts the audio signal so the wave shape becomes a mirror image of itself.

Before phase reversal

After phase reversal

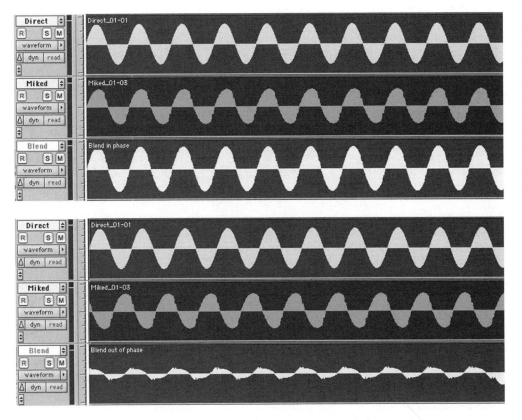

Fig. 14 Phase cancellation in action: A direct signal and a miked signal, when added together, can reinforce each other (top) or can partially cancel each other out (bottom). In each example, the bottom wave is the result of blending the other two waves, whose phase relationship makes all the difference.

other, rather than partially canceling each other out (see Fig. 14). In this scenario, flipping the phase of one of the mic signals could make a huge difference in the resulting sound. But even if your board has these switches, you'll probably never use them unless you find yourself recording two similar signals at once like this.

Effect Returns

As far as I know, every board with an effect send also has an effect return. This is a circuit that accepts incoming signals and assigns and blends them in somehow. Effect returns can be either mono or stereo. A mono effect return usually has one input jack, one level knob, and maybe a pan control. A stereo effect return usually has two input jacks (one for each stereo channel), one level knob affecting both channels equally, and perhaps a balance knob, which can tip the stereo effect-return signal to the left or right relative to its stereo destination. If the board has a bus section, there will invariably be assign buttons for each effect return as well: these allow you to assign the returning effect signal to a bus, the master stereo outs, or both.

An effect return is essentially one or two additional input channels, although it's not as flexible as an actual input channel. It usually has no EQ, and naturally it doesn't have its own effect sends. This may seem like a no-brainer—but sometimes I've wanted to take an effect-send line from the signal coming back from an effect. Suppose you have one effect send going to a delay and another going to a reverb. The reverb will

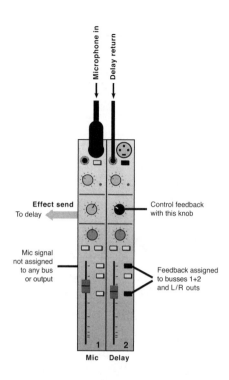

Fig. 15 By using a channel as an effect return, you can cause runaway feedback with effects. In this example, channel 1's dry signal isn't routed anywhere except to a delay, which feeds channel 2. By adjusting channel 2's send knob, the runaway delay can be controlled. The resulting sound is routed to busses 1 and 2 for recording (perhaps with reverb added), and to the main outputs for monitoring.

reflect the main, non-delayed signal only; meanwhile, the signal coming back from the delay will have no reverb on it. So you'll have the main sound with some reverb on it, and then you'll have a delayed version of that sound with no reverb on it. This may not be what you want, especially if it's a long delay. For this reason—and because going digital made available many of my board's input channels—I almost never use my effect returns anymore. Instead, I run the returning signal into one or two input channels of its own. This way I can EQ the returning sound (maybe I want the echoes to sound more muffled), and I can also take pre- or post-fader effect sends from the returning signals. In the reverb-plus-delay example above, I'd simply take a reverb send from both the original sound and the returning delay. The reverb unit would receive a blend of the original plus the delayed sounds, and it would output a reverb for that blend. Reverb therefore gets added to both the original sound and its delayed version, resulting in a more natural effect.

You can also get cool special effects by intentionally creating a positive feedback loop using effect sends. You might have the return from a delay, reverb, or pitch-shift feed back into itself, resulting in an interestingly chaotic, almost-out-of-control buildup of effect, which can be faded up or down—perhaps "encouraged or discouraged" would be a better way to put it—by working the return line's effect-send knob.

(See Fig. 15.) Make sure your send knobs are down before you try this, and *slowly* turn up the second channel's send until you find the point where feedback starts.

Effect returns are a great way for the Guerrilla recordist to get more signals going into the board—but if you have extra input channels available, using those instead will give you more flexibility and creative options.

Not Enough Inputs!

Since converting to digital, I've been spoiled by being able to work with as many as eight input channels on my board unoccupied. But I remember the days of running an 8-track analog machine into only a 6-channel board. How did I do it? I bought a separate mixer, an ancient thing, for $50. It had six ins and two outs, all RCA jacks. I used two tracks for drums and two for returning reverb, and I fed its stereo output into the main board's sub in jacks, which allowed me to blend a stereo signal straight into the board's outputs. I don't think there was a level control for those sub inputs, but it wasn't necessary—I could just set the drums' and reverb's levels on the second mixer.

In this arrangement, the second mixer is known as a *submixer*. (On my 6-channel board, "sub in" stood for "submixer in.") Submixing is a great way to add additional channels to your setup (see Fig. 16). If your board doesn't have sub in jacks—perhaps

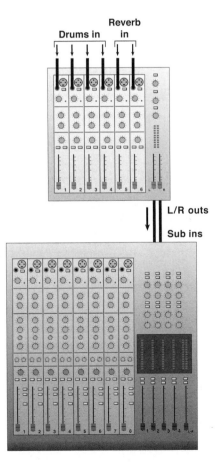

Fig. 16 Using a second mixing board as a sub-mixer for drums and reverb.

it calls them something else, like aux in—you can use a stereo effect return, or if need be, you can sacrifice two of its input channels. Then again, if you get a submixer that's nicer and more flexible than your main mixer, maybe you should use your new board as the main mixer and relegate the old one to submixing duties.

You may have to be a little creative getting all of your signals to come together, but do whatever it takes. It doesn't have to look pretty—as long as it sounds okay, who cares what it took to get the job done?

Digital Recording Media

see page 227

Let's continue on with our signal-chain tour. We've finally left the mixing board, let's say out of one of the bus output jacks. It's time to convert the signal to digital form so that it can be recorded. In the digital-recording world you have several options.

Standalone digital multitracks. Reminiscent of old 4- and 8-track machines that recorded on cassette tape, these record four, eight, or sixteen tracks to an internal hard drive or a memory card. They usually have their own limited mixing boards built in, which vary in quality from manufacturer to manufacturer.

Some standalones, particularly older ones, employ data compression schemes to cram a maximum number of track-minutes onto the drive or card. But when data compression is involved, you compromise the sound somewhat. This isn't a big problem if you're using the machine as an audio sketchpad. But as your ears improve, you'll begin hearing that sound files recorded with data compression don't quite make it to CD quality. If you're shopping around, consider going with a unit that can record without data compression. If it has an internal hard drive, make sure it also has a USB or FireWire port, because you will need a way to back up the data as the drive fills up.

What Sampling Frequency/ Bit Rate?

Your digital recording system likely lets you choose the sampling frequency and bit depth for your recordings. But actually, in terms of audible sound, the settings don't make much of a difference, provided you choose at least 44.1kHz sampling and 16 bits of resolution. Higher rates and depths improve the sound slightly (higher bit depths are easier to hear, especially in very quiet recordings, than higher sampling rates). But there's a tradeoff: Higher numbers require more disk space as well as more CPU power. For

example, a song recorded at 88.2kHz and 24 bits requires 2.5 times more disk space and CPU power than the same song recorded at 44.1kHz and 16 bits. While it's true that eventually all mixes must be reduced to 44.1/16 specs to be put onto a standard CD, many people insist that a recording just sounds better if it's tracked with higher specs. My advice: Use the best specs that your system and hard drive allow, but don't max them out. Your needs will probably change over time as your recording skills get more sophisticated, and there's nothing worse than wanting to add one more part, only to find your computer can't handle the added load.

Modular digital multitracks. This format exploded on the scene in the early '90s with the Alesis ADAT and the Tascam DA-88, opening the world of digital recording to the masses. Originally, MDMs recorded digitized audio onto videotape cassettes; a single machine could record eight tracks, and multiple machines could be cabled together to record 24 or more synchronized tracks. Tape MDMs, though available on the used market, are on the way out and aren't a great option anymore; they're less reliable than other formats, and it can be a huge pain to have to wait for multiple tape machines to sync up when you're doing repeated rewinds and playbacks. MDMs that record to hard drive are a much better option, although you'll almost certainly need a mixing board if you use them. As on standalone machines, you can't record MIDI on MDMs (although it's possible to sync them with a MIDI recording program on a computer), so that's an obvious disadvantage if you use a lot of MIDI instruments. Also, editing capabilities are limited.

DAW recording. This refers to recording on a digital audio workstation—a computer with recording software—and hands down, it offers the best combination of sound, convenience, and cost to the Guerrilla recordist. You may be able to record digitally using your computer's internal sound card, but a more powerful setup adds an external digital audio interface or a dedicated sound card for the computer. This interface or card does all of the digital encoding and decoding. Here's how it works: A signal enters one channel of the interface, it's converted to a digital data stream, and that stream is ported to the computer, which writes the data onto a hard drive. During playback, the process happens in reverse, turning a hard-drive data file into an analog signal. The number of channels on the interface determines how many discrete tracks can be recorded or played back at once, although many more tracks (more accurately called "voices" in desktop recording) can exist separately on the computer and get mixed within it during playback. On the computer, the process of recording and playing back tracks is managed with a MIDI-and-audio recording program that's set up to work with the interface.

 Audio vs. Data Compression

Don't confuse audio compression with data compression. Audio compression—that's the kind performed by outboard compressor/limiters and compressor/expanders—refers to intentionally reducing a sound's dynamic range to improve a recording's quality (explained in detail in Chapter 4). Data compression, on the other hand, is a necessary evil in some systems to increase the total duration of sound the system can record. Data compression involves running the digital data through an additional encoding process on recording and then decoding it on playback. Less disk space is used as a result, but it's a compromise: inevitably there's some loss of sound quality.

A complete discussion of the various DAWs is beyond the scope of this book—but wherever you are in your journey toward pro-quality recording, I encourage you to look into what's available. Take it from someone who has recorded on every one of these formats over the years: this kind of recording rocks. It's just so flexible and user-friendly, to name just a few of its advantages, I would never go back to any other method.

Recording & Playing Tracks

We've looked at the path a signal can take, from a mic or instrument all the way to the recording medium. Now let's record the signal. Whatever the actual recording medium, generally you record by "record-enabling" a track—which might be as simple as clicking a button marked "R" next to the track—and then hitting a keystroke or clicking a button that starts the recording process. Onscreen, a vertical line travels from left to right, and your audio starts appearing on the track, either as a rectangle or an actual waveform (or both). When you click the "stop" button, your audio is digitized on your hard drive and displayed onscreen, ready to be manipulated. Recording MIDI works the same way as recording audio, but instead of a separate file being written onto your drive, the MIDI data is stored inside the song file. Before you record MIDI, you may need to configure the track to be a MIDI track or to record MIDI data only.

Now that you've recorded a track, you can play it back. (Depending on your program, you may have to record-disable or unmute the track first.) You can then record onto a second track while you listen to the first, and continue in this manner, building up a multitrack arrangement. When recording multiple MIDI parts, you need to configure each track to send its data on a particular MIDI channel, and set up your MIDI instruments so that each receives only the channel corresponding to the sound it needs to produce. Once you've played and sung everything there is to play and sing on that song, you're done recording it. Now it's time to mix the song.

The Mixdown Signal Chain

Say you have recorded eight tracks of audio and you're ready to mix them. Let's look at how you could bring the various signals together, along with effects, on a conventional mixing board. (If you don't use a mixing board and outboard effects, you can skip ahead to the next section.)

During mixdown, your board's input channels (or at least some of them) accept signals from the digital audio interface or multitrack, outboard effects, and any hardware MIDI instruments that are running in real time (meaning you haven't yet recorded their audio to separate tracks). You output everything from the main L/R outs. Typically you monitor the stereo mix out of a separate pair of "control room outputs" or something similar. Mixing then becomes a matter of making sure the various levels of recorded tracks and MIDI instruments are balanced, setting the EQs and pan pots appropriately, adding effects with the send and return circuits, and adjusting all of these variables as the tracks play back and you record the mix in stereo. (See Fig. 17.) As an alternative

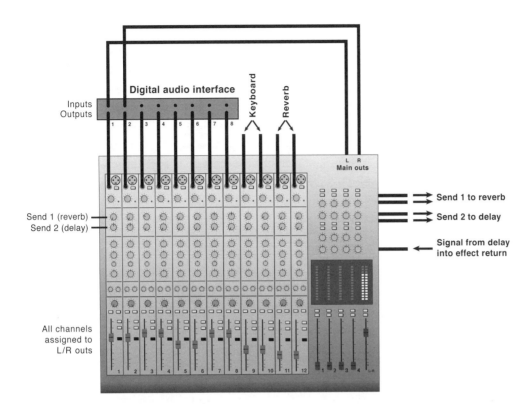

Fig. 17 An example of a mixdown signal chain using a hardware mixing board, effects, and a keyboard instrument. Everything is assigned to the main outputs, which feed inputs 1 and 2 on the interface, so the mix can be recorded in stereo.

to mixing to the main L/R outs, you could mix to busses 1 and 2 (sending those to the interface) and monitor on either busses 3 and 4 or the main L/R outs.

Mixing With A Virtual Console

Your recording program probably has a "virtual" (onscreen) mixing board incorporated into it. If you're accustomed to a hardware mixer, it can take awhile to get used to a virtual console, but it's worth it. By far, the best thing about a virtual console is that you can automate mixing moves with great precision—you can do things like ramp up the lead vocal level by a certain amount each bar, make a certain word pop out, or even change the delay time going from the verse into the chorus. The mix is then completely reproducible—a year after doing your mix, all of those fader and effect moves will still be a part of your recording file. The possibilities are unlimited; virtual consoles really appeal to the control freaks and tweak geeks among us.

Virtual consoles are designed to look and work like a real mixing console. Specifics vary by program, but generally there's one channel per recorded track, and you can assign each track to one or more virtual output busses, or simply to a stereo output. There are two ways to mix a digital recording. Some people (including myself) prefer to output separate groups of instruments to a hardware mixing board, blend the groups and add external effects on the board, and then record the resulting mix back onto the computer. Others prefer to mix within the digital realm, meaning all of the blending and processing is done inside the computer, using the virtual console and

Onscreen Meters Can Be Deceiving

One of the nice things about a virtual console is that it gives you a separate meter for every single channel or track, and even for things like effect sends and returns. These can come in really handy in gain-staging, but they can also provide a false sense of security. Unless your recording program allows you to specify otherwise, a meter on a track indicates the signal level *coming into* that track, not leaving it. As a result, even though a meter indicates that its signal is maxxing out at a safe –1dB, digital distortion may still be happening somewhere downstream.

I learned this the hard way. I like to reserve two of my audio interface's output channels for vocals, and at one point I was getting distortion in the vocals, even though all of the virtual console's meters indicated that my levels were safely under 0dB. What I didn't realize was that the *combined* level of the vocals was exceeding 0dB in places, so it was distorting those output channels—which (at the time) weren't set up to have their own meters. Since this happened, I've been sure to run my outputs through their own channels in the virtual console (Pro Tools calls these Master Fader tracks). That way, I have a visual check on the levels of all the combined-output groups of tracks, and since these meters are at the very end of the digital chain, they take into account all EQ, plug-ins, etc., that may be happening on the individual tracks.

the program's plug-ins only. The first method allows you to incorporate your favorite hardware effects without having to "print" (record) them beforehand; the downside is your music has to be converted to analog audio for the mixing board and then back to digital, which degrades the audio quality by a tiny amount.

The advent of digital mixing boards, which are plummeting in price like everything else digital, has made it possible to combine these approaches. Your sound remains in digital form as it leaves the computer, passes through the board, has effects added digitally, and then goes back to the computer. You get the feel of a real hands-on mixer with the automation of a virtual console, and your music stays entirely in the digital realm.

Using Busses To Group Tracks

You already know that on a hardware mixing board, busses are additional output channels that are situated before the main (stereo) outputs. In a virtual console, you use busses whenever you need an extra output channel or you want to pre-mix groups of channels for whatever reason. Whether real or virtual, you can use busses to help you mix. You could mix four drum channels to one stereo bus (pair of mono busses), four channels of vocals to another pair, and everything else to a third pair, for example. (See Fig. 18.) This would allow you to turn up or turn down all of the drums (or vocals, or everything else) by moving or automating just two bus faders. This technique makes it easy to do things like having everything but the vocals gradually fade out until the song is *a cappella* (vocals only). It also makes it extremely easy to make broad adjustments to a mix. If you decide that all of your vocals need to come down by 1dB, it's a lot easier to make that change to one stereo bus than to 16 individual vocal channels.

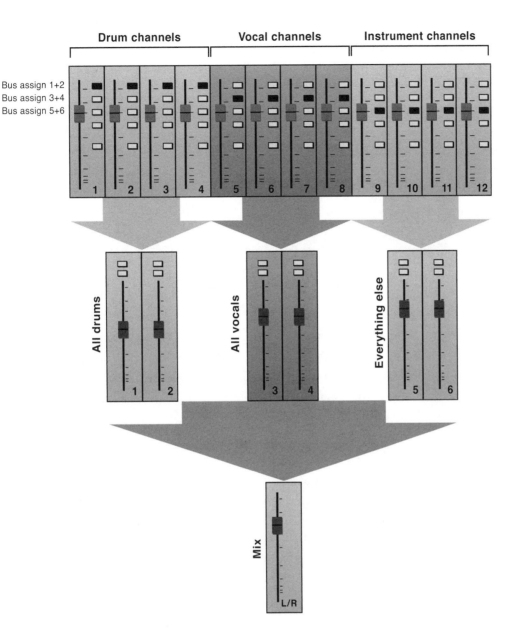

Drum channels   Vocal channels   Instrument channels

Bus assign 1+2
Bus assign 3+4
Bus assign 5+6

All drums

All vocals

Everything else

Mix

Fig. 18 Using three pairs of busses to pre-mix drums, vocals, and other instruments, which are blended into the stereo mix. This can be done on a virtual console as well as a hardware mixing board—but only if it has enough busses.

Recording The Mix

If you're doing desktop recording, typically you record your stereo mix back onto two open tracks in your recording program. Alternatively, you can mix the song digitally, entirely within the recording program. (Both methods are discussed in Chapter 10.) With a modular digital multitrack or standalone multitrack, you'd record the mix back onto the recording device—if you have two open tracks. If you don't, or if you've run out of voices in your desktop program, you can record your mix on another device. This could be a 2-track reel-to-reel analog tape deck, a DAT (digital audio tape) deck, or a standalone CD burner that has audio inputs. Of course, if you mix to analog tape, you'll have to digitize the file somehow and get it onto your computer's hard drive to burn it to CD.

Compact Disc & Internet

As I mentioned in Chapter 2, audio CDs and CD players use sound files recorded at 44.1kHz and 16-bit resolution. If your system is set to record to different specs, you'll need to convert the file first. To be burned to CD, the mix must be in the form of a single *interleaved stereo AIFF file*. This means it's one digital file in which the two stereo channels are woven together, in something called Audio Interchange File Format. Your recording program has settings that determine how the file is saved onto your hard drive. Be sure not to save your mix as two mono files; you won't be able to burn a stereo CD directly from these.

To burn a CD, just import the file into a CD-burning program—that's it. The program will allow you to set the order of songs on the CD and probably the duration of silence between them. This is great for throwing together a test CD of rough mixes. For final projects, though, you may want to use a more powerful program. (For more on that, see Chapter 10.)

Preparing a song for Internet distribution requires conversion to mp3 format (a highly efficient data compression scheme) so that it can be quickly downloaded. This can be done with iTunes or similar programs. The audio quality of mp3s is pretty good, although it does weird things with the high frequencies. Try different compression settings to see if one sounds better than the others.

Power Amp, Speakers & Headphones

We're finally at the end of the signal chain—the place where electricity is turned back into the sound of a mixed song. Whether you're listening to a CD or a mix in progress coming off the computer, you need to run the line-level stereo signal either to a pair of headphones, to a power amplifier feeding a pair of loudspeakers, or to a pair of powered loudspeakers (speakers with built-in power amps). In true Guerrilla Home Recording form, I've never used a dedicated power amplifier; I've always just run my mixer's master stereo outputs to a home-stereo receiver, a setup that works fine. I use the same home stereo when I'm listening to burned CDs.

As for speakers, I don't recommend using a pair bought from a stereo store unless that's all you have. You'll do better with a pair of good *near-field studio monitors*. Manufactured specifically for small recording studios, these are designed to be listened to at close range, so that almost all of what you're hearing is what's coming out of the speakers themselves, not a combination of that plus whatever is bouncing off the walls and other surfaces around you. Professional studio control rooms have monstrous speakers and perfect acoustics that allow for a near-flawless listening situation in locations all around the control room—but a Guerrilla studio doesn't. We need to listen carefully on near-fields and headphones, and we need to augment this monitoring setup by listening to rough mixes on other speaker systems, in other listening environments. I'll go into more detail about mixing and checking your mixes in Chapter 10.

Three Efficient Setups For Tracking & Mixing

Let's look at three sample setups for a studio with an 8-channel digital audio system: one with a modular digital multitrack and a smaller, cramped-for-space 8×2 board (eight ins, two outs), a desktop system with a 16×4×2 board (16 ins, four busses, and two main outs), and a DAW system without a hardware mixer—the mixing is done entirely within the computer.

Small-board setup. With an 8-track MDM and only eight input channels on the board, you've run out of channels before you've even begun recording. Each of the MDM's outputs needs an input channel (assuming you'll be recording on all eight tracks), leaving no channels open for tracking sources like microphone or direct-recorded bass. It's definitely possible to record on a setup like this, but you need to conserve your channels and make creative use of every input you have.

In such a channel-challenged situation, it helps to use a consistent tracking strategy from song to song that's conducive to your particular board setup. For example, you might get into the habit of recording all of your drum sounds in stereo on your MDM's tracks 7 and 8, and always have those tracks' outputs feeding your board's sub in or aux in jacks. That way, no matter what song you're tracking or mixing, you know the drums will be coming into the submixer inputs (you could say the drums had already been submixed). In this scenario you could send tracks 1–6 from the MDM into channels 1–6 on the board, leaving channels 7 and 8 available for tracking or (during mixdown) effects. Channels 1–6 would be perpetually switched to tape input, so that you can always monitor what you've previously recorded on the corresponding tracks. During tracking you might have a microphone feeding channel 7, with the return from a delay feeding channel 8, and a reverb running into a stereo effect return (see Fig. 19). If you wanted to

"print" reverb—record some mono reverb along with the signal—you could disconnect the reverb-carrying cables going into the effect return and plug one of them into channel 8, which also would allow you to EQ the reverb separately.

That's fine for getting signals *from* the multitrack—but what about sending signals *to* it? That can be tricky on a board with no busses. Most boards offer a direct out or line out jack on each input channel. Assuming that this jack is situated post-fader and post-EQ in the signal chain (which it normally is), you can just plug a cable into this jack on your mixer input channel, and connect the other end to the appropriate input jack on the multitrack. A downside to this arrangement is that each time you want to record a new track, you have to unplug the cable from the old track's MDM input and plug it into the next track's input.

If your board doesn't have direct out jacks, you could use an effect send to get a single mono signal out of the board and into the appropriate MDM input. Or, as a last resort, you could split the master stereo output into two mono channels: a monitoring side, and a bus to the multitrack. Here's how you'd do that: Pan all of the already-recorded channels hard-left, and pan your new signal(s) hard-right. In this case, one master output would go to your monitoring amplifier, and one would go to the MDM. This is hardly ideal, but the point is you can get it done. You just have to be resourceful, look at your options, and plan a course of action. If the situation is this dire, consider upgrading your mixer or converting to a desktop system—such extreme limitations get old fast!

Mixing with this setup is straightforward, since each MDM output is plugged into a corresponding board input channel. Switch all of the channels to tape, press play on the MDM, and have a go at it. Use the board's effect returns to blend in effects while the mixdown runs. (That's actually how the board was designed to be used!)

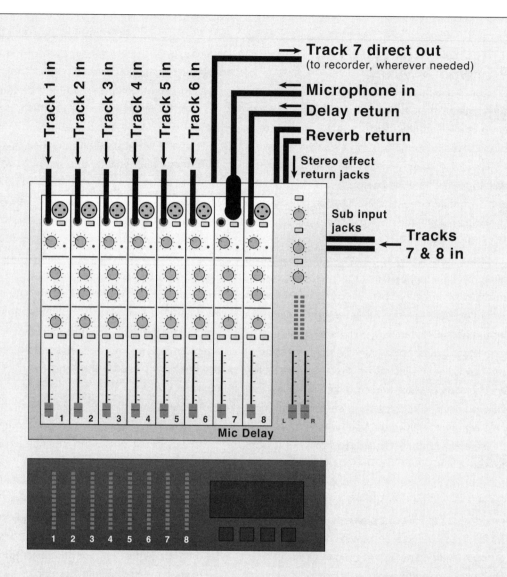

Fig. 19 Getting the most out of eight mixer channels and eight tracks on an ADAT-type recorder. Faced with a shortage of inputs, you could use the board's sub in jacks for tracks 7 & 8, and a stereo effect return for the reverb. Six of the board's channels could be used for monitoring tracks 1–6, and the last two channels could be used for tracking.

Large-board setup. It's much more convenient to record using a board with busses as well as more channels than your recording system—for example, a 12×4×2 board with an 8-channel digital audio interface. In that case, you could set mixer channels 1–8 to permanently monitor all eight outputs from the interface, leaving you four channels open for source inputs (mic, direct bass, etc.) or anything else you might need. You could use the four busses to feed the audio interface's eight inputs by doubling them up: bus 1 feeds inputs 1 and 5, bus 2 feeds inputs 2 and 6, and so on. This kind of arrangement is called *double-bussing*, and many boards have two or even three identical output jacks per bus for just this purpose (see Fig. 20). When you're double-bussing an 8-channel interface, though, you can record only four distinct channels at a time, even if the interface is capable of recording on all eight at once.

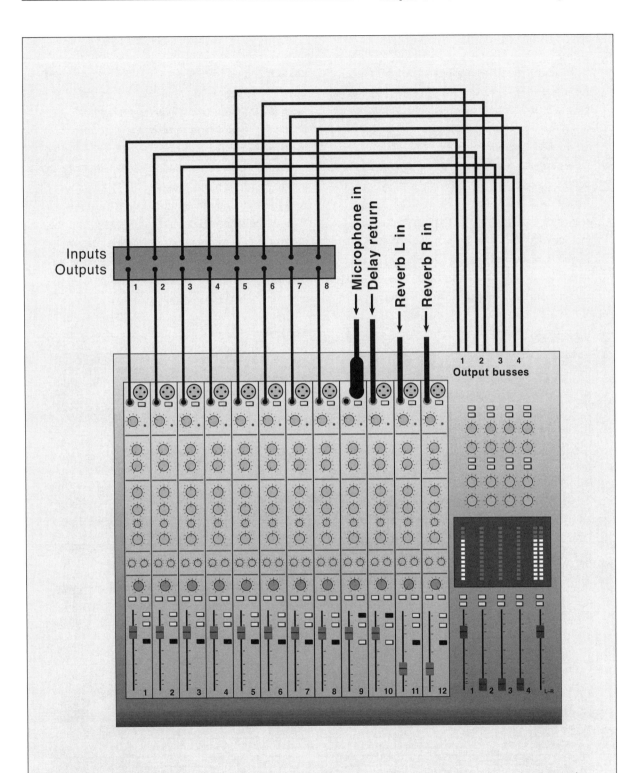

Fig. 20 There's considerably more elbow room—and flexibility—when you're using a digital audio workstation, and your board has busses as well as more input channels than your audio interface has outputs. From this 12×4×2 board, each of the four busses is feeding two channels on the interface; each interface output gets its own board channel for monitoring, and the reverb gets its own channel pair as well. In this case, a mic and a delay are being sent to bus 1, which is feeding interface inputs 1 & 5.

Having extra channels opens up your options for using MIDI instruments. In this 12-channel example, you could reserve channels 9 and 10 for a drum machine or sampler, leaving channels 11 and 12 available for source inputs.

For mixing with a system like this, you have a couple of options. You can mix entirely with the virtual console (see below), or you can set up your recording program so that it's outputting groups of instruments—for example, vocals on busses 1 and 2, guitars on 3 and 4, keyboards on 5 and 6, and the bass on 7 (see Fig. 21)—and bring these premixed groups into your mixing board. Alternatively, you could blend all instruments that are to be mixed "dry" (no effects) to channels 1 and 2, and all of the "wet" instruments (those with reverb and delay) to channels 3 and 4, and turn up the effect sends on those two channels appropriately.

I like to reserve an audio-interface channel for an automated reverb bus (see page 199); this doesn't contribute directly to the mix but instead feeds a muted, pre-fader effect send for a reverb. This lets the recording program's automation determine how much signal the reverb unit is getting at any particular moment, thus effectively automating the external reverb.

Fig. 21 In a virtual console, routing vocals, guitars, and keyboards through their own pairs of busses (highlighted), with each bus going to its corresponding audio output. Bass (far right) is going to output 7 in mono. Without a mixing board, you would output to two channels in stereo.

No-board setup. We've spent a lot of pages discussing recording with a mixing board, but it's becoming increasingly practical to record on a digital audio workstation with no board at all. In that case, you won't be able to run hardware effects or MIDI instruments in real time; you'll have to "print" them as a part of tracking. (Virtual instruments, such as software synths and sample-player plug-ins, do not need to be printed.) You will need something that's capable of accepting the various signals that mics, direct instruments, and MIDI instruments produce, as they all need to be brought up to line level so you can record them with your audio interface. A lot of interfaces have this capability, with ¼" and XLR jacks as well as input-level controls. If yours doesn't at least accept both mic and line signals, you'll need a separate mic preamp. (You may want one

regardless, especially if you need phantom power and your interface doesn't provide it. Plus, some mic preamps on audio interfaces just aren't that good.) Once your signal is at line level, all you need to do is make sure it goes to the appropriate input on your interface (see Fig. 22).

Mixing with this setup is even simpler. All of the mixing occurs, of course, in the virtual console. You can either internally bus the stereo mix so that it can be recorded onto two new tracks, or you can mix the song by making a digital bounce (or whatever your recording program calls it)—the entire mix is done by way of data calculation, remaining in the digital realm. In this case, during mixdown your digital audio interface serves no purpose other than allowing you to monitor the mix. More about these methods in Chapter 10.

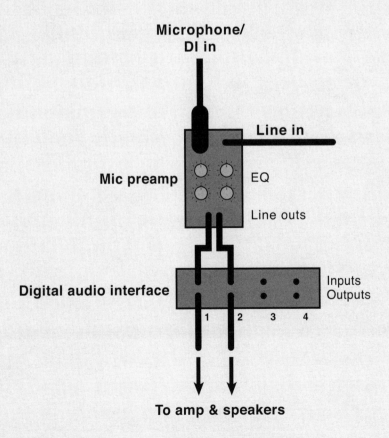

Fig. 22 The signal chain is simple when there's no mixing board: two inputs and two outputs. All of the mixing is done within the computer.

CHAPTER 4

Controlling Dynamics

In Chapter 2, I introduced the concepts of dynamics (variations in signal level between loud and soft) and dynamic range. Even with today's inexpensive recording systems, it's possible to achieve a dynamic range of over 90dB—in other words, the loudest sounds you record can be over 90 decibels louder than the background noise. Managing all of the "area" between these two extremes, for each and every sound you record, is a skill that's critical to making a good-sounding recording. Fortunately, there are devices called expanders, compressors, and limiters (collectively called dynamics processors) that help in this task. In this chapter I'll explain how to use them.

Using An Expander

Of the three types of dynamics processors, compressors are probably the most familiar—but let's begin with expanders, because they're a bit easier to understand. A lot of people record without using an expander in the signal chain, and I think that's a shame, because effective use of an expander can do an awful lot to clean up the tracks that you record.

Expansion refers to the process of increasing a signal's dynamic range—making it bigger. Isn't 90dB a large enough dynamic range, you ask? Certainly—but that number refers to a system's *potential* dynamic range, not necessarily the range you'll get if you plug in a mic and start recording. An expander is important in optimizing the *actual* dynamic range you get out of a system.

An expander operates at the low end of the dynamic range, where signals are at their quietest, or perhaps nonexistent. In other words, when audio is coming through the signal chain, the expander may be doing nothing at all. But when that audio stops coming through, the expander goes to work by lowering the signal further, expanding the background noise floor downward so that there's a larger dynamic range overall (see Fig. 1). Not surprisingly, this is called *downward expansion*. There is such thing as upward expansion, but you don't really need to know about it.

Fig. 1 Without expansion (left), the noise level in the signal chain can far exceed a stage's background noise. With expansion (right), the noise is brought down to the noise floor, without affecting the signal itself.

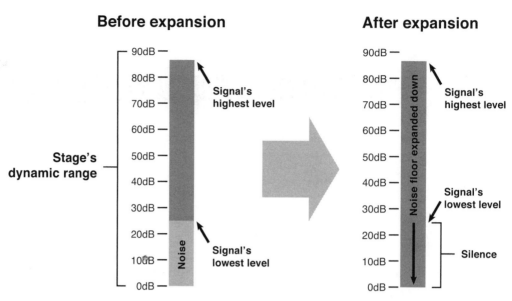

To understand this better, consider what happens when you plug a microphone into a mixing board and crank up the gain. If you talk or sing into the mic, you'll hear yourself coming through the headphones loudly. (Careful—you might also get a feedback shriek if it's too loud.) But if you stop singing, odds are you won't hear silence—especially in a bedroom or den Guerrilla studio. You'll hear the heating or air-conditioning system, planes going overhead, street traffic, or your kid brother's video game down the hall. This is all stuff that doesn't belong on your recording! Sure, domestic sounds are charming—if it's 1970 and you're Paul McCartney recording your first solo album. But we Guerrilla recordists are going after a slick, clean sound, and part of "clean" means not having anything on your tracks that you don't want there.

Here's where expansion comes in. You may have encountered a device called a *noise gate*, which is a crude form of an expander. In a noise gate, once the signal falls below a certain threshold, an electronic gate closes and no sound is allowed to pass through (noise or otherwise). However, when the signal begins to rise above that same threshold again, the gate opens up, allowing the signal to pass through once more. Naturally, this also allows unwanted noise to pass through along with the signal, but the idea is that noise is less troublesome when signal is present to mask it. Like faint starlight in the night sky, noise is most noticeable when it's by itself. Mix in a little signal (or sunlight in this analogy) and you're less likely to notice the faint background stuff. An expander works on the same principle as a noise gate, but an expander is a bit more subtle: it's not as obvious to the ear when it's doing its thing.

Here are the parameters that you're likely to find on an expander, or the expander component of a compressor/expander:

Threshold: This control sets the level at which the expansion effect begins to set in. Imagine a cymbal crash that begins at 0dB (the top of the dynamic range) and

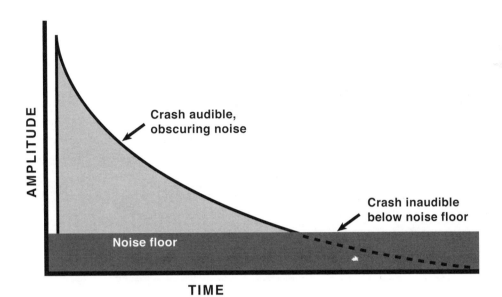

Fig. 2 As the sound of a crash cymbal decays, it eventually falls below the noise floor and becomes inaudible.

slowly decays to −∞ dB. At a certain point in its decay, the sound of the cymbal will get so quiet that you'll hear background noise mixed in with the cymbal, and at a still-later point you'll hear only background noise, as the noise masks what's left of the crash (see Fig. 2). If you were miking this cymbal by itself (perhaps to sample it for a collection of drum sounds), you might want an expander to kick in toward the tail end of the decay in order to take the background noise out of the sonic picture (see Fig. 3). The threshold control determines when this happens. If you were to set the expander's threshold to −30dB, the expander would begin to shut down the signal when the cymbal decayed 30dB below its initial peak. In this case you could get away with a lot more noise happening in or outside your studio without worrying about these sounds making it onto your cymbal sample. But if you wanted to make a long,

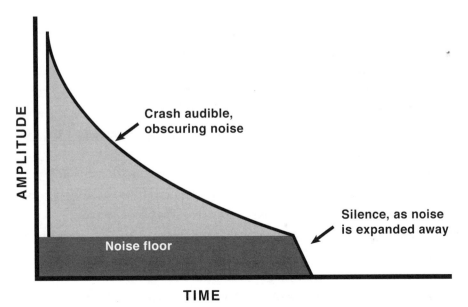

Fig. 3 When you run the crash-cymbal sound through an expander, the threshold level determines how much of the cymbal's decay makes it through before the expander closes down the noise.

Real-Time Dynamics Processing Plug-Ins

You may have compressor and/or expander plug-ins available to use within your digital system. These can be useful in some situations—but unless you have a lot of experience working with "real" compressors and expanders, wherever possible, use hardware versions of these effects instead. When you're setting up a signal chain, you need to be able to hear what a dynamics processor is doing in real time—and see what it's doing by

way of indicator LEDs—so that you can tweak the unit's parameters before you start recording, and without your recording system in the signal chain. Depending on your system, you may not be able to do this with a plug-in. Plus, some of these plug-ins offer so many variables, you may find yourself confused by them, unsure exactly which parameters are having what effect on the signal. Don't get me wrong; digital plug-ins are great for a lot of things. But learning how to apply compression and expansion isn't one of them.

realistic sample of the cymbal and capture a lot of its decay, you'd probably want to set the control lower—perhaps –60dB—and record it at a time when your studio is at its quietest, such as late at night. (Bummer for your sleeping housemates!) Since the expander is set to a low threshold, the signal chain will be more susceptible to noise coming into the mic or created by the mic preamp.

To learn how to set the threshold control, here's an exercise. Pretend you're about to record a fairly loud electric-guitar part using a miked amp. Set up your signal chain, with your mic in front of the amp, and gain-stage the chain (explained in Chapter 3) so you're exploiting the full dynamic range of all the stages without unwanted distortion. Next, put the expander into the signal chain, ideally by way of your mixer channel's insert jack. If the expander has compressor or limiter sections, bypass them by pressing the appropriate bypass switches or turning those sections' threshold controls all the way up. Turn the expander's ratio knob (which I'll discuss in a moment) all the way up, turn the threshold knob all the way down, and let your guitar sit on a stand with the amp running and the mic picking up the amp's background noise. Now put on the headphones, slowly turn up the expander's threshold knob, and listen to what happens. At a certain point in the knob's travel, the sound of the idling guitar amp will cut out—this is the point you're looking for. Set the threshold slightly above this point. Now, if you so much as touch the guitar's strings, you should hear the gate open up, with the amp sound (and perhaps some string noise) coming through. That's what you want—the expander is gating out the noise, unless some signal is present as well (you touching the strings), at which point the gate opens to let both signal and noise pass through. The expander's threshold is properly set, at least for now.

Ratio: In the exercise above, you probably noticed that when the expander's gate closes, no sound is let through—the gate closes completely. That's okay, but it isn't ideal. Setting an expander's ratio control properly allows the circuit to close more gradually as a sound decays, and it allows the expander to stay slightly open after the sound has decayed

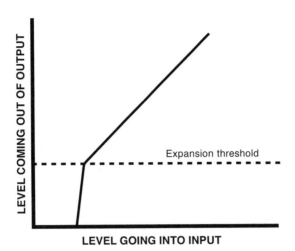

Fig. 4 Below the expansion threshold, the level coming out of an expander's output is much less than it would be if the expander weren't in the circuit.

below the noise floor. It's a bit like leaving a bedroom door open a little when you sleep: doing this lets in some of the light from the hall (similar to the background noise in this analogy) so you aren't in complete darkness (total silence). Fig. 4 is a graph showing how an expander reduces the level at the output when the input level is below the threshold.

Depending on the recording situation, setting up an expander to work like a noise gate—where it slams shut, resulting in sudden silence—can sound unnatural. This is particularly true with a gently decaying sound such as a crash cymbal, which would be abruptly cut off by noise-gate-like expander action (see Fig. 5). A hard-closing gate can mess with the sound in even worse ways, for instance chopping off consonants at the ends of vocal phrases. We need to set the ratio control to avoid these problems, while still allowing the expander to clean up the sound.

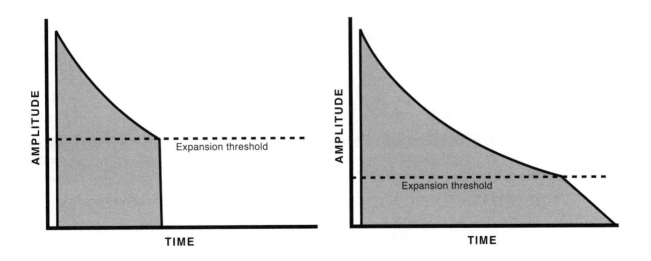

Fig. 5 Recording a crash cymbal through an expander set to a high threshold and high ratio (left) can cut off the cymbal's natural decay. Lowering the ratio and threshold (right) can result in a more natural sound.

With the guitar from the previous exercise still on its stand and the threshold control properly set, start turning down the ratio control and listen to what happens. At a certain point, you'll start to hear the sound of the idling guitar amp coming through—that's the gate opening up slightly. When the ratio control is all the way down, the amp noise should be exactly as loud as if the expander weren't in the signal chain at all; in other words, the gate is all the way open. When you record a track, look for a happy medium between these points. When the signal chain is idling, the gate should be closed enough to quiet the track significantly, but not closed so much that passages with no playing sound unnaturally silent next to played passages (unless, of course, that's the effect you're going for). You also shouldn't be able to hear the gate noticeably opening or closing when you start or stop playing. As much as possible, it should simply sound like your system is a lot quieter.

The trick to using an expander effectively is to find suitable threshold and ratio settings based on the sound you're about to record, as well as the song you're recording. You want the expander to be responsive to any sound you make during the performance—in other words, to anything that you actually want recorded on your track—but not necessarily anything else. Play lightly and let some notes or chords decay. Think about the performance you're about to record: Will you be playing full-out through the whole track? Is there a point where you'll need to hold a chord for several seconds? Will you be playing any passages very quietly? Test out any such critical performance moments and listen to how the expander reacts. If the expander seems to be too sensitive to what you're doing, turn up the threshold control a little. Adjust the controls one at a time until the expander is doing its job cleaning up your signal chain, without calling attention to itself. You may need to compromise—one pair of settings may be good for one part of the song while another is good for a different passage. Try to find settings that work as well as possible across the whole performance. If necessary, you can always punch in certain sections that require very different expander settings (see Chapter 9).

Attack & decay: Most (if not all) expanders have these controls. You'll recognize these terms if you have experience programming synthesizers: attack specifies how fast something rises, and decay specifies how fast it falls afterward. In the case of an expander, attack determines how fast the gate opens when its threshold is suddenly exceeded, and decay determines how fast it closes again when the signal suddenly goes away. You can usually set these knobs and forget them. Normally you want a very quick attack (so as not to cut off the beginnings of sounds) and a medium decay—perhaps around 200 milliseconds—to make sure the ends of sounds don't get truncated. The two sections of an integrated compressor/expander unit may have only one set of attack and decay controls but separate ratio and threshold; that's okay. Having the same settings for both sides usually works fine.

Indicator LED: This is a handy visual element that you can use in conjunction with your ears. One LED, or a series of LEDs indicating a range of levels, may light to show that the device is actively expanding the noise downward. When the gate begins opening, the LED may go dark, or a series of LEDs may progressively turn off as the gate opens wider. Indicator LEDs aren't really that necessary on the expander side—they're much more useful in compression—but they're nice to have anyway.

Compression

Unlike an expander, which increases dynamic range, a compressor reduces dynamic range. In recording, running a signal through both a compressor and an expander can be very effective. Why would you want to reduce and enlarge the dynamic range at the same time? Actually, you wouldn't. They don't both come into play at the same time; an expander does its thing when signals are at their quietest (or nonexistent), and a compressor does its thing in the louder part of the dynamic range. So if you're recording a cymbal crash through both a compressor and an expander, the expander will be working before the sound begins; then the expander's gate opens up immediately when the cymbal is struck, and the compressor takes over. The compressor works perhaps for a few seconds while the cymbal decays (with the expander doing nothing, since the signal is over the expander's threshold). Then the signal enters a kind of no-man's-land between the compressor's and the expander's active ranges, where neither circuit does anything to the signal. Finally, when the expander senses that the crash is decaying below its threshold, its gate begins to close again (see Fig. 6). This process accomplishes two things: the expander cleans up the noise before and after the crash, and the compressor tames the initial peak and thereby allows the whole signal to be brought up in volume, allowing it to have more punch and presence in the mix. If you were recording or sampling a series of cymbal crashes, one after another, the compressor would be even more beneficial: It would tend to even out the crashes

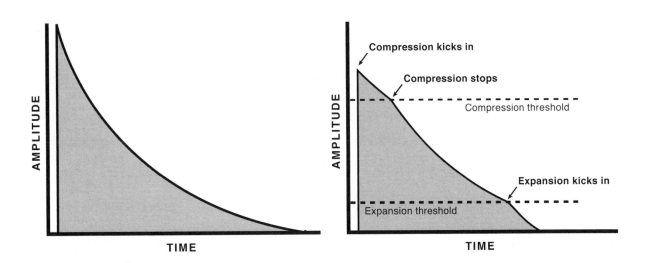

Fig. 6 A crash cymbal (left), and the same crash cymbal through a compressor/expander (right). The compressor and the expander come into play at different points of the cymbal's decay.

in volume, which would make the quieter crashes less likely to get buried in the mix and the louder ones less likely to overwhelm the mix. As a bonus, compression makes a sound less likely to overload stages downstream in the signal chain—which is particularly important if you're recording digitally.

Here's a look at a compressor's typical parameters and how to use them:

Threshold: To understand how compression works, it helps to imagine expansion upside-down. When a signal *rises* past the compressor's threshold, the compression circuit begins to kick in, and when a signal falls *below* this threshold, the compressor stops working. So compression happens only when the signal is above the threshold—just as expansion happens only when the signal is *below* the expander's threshold. Given a gradually rising signal, compression can kick in suddenly, which is called *hard-knee* compression, or the circuit can come into play gradually as the signal rises, which is called *soft-knee* compression. Some compressors allow you to specify which kind it performs; soft-knee compression tends to sound more transparent and natural.

Ratio: This term is a little easier to understand regarding compression. In an ordinary signal-chain stage, such as a mixing board's channel fader, the gain is linear: Any increase in level at the circuit's input will be matched by an identical level increase at the output. If it's a unity-gain stage (meaning that no amplification is occurring), three more decibels going into the circuit will result in 3dB coming out. This is a 1:1 ratio: what you put in is the same as what the circuit pumps out. A compressor changes this ratio, but only in the region of the dynamic range that's above the compression threshold. If the compressor is set for a 2:1 ratio, that means that when the signal level is above the threshold, increasing the level going into the circuit by 2dB will result in only 1dB more amplitude at the output. Likewise, pumping in an extra 10dB will result in only 5dB of output. But if the signal is below the compression threshold,

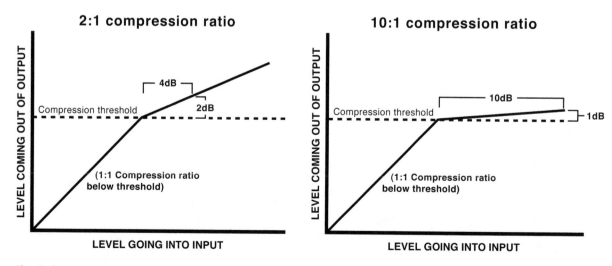

Fig. 7 Above the compression threshold, at a 2:1 compression ratio (left), a 4dB level increase at the compressor's input results in only a 2dB level increase at the output. With a high compression ratio of 10:1 (right), you need to put 10dB more signal into the input to get 1dB more output signal.

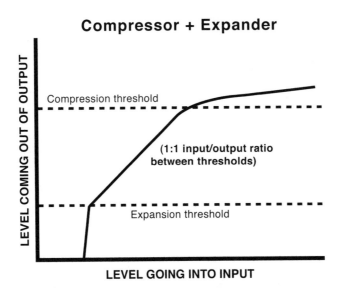

Compressor + Expander

LEVEL COMING OUT OF OUTPUT

Compression threshold

(1:1 input/output ratio
between thresholds)

Expansion threshold

LEVEL GOING INTO INPUT

Fig. 8 With both a compressor and an expander in line, the gain is unaffected only between the compressor's and expander's thresholds.

pumping in an extra 10dB will result in a 10dB increase at the output—the compressor is unity-gain (1:1 ratio) below the threshold. Fig. 7 shows how this works in graph form. It should be easy to see that if you set the compression ratio higher, you need to pump even more signal into the circuit to get the same rise in output: with a 10:1 ratio, a whopping 20dB of extra signal level will cause the compressor's output to rise by only 2dB. With an infinite compression ratio, you can't get the output to rise over the threshold no matter how much signal you put into the circuit. Any compression stronger than about 20:1 is considered *limiting*. A limiter is like the flipside of a noise gate—it's kind of black-or-white, either doing its thing or doing nothing (depending on the signal level at the moment), without much gray area in between.

Combining things, Fig. 8 is a graph showing how having both an expander and a soft-knee compressor in your chain affects a signal's dynamics.

Attack & decay: These parameters are essentially the same as in an expander. Attack specifies how fast the compressor gets to work when presented with a signal that's above its threshold, and decay specifies how fast it returns to a 1:1 ratio when the signal falls below the threshold. With a soft-knee compressor and a signal that slowly rises and falls in level, attack and decay may not come into play at all—but when presented with things like sudden transients, they can have a definite effect on a sound. As I mentioned, in a combined compressor/expander unit there may be just one set of attack and decay knobs; I tend to leave mine set to a very fast attack and a medium-length decay, which seems to work just fine for most sounds.

Indicator LEDs: A "compressor active" LED is a critical feature on a compressor, particularly if you don't have much experience working with compression. Since you can't always hear when compression is happening, particularly with a low ratio, it really helps to have an LED that lights immediately when the compressor's threshold has been exceeded. It provides great visual feedback as to how the compressor is operating with regard to the dynamic range of the performance you're recording. A compressor without this LED is much harder to use effectively, requiring more guesswork and listening skill. Some compressors have additional "gain reduction" LEDs or a gain-reduction VU meter; these are nice to have, but they aren't as important. If you're shopping for a compressor, by all means get one with at least a compressor-active indicator LED.

For the following exercise I'll assume you're using a compressor with ratio and threshold controls as well as a compressor-active LED.

Using A Compressor

Set up a microphone for vocals and run it into an input channel on your board. Put the signal through your compressor by way of the channel insert jack, and put on a pair of headphones. If you have an integrated compressor/expander, set up the expander section as described above—get it to clean up your studio's background noise, but don't let it chop off any final consonants or slowly decaying vowel sounds. If you find that the expander's gate is fluttering open and closed (which can happen if the threshold is right around the background noise level), try raising the threshold a bit, increasing the decay time a bit, or both. Now you can go to work setting up the compressor section.

Set the compressor's ratio knob to about 3:1 and stand in front of the mic, about where you'd be when you're singing. While you watch the indicator LED, make vowel sounds that start soft and increase in volume, and notice when the LED comes on. (If it doesn't come on at all, turn down the compressor's threshold knob and

---

"Manual Compression": Proper Mic Technique

If you watch skilled singers perform live, you'll notice that they constantly vary the position of the microphone relative to their mouth. During loud notes the singer may pull the mic away quite a bit, and during quieter passages the mic may be much closer. This way, the singer can "track" the mic's distance according to the level of the note being sung at that exact moment. This is an important element of mic technique, and because it tends to even out the notes' levels somewhat, it's a way of adding "compression" without using a compressor. The more of this "manual compression" you can

supply while you're recording a vocal track, the less electronic compression you'll require to achieve the same sound in the end. In a studio with a mic on a stand, it may involve simply backing up a foot or so for a particularly spirited phrase, or turning your head slightly away from the mic when you hit a loud note. You probably couldn't perfect your mic technique to the point where you never needed *any* compression; an electronic circuit is just better at tracking and adjusting levels than your ears and muscles are. But a little mic technique can go a long way toward reducing your dependence on compression, thereby allowing you to use compression in a more subtle and transparent manner.

try again.) A good starting position for the threshold is the point where your vocal starts to get loud—in musical terms, somewhere in the mezzo-forte range. If your compressor has a gain-reduction meter or LEDs as well, watch what happens when you sing even louder above the threshold. (When this kind of meter says that 6dB of gain reduction is occurring, it means at that particular moment, the output would be 6dB hotter if the compressor weren't there.)

Now try turning the compressor's ratio knob up or down and repeat the exercise, and try to hear a difference. You may notice that with a higher ratio setting (like 6:1), as you sing louder and louder above the threshold, the sound of your voice in the headphones may seem to get quieter. What's actually happening is that the sound of your vocal cords being conducted through the bones of your skull is overtaking the headphone sound, because the latter is being compressed while the former isn't. That's okay. If you want to hear what the compression really sounds like, record yourself. Record your vocals getting louder and louder first at 2:1, then 4:1, and then 8:1, and listen to the difference.

The best compression—and this applies not only to vocals but pretty much to every instrument—should do its thing without calling any attention to itself. If you recorded yourself in the above exercise, you may have noticed that the sound can start to get "squashed" near the top of the dynamic range, particularly with lower compression thresholds and higher ratios. How much "squashing" you can get away with depends largely on the context of the track you're recording. If it's a loud, rocking song with loud, rocking vocals, you can get away with a more "squashed" sound—in fact, very heavy compression is a cool effect frequently used on vocals, drums, and other sounds (see Chapter 6). On the other hand, if you're recording a soft tune with an intimate vocal, you need to be more careful about how the compression is sounding. If the compression in this kind of setting is noticeable, it can ruin a performance; it sounds unnatural and detracts from the performance's intimacy. Unless you're using heavy compression as an effect, try to make the compression as transparent as possible—it should sound like it's not even there. If you can hear the compression kick in during playback, try using a lower ratio as well as a slightly lower threshold. The lower ratio will make the compression sound less heavy-handed, while the lower threshold will bring down the hottest peaks' levels to about where they were with the previous settings. If you end up being the only person in the world who knows that a track was compressed, then you know you've done a good job applying compression.

Why Compression Is So Important

It might be a good idea to compress just about every track you record, before you record it. An exception is commercially sampled sounds (including drums)—first, because sampled sounds are often already compressed somewhat; second, because you may be bringing these into the mix by way of MIDI (see Chapter 1)

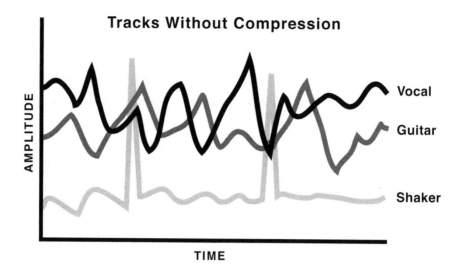

Fig. 9 Uncompressed tracks are hard to mix because their levels are constantly changing.

and therefore aren't actually recording them during the tracking phase; and third, because sampled sounds have more even, predictable dynamics than live acoustic sounds. For everything else, adding compression while tracking just makes everything much easier.

Here's why: Acoustic sounds, as well as many electronic sounds, tend to vary quite a bit in level. If you're recording a shaker percussion part without any compression, the loudest shakes may be a good 9dB louder than the softer shakes. Meanwhile, on your uncompressed rhythm-guitar track, some chords may be right up near the top of your system's dynamic range (0dB), while others are at −4dB. This kind of variation could be occurring on most of your song's tracks, including the all-important lead vocal, throughout the whole song (see Fig. 9). It's extremely difficult to create a consistently good mix of a song under these circumstances. Even if you could get the mix perfect for one moment in time, a half-second later the mix

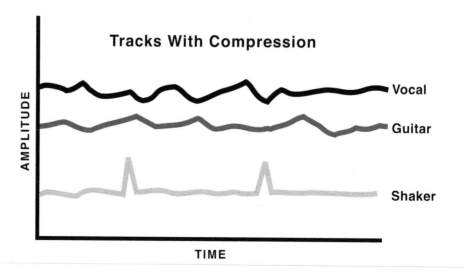

Fig. 10 The same tracks with compression can be mixed in a much more smooth, consistent way.

could be totally different—the rhythm guitar could suddenly get much louder and suffocate the lead vocal for a moment, which may have gotten suddenly quiet at that moment anyway, making matters worse. You have no real control over the blend, and the end result could be a random pastiche of obnoxiously loud moments and inaudibly buried moments.

Compression solves this by getting levels under a certain amount of control. If the levels of each instrument vary by only 2dB or 3dB, you can achieve a much smoother mix than if each instrument is varying by 9dB. From the song's beginning to its end, the mix will be much more consistent than a similar mix of uncompressed tracks (see Fig. 10). Simply stated, it makes things easier in the studio. And since we Guerrilla recordists mix as we go, we need to have the tracks compressed as they go down. Million-dollar facilities may be able to compress each track separately during the mix; we can't.

De-essing

The process known as "de-essing" is a type of compression. If you record a vocal track very bright, adding some top-end EQ, you'll get a very present, airy sound—two good qualities to have on a vocal track. However, moments where words have "s" sounds can cause an explosion of noisy *sibilance*. Sibilance refers to excessive high end associated with the sound of the consonants S, Z, etc. Sibilance can mess up an otherwise well-recorded track, and if you have an effective way to tame a track's sibilance, you should use it.

The most common way to do this is by de-essing the track (see Fig. 11). De-essing refers to compression based only on the signal's high-end frequency content. Here's how it traditionally works using hardware compression: An audio track is split into two parts, and one of the parts goes through a highpass filter, which removes everything but the highs—say, everything below 8kHz. This highs-only signal is then fed into a compressor's *side-chain input*. This is an input that allows the compressor to react to a signal different from the one it's actually compressing. Meanwhile, the non-filtered portion of the signal goes into the compressor's normal input. When there's

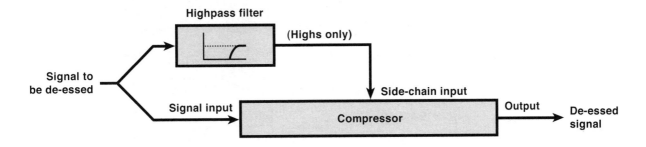

Fig. 11 In de-essing, the signal is split, and compression is applied based on its high frequencies only. This is done by sending a highpass-filtered signal into the compressor's side-chain input.

Watch That De-esser!

A good de-essing stage allows you to brighten up a vocal track considerably without making the "s" sounds harsh or spitty. The object of de-essing should be to return the performance to natural-sounding sibilance—nothing more, nothing less. After applying de-essing, listen carefully to the track and make sure it simply sounds natural. If you overdo or incorrectly set up the de-essing, you'll hear the vocal track "duck" or "breathe" every time there's an "s" sound: The track will seem to collapse in an unnatural way for a moment. Another possible by-product of de-essing is a lisping sound; "th" sounds are similar to "s" sounds, only with much less high frequencies. If de-essing is causing either of these side effects, it's doing more harm than good. De-essing, like good full-bandwidth compression, should not call any attention to itself. Experiment with the de-essing compressor's parameters until you achieve a natural-sounding sibilance while leaving the rest of the track untouched.

a burst of high frequencies from an excessive "s" sound, it easily passes through the highpass filter, goes into the side-chain input, and causes the compressor to attenuate the full-range signal going into the input jack. The result: the track is compressed slightly at the moment where the excessive sibilance occurred, thereby taming the sibilance. Theoretically, you could achieve the same result by manually pulling down the fader whenever the harsh "s" sounds occurred, and then immediately returning the fader to its original position—but this would be difficult or impossible (particularly if you're singing at the same time!). De-essing, like ordinary compression, makes this process automatic, so you don't have to worry about it.

In a digital studio, the simplest way to de-ess a track is to put a de-essing plug-in on it. The plug in will probably allow you to specify a threshold for the de-essing

Fig. 12 A de-esser plug-in. Level indicators are always helpful; this plug-in has one for gain reduction (GR) of the sibilance.

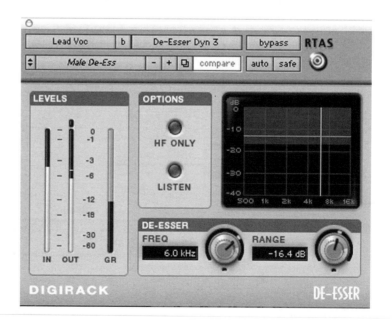

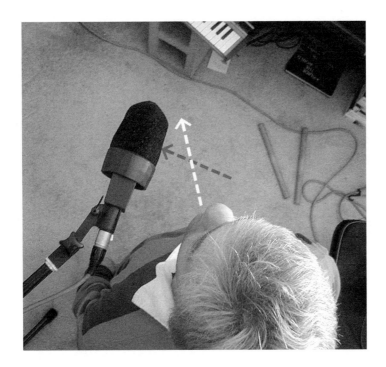

Fig. 13 Singing slightly past a microphone (white arrow), rather than straight into it (gray arrow), reduces problems with breath noise and also softens sibilance. This mic has a pop filter installed.

compression circuit, and perhaps also a cutoff frequency, which specifies how high the highs must be to trigger the de-esser (see Fig. 12). If you don't have a de-essing plug-in or you're recording analog, you could use an outboard compressor to do ordinary compression while tracking, and then run the track through a de-essing configuration during mixdown. Or, you could buy a second compressor. Some compressors have a built-in "de-ess" button which, when pressed, turns the compressor into a de-esser (mid- and low-frequency dynamics remain unaffected). No matter how you employ de-essing, be sure to experiment with various settings to see what sounds best.

Of course, it's better to avoid excessive sibilance on a track in the first place. With many condenser mics, singing too closely to the mic, or too directly into the mic, can enhance sibilance in an unnatural way. By backing off the mic and singing a little off-axis—meaning you're kind of singing *past* the mic rather than directly into it (see Fig. 13)—you can achieve a more natural sound with fewer sibilance problems.

P-Pops

"P-pops" aren't really related to controlling dynamics, but in terms of the frequency spectrum they are the polar opposite of sibilance, so I'll mention them here. A P-pop results when *plosive* consonants—the sounds of the letters P and B—produce a puff of air that hits the mic diaphragm, causing a low-frequency thump on the track. At worst, this thump can have so much energy it causes the signal to distort one of the downstream stages—but usually it just sounds annoying and unprofessional, and often it causes a compressor to make the signal "duck" for a moment, which sounds unnatural. The simplest way to prevent P-pops is to install a pop filter in front of the microphone. These are available commercially, either as a cover that slips over the mic itself, or as a two-layer fine-mesh screen stretched over a ring, which attaches to the mic stand and can be positioned with a flexible assembly. For a while I used a piece of silkscreen stretched on a wooden frame with good results. And similar to taming sibilance, you can go a long way toward preventing P-pops just by singing a little off-axis. There's really no reason you need to sing directly and closely into a mic, unless you're recording background vocals consisting of pure vowel sounds and you want to make them sound as airy and intimate as possible. (More on recording vocals in Chapter 7.) You'll get a more natural, balanced sound if you back off the mic a bit and sing over it or past it a little.

CHAPTER 5

Separation

One characteristic common to all good recordings is *separation*. In a recording with good separation, you can clearly hear each individual track or part; even if one instrument or voice is much quieter than others, you can still hear it as you're listening to the mix. Some of the sounds are intentionally blended together. For instance, you might not want to be able to hear the individual performances in a six-part background-vocal arrangement; instead, you'd blend them together into a unified but distinctly audible part of the whole.

The result of good separation—assuming the recording is also free of excessive noise and unwanted distortion—is a sound that many people describe as "clean." If, on the other hand, the recording was made with poor separation, the instruments tend to blur together into a kind of ambiguous glob of sound, and the listener's ear doesn't really go anywhere in particular. Sometimes, this may be what you want. But in most cases, recording musicians want a clean-sounding, clear mix where the individual parts have good presence, and this means the separation needs to be good.

Separation Fundamentals

What contributes to good separation? Actually, all three of the "dimensions of sound" that I've been mentioning—dynamics, frequency content, and pan position—are the keys to getting sounds to separate effectively in a mix.

Dynamics. If the individual parts' dynamics are uncontrolled and fluctuating all over the place, a sound can disappear for a moment while it's masked by other instruments; then it may reappear and mask other instruments, causing them to disappear. Even if the instruments are otherwise well separated, the mix will be uneven, and you'll have trouble picking out one sound in the mix for any length of time. The solution is to control the dynamics through compression (see Chapter 4). If you give each instrument its place in the mix by settling down its dynamic fluctuations, it has a much better chance of being heard consistently as the song plays.

Frequency content. One way to make an instrument fall back or recede in the mix is to cut its high-frequency content. Highs and upper-mids make things sound more up-front, so cutting these frequencies tends to make an instrument less "present"—and in a dense mix, that can mean the sound practically disappears. This may be what you want; by no means does every instrument need to be at the forefront of the mix. Some sounds work well as minor elements in an orchestration, contributing to the mix almost subliminally. But if it's an important part, like a funky rhythm guitar, it should be up where it can be heard—and that means it may benefit from a little high-end boost. However, inexperienced recordists often pile the highs onto lots of the sounds, thinking this is what's needed to make all of them "pop." But instead, it only causes them all to wash out equally, resulting in a mix that fatigues the ear. It's a matter of balance and taste. A large part of learning to record and mix involves learning how much upper-frequency content is appropriate for each part—as well as learning when you've gone too far, like a cook with a jar of curry powder and a heavy hand.

Actually, the *entire* frequency spectrum is important in achieving separation, not just the highs. A huge factor in getting sounds to separate is a concept called *frequency slotting*. Frequency slotting means making sure each instrument has a "niche" in the frequency spectrum, and as much as possible, keeping the sounds out of each other's way frequency-wise. More on how to achieve this in a moment.

Pan position. In terms of separation, this is the simplest "dimension" to understand. On a monophonic recording, all of the instruments are bunched up together in the middle of the (non-) stereo image. Panning the instruments in various ways between the left and right channels is a simple way to almost physically separate them from each other. If a recording consists entirely of piano and guitar, even if their dynamics are all over the map and they occupy the same zone of the frequency spectrum, all you have to do is pan them left and right somewhat and they'll separate from each other. It might still be an ugly recording, but at least the two instruments will be clearly distinct, coming differently out of the left and right sides.

Determining pan positions is a matter of personal taste and artistry. I'll discuss pan position as it relates to individual sounds in Chapter 7.

Frequency Slotting

Frequency slotting is an important part of the process of creating a clean, balanced, and crisp-sounding recording. Even among those who put slotting into practice, some think about it only when it's time to mix. But unless you have mountains of outboard gear and plug-ins and processor power for mixdown, you may want to try to get ahead of the game. Think about frequencies *before* the sounds get captured on your hard drive in the first place.

Consider a painter creating a still-life of a bowl of fruit. If he used only one color for all of the fruit, the table, and the background, it would be pretty hard to distinguish the various elements depicted in the painting. They'd all kind of blur together, and you might have to squint or look closely to tell them apart. But if each element has a distinctive hue and shade, there will be contrast and a heightened sense of drama. The composition's strengths will be enhanced, too. These hues and shades are not unlike the tone "colors" on an audio recording: they create a more detailed, more interesting, less homogenous sound-image of all of its various elements.

If your mix consists of ten different instruments, allowing each one to "specialize" in a particular neighborhood of the frequency spectrum will allow it to be more present or audible in the final mix, because the instruments won't have to compete against each other as much. The flipside of this is also true. If you don't want the instruments separated out—if you want a "wall of sound," like the kind producer Phil Spector made famous in the 1960s—you can employ a kind of anti-frequency slotting. Just bunch all of the instruments together in a similar frequency range through your choice of tones, EQs, etc. You'll get more of a unified, sonically amorphous texture than a blend of distinct instruments.

You might also ask: On a good record, the instruments sound tight and together, like they're a unified and blended (not separated) whole, right? Absolutely. But certainly a big part of that kind of mix relates to the performances themselves, not necessarily

---

The Peek-A-Boo Principle: Arranging Comes First

This book is about recording songs, not writing or arranging them. But when your goal is instrument separation, it really helps to put some thought into the song's arrangement before you start recording. There's probably no better way to separate two instruments sonically than by separating them in time. If you have a piano and a guitar in a mix, and the piano is playing on the downbeats and the guitar is on the upbeats, they're automatically separated—you will hear them as distinct sounds, even if they're panned together and occupy the exact same frequency space. You'll be able to hear both instruments clearly.

A whole book could be written on this topic, so it's something to keep in mind either when you're arranging a song or laying down a track. The great hit-making studio rhythm sections of the '60s, like the Funk Brothers with Motown or the Bar-Kays with Stax, understood this well and used many tricks to achieve the goal of keeping the instrumental parts together yet distinct—for example, everyone laying out on beat *two* so that the snare-drum backbeat could really pop out of the mix. You can put this into practice, too. If you're recording a bass line, for instance, don't put that slick upper-register fill during the lead vocal's climactic moment or even during the triplet-16ths drum fill. No one will hear it, and it'll probably just make that moment of the song unnecessarily busy. Instead, *pick your spot*— listen for a place, perhaps between vocal phrases, where something is needed. That way, when you mix your song, you won't need to reach for an EQ knob or something to make sure the listener catches your slick fill. It'll be the focus of attention at that moment. As a bonus, a song that shifts around its focal points in this way—where the various parts are essentially playing "peek-a-boo" with the listener—is more interesting than one where all of the parts are monotonously consistent. Take a close listen to the classic recordings on Stax or Motown to hear what I mean. Better yet, "re-produce" one of them (see Appendix C).

the sounds. Performances affect the sound of a mix in ways that are more time-related (or rhythmic) rather than sonic. A well-performed song can be rhythmically tight but sonically mushy, and a badly performed song can have great sonic separation but still be a complete mess. It's important to understand the distinction, and to know whether what you're hearing is performance-related slop or sound-related mush.

Even assuming you're recording performances that are tight and together, before you get them to blend into a unified whole, each sound needs to be separate and pure. It's like a recipe. Imagine if you had to bake chocolate-chip cookies but there was salt in your brown sugar, eggs in the flour, and flour in the butter. The cookies might still turn out all right, but you'd have less control over the final product than if all of the ingredients were originally pure and high quality. Mix good ingredients together in the right proportions and you'll get good cookies. It's similar with recording music: get clean, good-sounding recordings of your performances first, and then blend them together just right. More about how to get the perfect blend in Chapter 10.

Frequencies & Their Roles

Each region of the audio frequency spectrum has a function in music. All of the frequencies—at least in the audible 20Hz to 20kHz range-are important, and they should all be represented in some way in your mix.

If your recording is a solo acoustic guitar performance, you'll want to capture the sound with a mic that covers a broad range of frequencies, from the very bottom to the very top. If you were recording solo didgeridoo (a low-sounding aboriginal wind instrument from Australia), you'd certainly want to feature the bellowing fundamental on the bottom, but you'd also want to get that airy breath and wind noise in the top end. If you recorded only the didgeridoo's distinctive lows and cut off everything over 1kHz, the recording would be dull. The upper half of the frequency spectrum has a function—in this case, to add life and excitement to the performance. Then again, sometimes the low end has the function of supplying excitement; it depends on the instrumentation, the musical style, the tempo—lots of things.

When you're recording an instrument, take a moment to think about how it should sit in the frequency spectrum. For example, a fingerpicked acoustic guitar (see Fig. 1) has a lower region that represents the "body" or "fullness" of the sound; a middle that covers the fundamentals of the upper, more melodic notes; an upper region that makes up the picking sounds and the "zing" of the strings; and finally a high region for that hard-to-describe "air" or "openness." To hear what I mean, record a simple fingerpicked acoustic-guitar part with a condenser mic and flat EQ. Then, as the track is playing back, give the mid EQ a generous boost (either with your mixing board's sweepable-mid EQ or with a similar EQ plug-in in your virtual console). If there's a "Q" or bandwidth control, give it a mid-to-narrow setting. Slowly sweep through the frequencies and listen to how this enhances different aspects of the sound. Also notice where, in terms of hertz and kilohertz, these aspects reside. (If your mid-EQ doesn't

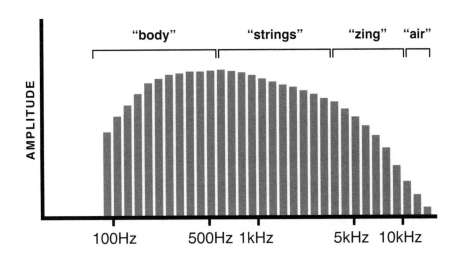

cover a broad-enough frequency range, use a graphic EQ or outboard parametric EQ instead.) Achieving this kind of familiarity with sounds is a major step in learning to record, because if you're mixing a song and you decide the acoustic guitar should have more "body," it helps to know exactly how to get it.

That said, it's important that you learn how to record instruments "flat," with as little EQ as possible, as well. Don't fall into the common habit of recording tracks haphazardly, thinking you can always "fix it in the mix" later. For example, recording an acoustic guitar with the mic too close to the soundhole may yield an overly boomy sound with insufficient note-definition and highs. If you subsequently try to balance out the sound by cutting the lows and cranking up the highs, the lows may be tamed but may sound thinner or less natural than they should—and while the highs may be enhanced somewhat, they won't sound as natural as "real" highs. (Of course, boosting the highs means there will be more noise as well.) You'd be better off playing around with the mic's positioning before you record the track. Record a short segment with the mic in one place, then listen back, move the mic a bit, and repeat until you get something that sounds, to your ears, as much like a professional acoustic guitar recording as you can get. This ability to judge what sounds natural will develop over time, but you should at least approach the situation with the proper mindset.

As your ear and recording skills develop over time, you will refine this approach. Increasingly, you'll base your sonic choices not only on the instrument you're recording but also on the song you're working on. As a rule of thumb, the sparser a song's arrangement, the flatter and more full-range each sound can be. But if an arrangement is very full and many sounds are competing for space, that's when frequency slotting becomes most necessary. Eventually, when you're working on a song, you'll have a sense of where each sound most effectively needs to live, and this knowledge will affect the choices you make as you're recording each track. But when you're starting out, simply concentrate on recording a solid-sounding track with minimum EQ. You can always change the EQ as you go along.

GUERRILLA TACTIC	*The Kick-Drum Click Trick*

Everyone knows that drum sounds are important in recording, and of course, the kick drum (a.k.a. the bass drum) is one of the most important drum sounds. But it's often a challenge to give the kick drum a distinct sound in a busy mix; often it just gets buried, and if you try to turn it up, you just get a lot of woofy energy in the lows, not necessarily a more audible kick drum. To solve this problem, think of a kick-drum sound as actually two sounds at once. There's the sharp *snap* or *click* of the beater hitting the drum head (the attack), along with a full *thud*. Often, getting the kick drum to pop out of the mix better simply involves enhancing the first part of the sound. You can do this in a couple of ways. You can enhance the clicky aspect of the beater sound with EQ; try a narrow boost somewhere between 1kHz and 2kHz. Or, assuming you're using sampled drums, you can blend in a separate sound that's all click—perhaps it's a different kick-drum sound with all of the lows rolled off—and trigger that sound with every kick-drum event. (Just make sure the attacks of both sounds coincide exactly; otherwise the overall sound will lose its tightness.) When I was doing drums with a sampler keyboard, I had a "click only" sound ready on the keyboard's hard drive just for this purpose, and I would blend it into most of my kick-drum sounds. It was a very effective way to make sure the critical attack of the kick sound was always audible in the mix.

Separating A Simple Mix

Let's consider how you would go about enhancing separation on a simple recording: just acoustic guitar, recorded with one condenser mic, a male lead vocal recorded (in a separate performance) with the same mic, and a shaker percussion track. The three performances exist in mono on three separate tracks. The vocal has already been compressed somewhat during tracking, so that the louder part of its dynamic range is more even and present and its softer moments are more audible, and the guitar has been compressed just a bit to bring down its loudest moments, allowing the instrument to be more present in the mix overall. The shaker track has been compressed considerably, as its levels were varying greatly before the compression was added.

It's possible you could get excellent results simply by blending the three tracks in mono, particularly if the three parts play off each other rhythmically so that each gives the others space. You may not even have to think about frequency slotting or panning. If, however, the vocal and guitar often crash into each other (particularly at key lyrical moments), then the mix would benefit from a little frequency slotting. Here's how to proceed if you like the levels of the vocal and guitar against each other but some of the words aren't as intelligible as you'd like, or if the vocal just seems a bit sonically "crowded" by the guitar.

Think about the goals of the recording. Is the song a showcase for the guitarist, with the vocal serving merely an atmospheric or embellishing function? If not, you'll probably want to think "vocals first." You can assume the audience will be listening to vocals closest; typically, a vocal is what most listeners' ears latch onto. Therefore, craft the mix so as to feature the vocal, without neglecting the guitar.

Vocals—particularly male vocals—have a broad frequency range, with fundamentals in the low-mids and breath sounds and sibilants ("s" sounds) extending well past 10kHz. But vocals tend to be "centered" somewhere around 2kHz. This is the area that gives vocals presence; it's where you'll find most of the voice's formants—the harmonics, as resonated and enhanced by the singer's chest and head. You can think of this frequency region as the track's "signature" frequency band. Simply put, gently boosting this area (or cutting this area in competing sounds) will give the track more presence and make it seem more up front. Boosting or cutting other frequency bands will have different effects, but they won't necessarily enhance the vocal's presence.

Acoustic guitar, on the other hand, has a somewhat lower "signature" frequency region—let's say somewhere around 800Hz. That's one of the reasons why vocals and acoustic guitar go well together: Their frequency characteristics tend to naturally separate from each other somewhat. Recorded, the guitar needs to provide the song's foundation frequency-wise. There needs to be some bottom end to anchor the recording; the vocal doesn't "live" down in that region enough, so the guitar should provide that function. Also, the sound of vibrating acoustic guitar strings contains plenty of harmonics, but they're subordinate to the fundamentals. A guitar doesn't have the resonating chambers that a human head and chest do, so it has ordinary harmonics rather than formants.

The shaker, meanwhile, is very much a high-frequency part. In fact, there may be nothing substantive below about 5kHz. That isn't to say there's *nothing* below 5kHz, though—it's just that there may not be anything good or useful down there. To hear what I mean, try recording a shaker part with a condenser microphone. Then, while listening back, give everything under 5kHz a hearty EQ boost. What do you hear? Chances are, it's a fairly ugly sound, one that doesn't sound much like a shaker at all. The reason is that you boosted frequencies that weren't characteristic of the shaker; they aren't the frequencies you want to get out of a shaker on a recording. The shaker's signature frequencies are above 5kHz, and all of the other frequencies just tend to get in the way. You could certainly record the shaker full-range, but the resulting mix wouldn't sound as clean as one that highlights the shaker's best frequencies. Equalization is one way to make this happen—particularly on high-frequency-specific sounds like this (as well as hi-hat, crash cymbal, etc.), where you can simply roll off the less-useful frequencies.

So now we have figured out roughly where all three sounds' "signature" regions exist: around 2kHz for the vocal, 800Hz for the guitar, and perhaps 8kHz for the shaker (see Fig. 2). If you wanted to do some gentle frequency slotting with this arrangement, you could use either the EQ on your mixing board, or EQ plug-ins in your virtual console. Start by giving the vocal a slight boost (1dB may be plenty) at 2kHz, with a similar cut to the guitar at the same frequency. Since the guitar needs to supply a solid bottom end, listen to hear if the vocal's low notes are muddying up the mix as they coincide with the guitar's frequencies in that region (somewhere around 400Hz). If so, you might try gently cutting the vocal's low mids. You don't want to cut a vocal's

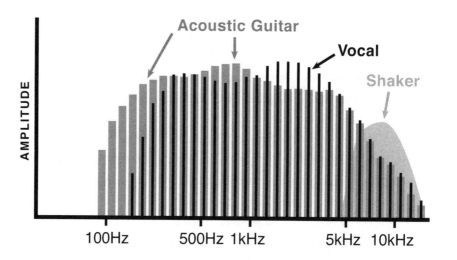

Fig. 2 The frequency profiles of an acoustic guitar, a vocal, and a shaker can be gently shaped to give each sound more "room" in the frequency spectrum—and therefore, better separation.

lows too much, though, as that can remove its "body"—almost literally—and make it sound detached, thin, and less warm. Slotting the shaker is easy: just roll off everything below 5kHz. If that seems too extreme, try a lower cutoff frequency, or a gentler cut.

Since you're "mixing as you go," you should have already set rough levels for the three tracks. Level-wise, the vocal will probably sound like it's a little in front of the guitar, to highlight the singer. The shaker, though, will probably be much lower in level than the others—maybe by 12dB or more—because nobody wants to hear a shaker track in their face on a nice guitar/vocal tune. It's an accent, a spice, a background element. Also, since the shaker is both percussive and heavy on the highs, you'll be able to hear it easily, even at low levels. An acoustic guitar just doesn't produce that much energy above 5kHz, and vocals do only during sibilant moments, so the shaker is very much by itself in that frequency band 95 percent of the time. There's no need to make the shaker loud at all; comfortably audible in the background is sufficient.

By now, the guitar, vocal, and shaker are living in their frequency "homes" and are conflicting less with each other than when we began. In terms of frequency, they're separated. Now we can use pan position to enhance this separation further. We have three tracks—if we pan all of them to the center, then the recording will be monophonic, except perhaps for some reverb we might add. Can we pan the guitar and vocal, say, to 9 o'clock (left) and 3 o'clock (right)? Sure—but this is kind of unconventional, because the all-important lead vocal is typically panned to the center, and listening to a left/right mix like this won't exactly conjure the feeling of sitting in front of a singer while he's playing a guitar. How about panning the vocal to the center while the guitar is off to the left and the shaker is on the right? Okay, but now the mix will be lopsided in the stereo field—one channel (the left) will have a much higher level than the other, because the guitar is some 10dB louder than the shaker.

What to do? You have several options. If you had recorded the guitar on two tracks with two mics (discussed in Chapter 7), or a mic and a pickup on the guitar on two tracks, you could pan them left and right somewhat, with the vocal in the center.

But let's say you didn't. One idea would be to pan the guitar to about 11 o'clock and the vocal to 1 o'clock; this would separate them a little spatially, but they'd still both sound more or less like they're coming from the center. Or, you could pan them both to center and give them different reverbs. You could pan the vocal to center and the guitar to 10 o'clock, with a slight echo or tasteful chorus effect (see Chapter 6) that's panned to 2 o'clock or 4 o'clock. Or, you could combine the above approaches. As for the shaker, since it's a very quiet part, you could pan it almost hard-left or hard-right. Personally, I like the sound of a percussion part way off to the side with a slapback echo or reverb of the part in the same location on the other side; it offers a nice balance plus an enlarged sense of space in the recording. Fig. 3 is a visual representation of some of these stereo images.

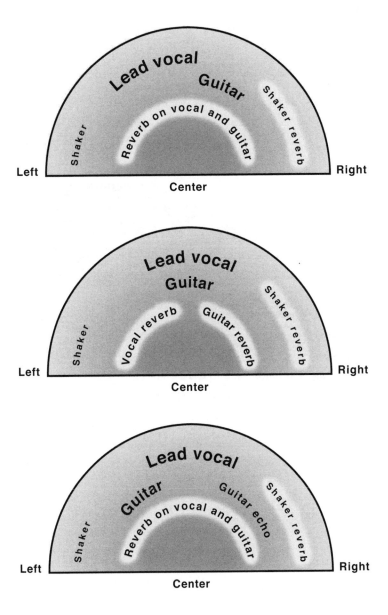

Fig. 3 This kind of diagram illustrates a way to think about the panning of sounds and effects—in this case, three possible ways to separate out a vocal, guitar, and shaker through different pan positions.

Effects such as echo and chorusing offer many opportunities to enhance separation by altering the stereo-field placements of sounds. I'll cover them in detail in the next chapter.

Separating More Complex Mixes

The concepts described above apply to complex mixes, too. The more complex the mix—the more stuff is going on all at the same time—the more that separation is needed. For a really complex mix with drums, bass, several guitars, keyboards, vocals, and who knows what else, you may have to use every technique available to keep the mix separated and clean-sounding. That may mean heavily compressing everything, giving each sound (including each individual drum sound) its own pan position, frequency-slotting most of the tracks, and using multiple reverbs.

Fig. 4 shows a chart of the frequency spectrum, with highly approximate key frequencies of instruments in a complex rock mix. Use this only as a guideline, not a recipe—every sound you record will have its own unique frequency characteristics.

Fig. 4 A visual representation of the way instruments can separate out by frequency in a very dense mix. Note that the acoustic guitar and piano, which can produce a lot of low frequencies on their own, work better in a mix when their lows are EQed so they compete less with things like crunch guitars.

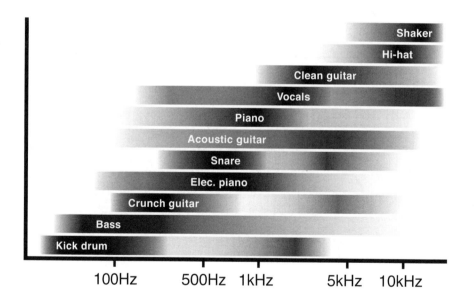

CHAPTER 6

Effects:
The Recording Spices

Many home recordists think effects are like the frosting on a cake: they're kind of an afterthought, slopped on top after the cake is finished baking, perhaps to help mask inadequacies in the cake itself. But I recommend thinking of effects more like spices—intrinsically important parts of the whole, to be added with care and good taste. If you think of effects this way, you'll be less afraid to add an effect to a track during the tracking process (i.e., "printing" the effect), a technique that can serve you very well.

Let's take a close look at all of the effects you're likely to have at your disposal: what they are, how to get them, and how and why to apply them. (Most of these effects are available as digital plug-ins, but for simplicity's sake I'll assume you're working with outboard devices.)

Reverb Effects

Reverb is the king of recording effects. It refers to the smooth, gradually decaying sonic texture that occurs after a sound is made in an acoustically reflective space. If you go into an empty concert hall and yell "Hey!" you'll hear reverb for a few seconds. People sometimes refer to this as "echo," but technically, echo and reverb are very different (see Fig. 1). Echo refers to discrete, repeating reflections of a sound, similar to what you'd hear if you yelled "Hey!" between two cliff sides 100 yards apart. In a concert hall, however, there are so many reflective surfaces that the individual random echoes almost immediately blend into a smooth sound that's pleasing to the ear. That's reverb.

Types of reverbs. Decades ago, the only ways a recording engineer could add reverb in the studio were to use either a real acoustical space (popularly called an "echo chamber") or a mechanical device to simulate real acoustical reverb. In the first method, a sound was fed into a loudspeaker situated in a room with highly reflective surfaces. On the other side of the room was a microphone, which fed a reverb signal back to the studio's control room. The invention of the *plate reverb* (and to a lesser degree the *spring reverb*) provided an alternative to the actual reverb chamber. A plate

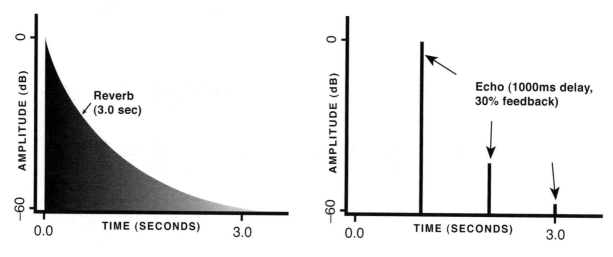

Fig. 1 When you apply reverb to a short sound (left), the result is a smooth decay. Echo (right) creates a discrete delay that can repeat if some of its output is fed back into the input.

reverb—still used in some studios—consists of a suspended sheet of metal with a transducer at either end. One transducer causes the source signal to create vibrations in the metal; myriad reverb-like reflections then bounce back and forth across the sheet, and another transducer picks up these reflections and turns them back into an electrical signal. (Two receiving transducers can generate a stereo reverb signal.) A spring reverb is similar but uses a set of metal springs. Spring reverb doesn't sound as authentic as plate reverb, but spring reverbs can be small and cheap to manufacture,

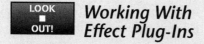 ## Working With Effect Plug-Ins

Digital plug-ins offer an extremely convenient alternative to hardware (outboard) effects: You just load one into a channel on your recording program's virtual mixing console, and away you go. This is great for speeding up the creative process, particularly with simple effects like delay, which can be thrown onto a track in seconds. Even better, some plug-ins allow you to synchronize the effect with the song's tempo. For instance, you might get a tremolo to cycle exactly twice per beat, always in time with the music—something that wouldn't be easy to achieve with an outboard effect. Plug-ins are also a godsend when a track just needs *something*, but you're

not sure what it is; just cycle through a bunch of plug-ins one after another and you're bound to hit on something that inspires your creativity. At that point, you can tweak the effect to get it just right for that track and that song.

If the sound of a needed effect is complex and demanding, though, be wary about grabbing a plug-in simply because it's quick and convenient. Sometimes, plug-in versions of things like reverbs and phasers just don't sound that good—or if they do, they can be a serious hit on your CPU's workload. Unless you have a really good bundle of plug-ins and your computer system can handle anything you throw at it, reserve plug-ins for basic grunt-work effects like delay, auto-pan, and tremolo, and get your more demanding effects from dedicated hardware processors.

which is why spring reverb "tanks" are found in many guitar amplifiers. Spring reverbs also don't respond very well to quick transients like drums or handclaps; the result is an otherworldly, shooting *ping* that reminds me of the sound I heard as a kid when I'd toss rocks onto a newly frozen lake. Pump a very percussive sound into a guitar amp with spring reverb and you'll hear what I mean. It's a cool effect with a unique, lo-fi sound that can be useful sometimes, but it's nothing like authentic reverb.

Of course now we have digital reverbs (including reverb plug-ins), which have made mechanical reverbs nearly obsolete. While pro engineers still get real room reverb by putting mics around a specially designed performance space, in Guerrilla Home Recording this is usually unfeasible—so this is where digital reverbs save the day. A digital reverb digitizes a source signal and runs it through a mathematical algorithm that simulates the generation of reflections of the sound (and reflections of the reflections) and blends them together. The great thing about digital reverbs is they're small, inexpensive (compared to plates), and highly versatile. Even some downright cheap reverbs sound pretty good. Digital reverbs offer different programs to simulate acoustic hall reverb, small-room reverb, and plate reverbs, plus other specialty effects.

Choosing a digital reverb. In Chapter 1 I mentioned that there are awful digital reverbs and there are great ones. Simply put, a bad reverb is one that doesn't sound real, and a good reverb is one that does. This isn't something you can tell from a magazine ad or even the price tag; you've got to listen to a reverb to judge it. You can choose a reverb based on recommendations, or you can use your ears. My own reverb, a first-generation Yamaha SPX90 circa 1986, is also the first one I bought—I got lucky. (I later bought a second, used SPX90.) As it turns out, this classic piece of gear is still found in many pro studios. I knew I had something good when I read that Peter Gabriel had two of them in his own super-high-tech studio.

Blend At The Board— Not In The Box

Many effects, such as reverbs, allow you to specify the blend of dry and effected ("wet") components being outputted. But if you're feeding the effect by way of an effect send on a mixing board, this "feature" can cause trouble. You don't want the effect to output any dry signal at all, because you've already got the dry signal coming through the channel for that track. Make sure the effect is outputting 100 percent effected signal all the time, and *then* blend in however much of it you want.

Yes, you could send all of your source to the effect and determine the blend there—but why? Doing so only introduces another stage where the source signal could be corrupted by distortion and noise. You'll get a cleaner sound by keeping the source pure and unadulterated within its mixing channel, taking a feed from an effect send, and then blending in a small amount of the effect (or a large amount, as the case may be) with an effect return or a separate pair of channels. Any noise or distortion created by the effect will at that point be brought down in level, ideally below the noise floor of the overall mix.

Poor reverbs don't create as smooth a sound as a good reverb. A simple way to check for this is to run an extremely short sound through the effect, such as a finger-snap. A finger-snap is basically a sharp transient and nothing else—so it will help expose where on the cheesy-to-complex continuum the reverb's functioning falls. A good reverb will do an okay job generating a smooth, realistic-sounding reverb "tail" from a finger-snap. A poor reverb will not; it will sound gritty and grainy, especially as the reverb tail fades to silence. Longer sounds like strings might sound good through a crappy reverb, but they'll sound better through a good reverb—and a good reverb will be able to perform well with more percussive sounds like drums and handclaps (and maybe even finger-snaps).

Another thing to check is the reverb's high-frequency response. Some reverbs are designed with a hyped-up high end in order to provide a crisper, more dazzling sound, but this can create a sizzling, unnatural-sounding response to bright source signals. Try feeding quick "s" sounds into a reverb from a condenser mic and listen to how the unit reacts. Does it sound like an "s" sound in a room or concert hall, or does it sound like someone started frying a huge pan of bacon? There are a lot of "s" sounds on any lead vocal track, and if your reverb reacts to each one with a little explosion of sizzle, it's not going to make the track sound very much like a live performance in a real space.

Applying reverb. Don't make the mistake of thinking that reverb's function is to cover up flaws in a track. Going back to the spices analogy, that's like using hot sauce to cover up the taste of rotting meat—the end result could be even worse. Also avoid the temptation to apply it heavily; a song drenched with reverb is like a salad drenched with goopy dressing. In most cases, reverb sounds best when it provides just a tasty "aura" or "glow" around a sound—cushioning it and giving it a subtle spatial context, not overwhelming it.

Then again, there are times when you want a track to be mostly reverb, or even all reverb. For a lush, pillowy texture on a sustained sound like strings, crank up that

Reverb As A Fickle Fashion

The use of reverb on recordings seems to go in and out of fashion. In the '60s, particularly in psychedelic rock, reverb was hugely popular. In the '70s it became fashionable for drums to be recorded very dry, almost dead-sounding (think of the sound on most disco records). That sound carried into early '80s new wave—but soon afterward, heavy gated reverb on drums became the rage, resulting in a near-arms race of reverb and huge drum sounds on pop-music recordings (reaching a zenith with INXS). Then in the '90s, with the rising popularity of drum loops, reverb began to wane again in popularity. By the 2000s reverb had reached another low in popular music, as bold, heavily compressed, in-your-face sounds became the way to go.

reverb. By "crank up" I don't mean send more source to the reverb box; as always, observe proper gain staging (see Chapter 2). The reverb generator should always be receiving a near-maximum level of source, and you should be controlling the reverb level after it comes back from the reverb device, not before it's even been generated.

One of my favorite sounds is a vocal with no "dry" signal, consisting of reverb only. Perhaps slowly panned around a mix, it can create an ethereal, detached sound that seems to be coming from another dimension. A good way to achieve this sound is to set the vocal channel's effect send to pre-fader and then mute the channel. The "dry" signal will therefore be muted, but the reverb unit will still receive a source signal. Blend the resulting reverb into the mix with an effect return or a pair of input channels dedicated to the reverb.

The proportion of reverb to "dry" signal is largely responsible for a sound's perceived distance in the mix. If you want to make a sound seem to fade off into the distance, switch the send to pre-fader and start fading out the source, and after the source is partially faded out, begin fading out the reverb. If the whole mix is fading out at the end of the song, you can make the fade-out a bit more "organic" by boosting the reverb returns while you're bringing down the master fader; this will make the song seem to go off into the sunset rather than simply getting quieter and quieter.

How about no reverb at all? That can be a great effect (or non-effect). Bass guitar, unless the song is slow and/or sparsely arranged, usually sounds best with no reverb; reverb tends to reduce the instrument's tightness and punch, and it also makes it muddier (neither is good for a bass track). By all means, don't feel you need to apply reverb to all of your tracks, or even to most of them. A mix is more interesting when it has an artful combination of "wet" and "dry" tracks. Put on your headphones and listen to how it's done on your favorite recordings.

Also, avoid using the same amount of the same reverb on several instruments at once. Putting the same reverb on a lead vocal, guitar, and drums tends to make the reverb space flat and uninteresting. Your mix will be better if certain tracks get some

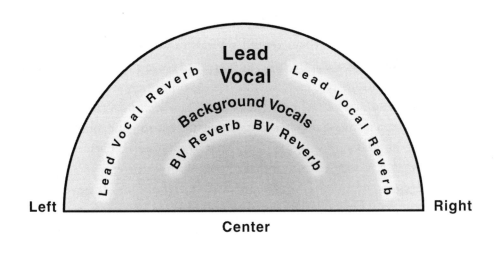

Fig. 2 Here, the lead vocal is panned to center with its reverb spread across the stereo field; the background vocals are spread across the central region, with their own reverb spread slightly wider.

reverb (say, the lead vocals), certain tracks get just a hint (maybe the guitar and snare drum), while other tracks get none at all (the bass and hi-hat, for instance). And if you can tastefully bring in a second or third reverb, either by "printing" reverb onto tracks or using additional reverb units or plug-ins during mixdown, you can really enhance the spatial influence that this effect brings to a mix.

Reverb return channels need not be panned hard left and right. For instance, you can get interesting stereo-image effects by bunching a background-vocal's reverb more toward the center while the lead vocal's reverb spreads across the whole stereo field (see Fig. 2), or vice-versa. Another great sound is to pan a "dry" track to one side and all of its reverb (or maybe just one reverb channel) to the other side. This can create the impression of having a large acoustical space way off on the opposite side from a nearby instrument. It's similar to a surround-sound effect you might hear in a film: the sound seems nearby (from one direction), yet distant (from the other direction) at the same time. So much can be done with reverb; it offers a ton of potential for artistically creative techniques. Have fun with it!

Reverb parameters. The primary variable in a digital reverb sound is the *decay time*. This represents the time, in seconds, for the reverb to drop to 60dB below its starting point. Two to three seconds is about right for a lead vocal; four seconds can be useful for a more lush, expansive effect, although be careful—the longer a reverb lasts, the more it tends to pile up in the mix, leading to clutter and mud. Rolling off some of the lows or low mids can remedy this somewhat. I've found that in general, the faster and busier a song is, the "tighter" (shorter and less muddy) the reverbs need to be. A fast ska song is no place for a languorous five-second reverb! But in a sparse, ambient type of recording, the same reverb may be perfect.

Below two seconds, a reverb can begin sounding metallic or "hard." This is where other parameters, such as "liveness," "diffusion," and "lowpass filter," can help give the reverb a more natural sound. A reverb shorter than one second can create interesting special effects—try it and see what you come up with.

Other than delay time, reverb parameters are not standard and therefore vary quite a bit. For example, some advanced reverbs allow you to specify the dimensions and materials of the room being simulated. With a unit like this, it's a blast to "build" a concrete room that's ten feet square and several hundred feet tall and hear what it might sound like at the top. But as with many effects, don't get caught up in the meaning of all the various parameters. It's helpful to know how to get sounds that you're imagining, and arcane technological details can be fun to play with, but too much knowledge can also bog down your creativity. Just run your sound through the thing, tweak the numbers in real time, and listen to the results. Eventually you'll hit upon something that works well—and that's really all that matters.

Early reflections. Many reverb generators have programs for *early reflections*, kind of a cross between reverb and delay. Early reflections represent reverb's first-occurring component: the direct echoes from the walls of a concert hall, for instance, before

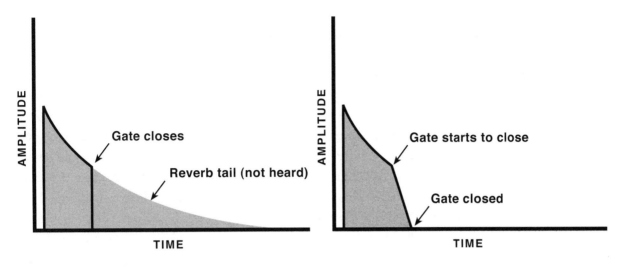

Fig. 3 Gated reverb cuts off soon after the reverb has begun to decay. The cutoff can be made to sound less abrupt by increasing the "release" parameter.

the echoes become so numerous and so diffuse that they blend into a smooth reverb sound. It's a dense, stuttering delay; the number of echoes and the spacing between them can be specified with the effect's parameters. You can use early reflections to create a robotic, gated-reverb-like sound on a snare drum, and I've also laid it thick onto a voice-over to spoof an aggressive radio commercial for a monster-truck rally. Used more delicately, it creates a nice atmosphere behind a strummed acoustic or electric guitar. Because it's a wide stereo effect, it could work well on anything that needs broad ambience where reverb might sound too simple, obvious, or cluttered.

Gated reverb. This effect, which combines reverb and noise gating, is generally attributed to engineer Hugh Padgham in his work on Peter Gabriel's 1980 self-titled

---

GUERRILLA TACTIC *Samples Plus Sampled Reverb*

Paul Simon's song "You Can Call Me Al" features gated reverb tastefully applied to each tom-tom drum. At one point, I wanted to create a similar sound using sampled drums. Putting one gated reverb on all of the toms at once didn't work out; the toms had individual pan positions, but the gated reverb's panning remained static—it didn't follow the toms through a fill. My solution was to create a separate gated-reverb sample, in stereo, for each tom. Instead of just the tom sample sounding,

the reverb sample for that tom sounded as well. In order to create the impression that each tom's reverb had its own position in space, I tightened up the panning so that the reverb "surrounded" the tom. For instance, if a tom was panned to 2:00, I panned the left and right reverb channels to around 12:00 and 4:00. This way, when all of the toms sounded in succession, their respective stereo reverbs "followed" along, creating a large, spacious sound with a complex stereo image. This can produce a bigger, cleaner sound than what you'd get with just one reverb panned hard left and right.

"Melting Face" album. It subsequently became the effect that essentially defined the huge drum sounds of the '80s, and it's still often heard today. By following a reverb with a high-threshold noise gate, you get a reverb that abruptly cuts off after it has decayed slightly (see Fig. 3). Applied to drums (or perhaps only the snare), this allows you to use a "big room" reverb time of two or three seconds—but the gating cleans up all of the reverb between each drum hit, allowing the hits to sound tight and individual, as opposed to blurred together. Basically, a drum sound with gated reverb results in an explosion of reverb for a moment, followed by silence. Listen to any dance hit from the mid '80s and you'll likely hear gated reverb in action.

Many digital reverbs have gated-reverb programs built in, which is obviously more convenient than following a reverb unit with a separate noise gate or expander. These programs often allow you to specify the reverb time as well as a "hold" time (the duration that the gate is held open after a sound exceeds the gate's threshold). A "release" time parameter slows down the gate-closing speed, which makes the gate's cutoff a little less abrupt and artificial-sounding.

If you have only one reverb and want to use gated reverb on your drum track as well as conventional reverb on the vocals and other instruments, you have a couple of options. If you're recording your drums (rather than having them play along with the recording program via MIDI), just "print" the gated reverb by itself, so you can blend it in with the dry sounds and alter the balance at any time. Another option is to build the gated reverb into the drum sample (see the box on Sampling Gated Reverb).

Reverse reverb. Sometimes called "preverb," this sound was made famous in the 1982 film *Poltergeist*; its most familiar musical application is probably in Pearl

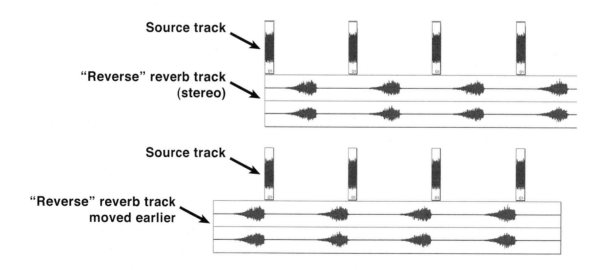

Fig. 4 Using a reverse reverb effect to create "preverb": Record the reverse reverb on a separate track (top), and then shift it backward in time so that it peaks immediately before the source sound (bottom).

Jam's "Even Flow." By running a tape backward, recording reverb from a track onto the backward-running tape, and then playing the tape forward, the film's engineers got reverb that *builds up* to a sound rather than trailing off after it. The effect can be startling, but use it tastefully—reverse reverb gets old fast. Some digital reverbs offer "reverse" reverb programs, but since even the most expensive reverb generator can't predict the future, the reverse reverb doesn't begin until *after* the sound occurs. As a result, you hear your source sound, then a swell of reverb that builds to a peak, but the source sound doesn't occur at the peak. But digital recording makes it easy to use reverse reverb to approximate true preverb: print the reverse reverb, and then shift the reverb track earlier so that it builds to the source sound rather than to nothing (see Fig. 4).

Delay-Based Effects

Along with reverb, delay is one of the most useful effects. The basic idea is simple: a sound is recorded digitally, held in memory for a predetermined time, and then played back. The first studio effect I bought (even before I had a cassette 4-track) was an Ibanez digital delay, and I still use it sometimes—unlike reverbs, all digital delays sound pretty much equally good, so I've never felt the need to upgrade.

Delay effects come in many forms, which is what makes delay one of the most powerful tools in a studio. The factors that determine what a delay does are the delay time, *feedback* (sometimes called *regeneration*), and *modulation*. Feedback refers to adding some delayed signal back into the input, which causes an echo to repeat again and again, softer each time. Modulation refers to altering the digital playback speed, which can do various things to a delay effect, as we'll see.

Basic echo. With a delay set to, say, 300ms (milliseconds) and its feedback set to zero, you'll get a single repeat of everything the delay "hears" at its input, three-tenths of a second later. Turning up the feedback will result in multiple echoes; the higher you set this parameter, the more echoes you'll get and the closer in volume they'll be to each other. On some delays, cranking up the feedback all the way pumps more sound back to the input than what you started with, causing the echoes to build and "run away" into distortion. Neat.

Medium to long echoes are usually best applied as "spot" effects. A good way to do this is to keep the effect-send knob for the delay all the way down for most of a vocal and turn it up just before the last word or syllable of a phrase. This way, only that word or phrase is sent to the delay, and its echo or echoes occur when the vocal track is otherwise silent—the delay doesn't obscure the lyrics. (Think of Pink Floyd's "Us and Them.") If you try to bring the echo in and out using the effect-return knob, you kind of have to guess where the echoes will fall. Also, if there's feedback on the echo, the word or syllable you want to repeat could be contaminated by previous sounds on the track. Working that effect-send knob instead will send what you need delayed to the delay, and nothing else. (If you do run a long delay through an entire vocal, keep it much lower in level than the source, unless you want a psychedelic effect with an obscured vocal melody and lyric.)

Down around 100ms is where you get what I call the "John Lennon delay." On many of Lennon's early-'70s solo recordings, producer Phil Spector used a tape-echo device (the precursor to the digital delay) to add a short single echo to Lennon's vocal. Echo in this timing range is called *slapback* echo; the dry and delayed sounds are close enough in time that you can mix the delay at a fairly high level through a whole track without obscuring the lyrics. The amount of delay you use in the mix determines the effect's intensity.

Shorter than about 50ms, and with a good amount of feedback, you get what's called a *hard reverb* sound—it's similar to reverb in the way it decays, but you don't get the random blending together of a real reverb into a smooth sound. Rather, it's the sound you might get if you shouted while standing between two large, parallel concrete walls. Hard reverb is a distinctive vibrating, metallic effect that can be cool on the snare drum and other sounds. It can quickly become obnoxious, though, so use it with taste.

When you're using a delay, pan positioning can make a big difference in the results you get. With longer echoes it's often effective to pan the echo away from the source—a vocal snippet can appear at left and echo to the right, for instance. With shorter echoes, though, it's usually better to pan the dry and delayed signals together; otherwise the sound bounces around in a disconcerting and confusing way, and you get what seems like a tight performance from one direction and a lagging-behind performance from another direction. Stereo separation allows the listener to hear the delay as a distinct sound; it doesn't blend in with the "dry" sound. But maybe that's what you want—try each approach and see which works best for your song.

Multi-tap delay. With a simple delay, you get an echo that may or may not repeat, depending on the feedback setting. A *multi-tap delay*, though, is like having several delays in one: you could tell it to provide an echo at 100ms, another at 150ms, a third at 350ms, and finally a fourth echo at 600ms. Often these delays are entirely independent, each with its own parameters for feedback and perhaps EQ. A stereo multi-tap lets you assign a different pan position for each delay, so you can have echoes appearing all over the stereo field. (The term *ping-pong delay* refers to a multi-tap in which the echoes are programmed to bounce back and forth across the stereo field.) This effect is so cool it's easy to overuse; unless your mix is sparse or even *a cappella*, your song will be best served if you use a multi-tap subtly, or in a few carefully selected spots. Otherwise your mix can clutter up fast with seemingly random echoes everywhere. Remember, just because you have an effect doesn't mean you need to use it!

Doubling. When a delay is short and by itself (no feedback), it tends to blend into the source sound and disappear somewhat; your ear is unable to distinguish between the original and delayed sounds. This is where modulation can make things happen. When the delay is modulated, its playback speeds up and slows down in a cyclical fashion, like an off-center vinyl record. This makes the delay's pitch go up and down. Applying a small amount of slow modulation to a delay of around 20ms results in a "doubling" effect. It roughly simulates what you'd get if you recorded the performance a second time on a different track: the timing and pitch wouldn't be exactly the same, but close. Doubling with a delay is an okay way to thicken a track, but it never sounds as good as actual double-tracking. You can increase the thickening effect by adding a little feedback, but not too much—the repeats will accentuate the pitch-shifting effect, so just a few low-level repeats can smear the performance's pitch and timing into ugly-zone.

Modulation is controlled by two parameters: width (or intensity) and speed (or rate). Width controls how far from normal the delay's playback speed varies; a low width results in a subtle pitch variation, while a high width causes more extreme fluctuations. The amount of width you can get depends on the delay time parameter; longer delays allow for broader modulation. The speed parameter determines how fast the modulation occurs; like sound itself, it's often measured in hertz (cycles per second), only using much lower numbers. A moderately fast modulation rate of 2Hz means the circuit will go through two speed-up-slow-down cycles every second; a 0.1Hz rate means it takes ten seconds for the cycle to repeat, which is a very slow modulation. Anytime you're working with a modulation delay effect, spend a little time tweaking these two parameters, as they often have a huge influence on the resulting sound.

Chorusing. Similar to doubling, this effect attempts to simulate the sound of a group of singers or instrumentalists performing in unison. Really, though, it usually just adds some movement and interest to an otherwise static sound. Compared to doubling, chorusing delay times are usually a bit shorter (maybe 10ms or 15ms), the modulation is wider and perhaps faster, and there may be some feedback to thicken the sound. Chorusing is popular on synth pads, clean electric guitar, and bass guitar (particularly fretless).

 Chorusing Bass Guitar

Electric bass is an instrument that doesn't get along well with many effects; for whatever reason; it usually sounds best dry and panned straight up. Chorusing is one effect that can work well on bass, but there's a catch: chorusing can have a "blurring" effect on the pitch, particularly if the part is in a low register; with bass you normally want the low end to be tight and solid. One way to get around this (aside from using a plug-in or hardware chorus specifically made for bass) is to split the signal into two, roll off the lows on one of the sides, and chorus this high-frequency side only. When you combine the thinned-out, chorused side with the dry side, the bottom will remain tight and solid, while the top will have some motion and animation. In fact, many chorus effect pedals made for bass have this splitting circuit built in.

Delay is normally a monophonic effect: one channel goes in, and one delayed channel (or a dry/delay blend) comes out. But effects with short delay times can be produced in stereo—two output channels that are slightly different—provided the delay has stereo outputs. Here's how: The delay splits the signal into two channels and flips one channel's waveform over, so that it's a mirror image of the first. (An engineer would say it's "180 degrees out of phase.") Both sides are then delayed by the specified time. When the dry sound is blended back in with the two-channel delayed signal, frequency cancellations occur in the out-of-phase side, causing the frequency makeup of the two stereo channels to be different at any given moment. The ears therefore perceive a subtle difference between the two sides, creating the impression of a "wider" sound. That's why stereo chorusing is a popular way to "widen out" sounds that might otherwise seem thin and one-dimensional.

Although chorusing is useful, it doesn't sound particularly authentic. So, for background vocals and other applications where you need a more symphonic, layered texture, you're usually better off just building up multiple takes. If you need to conserve tracks or CPU power (or just want to make mixing a little simpler), you can bounce them down to stereo (see Chapters 1 and 9).

Flanging. When delay times get into the single-digit millisecond range, an effect called *flanging* occurs. Flanging is commonly described as a "whooshing" or "jet airplane" sound; it creates a kind of filtering or resonance that audibly seems to climb up or down in frequency depending on what's happening with the modulation. If a sound is delayed by five milliseconds or so and then combined with the source sound (particularly if feedback is added), certain frequencies cancel out, resulting in a peaks-and-valleys pattern across the frequency spectrum called *comb filtering*. With modulation applied, the delay time either shortens or lengthens, causing this

GUERRILLA TACTIC *True Flanging with a Sampler*

You don't really need two analog tape machines to get the sound of true flanging. You can do it with a sampler. Sample a sound that has already been recorded—either a portion of a track or a portion of a whole mix—and then duplicate the sample in the sampler's memory, or sample it again the exact same way. Detune one of the versions by just a few cents so that it plays a bit faster or slower than the other, and experiment with starting both samples at *almost* the same time—offset them by the tiniest

amount, so that the slower sample starts first and the faster one starts immediately afterward. If you do it right, as the two samples play in unison, you'll hear the samples crash together and flange, with the flanging sound going "up." At the moment where the faster sample catches up exactly, you'll hear that "flange nirvana" moment where the frequencies go through the ceiling—a sound unattainable with delay-based flanging. Analog purists will argue that true flanging is achievable only with two analog tape machines, but sampler-based flanging can still produce a cool sound.

comb-filtering pattern to shift up or down. This shifting is what you perceive when you hear flanging. As the delay times shorten the flanging appears to go "up," and as they lengthen the flanging seems to go "down."

Flanging got its name in the 1960s, when engineers learned that if they recorded the same sound on two tape machines and played them simultaneously—one slightly delayed relative to the other—the two recordings would react with each other with frequency cancellations. By touching the flange of one of the machines' tape reels, that machine would slow down, causing the delay between them to change. The result is a true flanging sound, because the two sounds actually cross in time. If the machine that's ahead is slowed down, eventually the other machine's recording will pass it by, like a runner in a race. At the moment where they cross, the delay time between them gets infinitesimally short, causing the flanging to sound like it's shooting through the roof. Effect-box flanging can never achieve this state of "flange nirvana," however, because it relies on one source sound and one delayed sound; the two can come close to each other in time but never actually cross. That's why many engineers still prefer true flanging. A famous example of this sound, expertly applied to a whole mix, can be heard at the 2:20 point in the Doobie Brothers' "Listen to the Music."

Flanging is kind of a special effect; it has such a distinctive sound, and the sound is so bold, it's easy to overuse to the point where it becomes gimmicky.

Phasing. *Phasing* occurs with even shorter delay times than flanging—from 2ms down below 1ms. Essentially, phasing is the high-in-the-stratosphere component of flanging—pretty much only the highest frequencies are involved in the frequency cancellation. It results in a "liquidy" sound; that's truly the best way to describe it. (A good example of phasing can be heard on the main guitar riff of the Rolling Stones' "Shattered.") Phasing isn't really audible unless you apply a lot of modulation, with modulation rates in the faster range. But because phasing delay times are so short, to get a good sound, the delay needs to be very precise. Interestingly, dedicated analog effect-box phasers usually produce a better phase sound than most all-in-one digital delays. In fact, the famous Small Stone phaser, manufactured by Electro-Harmonix in the 1970s, might have the best phase sound ever made.

Phasing is good as an ear-catching special effect or a subtle texture, but it also works well as a first stage on lead guitar, meaning between the guitar and the first distortion stage. Not surprisingly, the effect doesn't sound much the same after the signal has been distorted—but the phasing adds a cool extra dimension to the lead tone, with frequencies gently whipping around, that rarely seems out of place.

The Many Faces Of Dirt: Distortion

As any guitarist knows, distortion is one of the most popular effects around. But distortion is like the witches of Oz: There are good kinds and bad kinds. There's distortion that you intentionally apply because you want it, and there's the kind that happens by accident because you've done something wrong—improper gain staging is the most common cause. I mentioned distortion in Chapter 3, but when people speak of distortion as an effect, they're usually referring to a type more complex than simple wave clipping (see the diagrams on page 50).

For our purposes, we can think of distortion as the electronic addition of frequencies due to some stage being overdriven. Thinking back to our distorted sine wave from Chapter 3, the sine wave by definition has no harmonics (higher-frequency components), but the square wave that resulted from extreme clipping has plenty. Therefore, the process of distortion has actually added harmonics—specifically, odd-numbered harmonics—to the sound. Where a sine wave sounds like a muted whistling tone, a square wave sounds more like a clarinet. Distortion has changed the tone.

In a different kind of distortion, a raspy, gritty, or buzzing quality is imparted to the signal. Digital distortion—by far the worst-sounding variety—involves the creation of sudden discontinuities or sharp corners in the wave shape, resulting in an obnoxious ripping or popping sound. Unless you want listeners to go running for the nearest exit, that's not the kind of distortion you want in a recording. But you may not want the strictly square-wave kind, either—unless you're going for something like the ultra-smooth lead guitar sound on the Guess Who's "American Woman." In most cases, good distorted guitar tones contain both even and odd harmonics; the proportion in which they occur, and the ways in which they're added, largely determine the distortion's effect on the original tone.

A complete treatise on guitar distortion is beyond the scope of this book, so I'll offer just a few observations about generating and capturing distortion in the Guerrilla studio. (More about recording and distorting guitar tones in Chapters 7 and 9.)

Distortion sources. Before the mid '90s, you could get distortion in one of two ways: with a tube circuit, or with a solid-state circuit. Most guitarists feel that amps using old-style vacuum tubes produce distortion that's more pleasing to the ear. Solid-state amplifiers use transistors instead of tubes; for decades electronic designers have tried to emulate the tube-distortion sound with solid-state circuits, with mixed success. (The famous Ibanez Tube Screamer pedal is one of the better such circuits.)

Even an all-tube amp, though, can produce fairly bad-sounding distortion. If you overdrive only the preamp tubes, for instance, you may get a buzzy, electronic-sounding grit that doesn't sound much like anything you hear on records. Better-sounding distortion often happens only when you overdrive the amp's big power tubes and push the speakers hard. This means you need to crank up the amp *loud*. That may or may not be possible in your Guerrilla studio—if not, you can use a device called a *power soak*. This acts like a speaker electronically (a power amplifier can self-destruct if you send its output to anything other than an appropriate speaker or a power soak), but instead of producing acoustic loudness that must be captured with a mic, the power soak generates a balanced electronic signal that can be recorded directly. A power soak allows even apartment-dwelling Guerrilla recordists to crank up a 100-watt Marshall stack and push record.

In the mid '90s, the first *modeling* circuits came along. These use digital technology to shape waveforms based on the analysis of real sound waves from specific sources. The Line 6 POD was the first portable modeling device, and right off the assembly line, it blew away all other strictly solid-state circuits, both in terms of mimicking actual tube sound and sheer versatility. The POD included models of not only real vintage tube amps but also speaker cabinets and effects, allowing you to mix and match them at will. Since then, many other manufacturers have joined the modeling fray, and some of the products out there sound so authentic it's scary. It should come as no surprise that modeling circuits are extremely Guerrilla-friendly: They allow you to build big-studio sounds even in a small, low-budget studio—particularly if you employ some special techniques, which I'll discuss in Chapter 7.

Getting good distortion is tricky; I've always relied on trial and error to determine what combination of effect-box, modeling-unit, and amp settings result in a tone that's most useful for the situation. In other words, I tweak, listen, tweak, listen, and so on, until I'm satisfied. Perhaps more than any other sound, distorted guitar requires you to actually record and play back a segment of a track to hear what the tone *really* sounds like. Listening live through headphones or speakers often just doesn't cut it—probably because there's usually a live amp blasting somewhere nearby, interfering with the monitoring process. But there's also something about playing guitar that makes it harder to simultaneously judge the tone you're getting. If you're recording by yourself, this makes the trial-and-error process more tedious, but that's the price you pay in the pursuit of great guitar tones.

Bass distortion. This isn't as ubiquitous as guitar distortion in rock & roll, but it's still quite popular (especially, for some reason, in commercials for pickup trucks). In fact, a bass version of the Line 6 POD came out shortly after the guitar version, offering models of classic overdriven bass rigs like the Ampeg SVT. Bass distortion is most easily achieved with a plug-in specific for bass. If you're setting up a distortion signal chain with a guitar plug-in, or using a guitar stompbox or other hardware effect, the trick is to make sure you don't lose that critical low end. Run bass through most guitar-distortion circuits and you'll hear a noticeable thinning out of the tone—almost never a good thing when recording a bass track. If you don't have a bass-specific distortion unit or plug-in, one solution is to split the bass signal into two; you can then add distortion to only one side, and when you recombine them, the clean side holds up the low end. In the hardware world, the best way to do this is with an effect send from a mixing board. A slightly more complicated alternative involves splitting the signal coming out of the bass, running one side to a cranked-up and miked bass amp, and running the other side to a DI box. Pro studios commonly use this approach, although they usually record the clean and dirty sides as two separate tracks, so the blend between them can be altered later at mixdown. If this isn't feasible in your studio, obviously you'll need to commit to a blend on one track. Recording the bass late in the tracking process and mixing-as-you-go (see

Good Digital Distortion?

You hear everywhere that digital distortion is horrible and unmusical—something to be avoided at all costs. Actually, that's only true *almost* all of the time. I've gotten useful distortion from a sampling keyboard by intentionally boosting and resampling a sound—in other words, applying a destructive edit that overwrites the original sample with one, say, 40dB hotter than the original. On that particular keyboard (a long-obsolete E-mu Emax II), the result was a completely blown-out sound, but for whatever reason, it sounded great—there was none of that ripping clatter typical of digital distortion. If you have a sampler that allows this function, give it a whirl and see what you get—digital distortion just might end up playing a prominent role on your next recording.

Chapter 1), or recording only a clean signal and later re-amping (see Chapter 9), will make it easier for you to get this blend right.

Distorting other instruments. Since the mid '90s or so, we've heard more and more instruments being subjected to distortion. A Hammond B3 organ run through a Marshall stack (or a modeled equivalent) can result in a massive, monolithic sound. You can give a drum loop (see Chapter 7) more aggression, and also make it sound less generic, with some good distortion. Vocals can sound very cool when given a crunchy edge, although bear in mind the lyrics might be made unintelligible (which may or may not be a good thing). As long as it works artistically, distortion can be applied to pretty much any instrument or track—give it a try and see what happens.

In most cases, though, avoid putting two sounds through the same distortion circuit at the same time. Doing so will mash and mush them together, and things can get ugly fast. Of course, maybe that's what you want. If your goal is to make a held vocal note seamlessly morph into the first note of a guitar solo, blending the vocal and guitar signals pre-distortion will do the trick. But if you want to maintain separation and keep the sounds distinct—messed up though they may be—give each instrument or track its own particular distortion, and either apply distortion to one instrument/track at a time, or use different distortion units to grunge up two or more sounds at once.

Pitch-Change Effects

One of the greatest feats of digital signal-processing technology is the ability to change a sound's pitch without altering its speed or tempo. On analog equipment (as well as on digital), you can easily slow down or speed up playback, and the pitch will change in exact proportion. If you record something on tape at 15 inches per second (IPS) and play it back at 30 IPS, it will naturally be twice as fast, and the pitch will be exactly one octave higher. But digital pioneers quickly realized the usefulness of being able to

GUERRILLA TACTIC *How To Shred Like Yngwie Malmsteen*

I've never been a fast guitar player—but there have been a few occasions when I needed to *sound* fast. Here's a trick I developed to double your apparent playing speed on any instrument using technology (and no drugs): slow down the appropriate section of your song to half-speed and create a half-speed mix. Your recording program may allow you to do this easily; if not, record the full-speed mix on a sampler and play back the mix one octave lower, or otherwise digitally slow it down by half. While monitoring the half-speed mix, play your solo—transposed down by one octave—and record it. Then either double its playback speed digitally, or sample it, play it back an octave higher, and re-record it (you may need to slide it into its proper position in time). Instant Yngwie!

The first time I did this, I had to use two different analog tape machines and a ridiculous monitoring setup involving a cassette deck. These days I can do it in minutes, right inside a recording program that allows for not only half-speed playback but half-speed recording, as well. This is especially effective with MIDI performances—you're doubling the speed at which notes play back, but you aren't altering the sounds of the notes themselves. The many conveniences of digital recording!

Tip: When playing an instrumental part that you intend to speed up later, you'll get a more authentic sound if you think "slow." Slow down your vibrato, slides, etc., to about half-speed, trying to make your part sound like one that's been slowed down by half. That way, when it's sped up, it will have less of a "sped-up" sound.

---

change pitch without changing playback speed—or, being able to alter pitch in real time, while the performance is happening. Several useful effects are based on changing a signal's pitch in this way.

Octave division. *Octave divider* or *octaver* effects, which typically come in pedal form, generate a note or notes that are one and/or two octaves below the input signal's pitch, and they output a blend of source, one-octave, and two-octave tones. A bit of a backtrack, though: The first octave dividers were not digital but analog. They produced rather crude, synthesized square waves for the octave tones; the waveforms weren't based on any of the source wave's characteristics other than its fundamental frequency. (This approach has made a comeback in the form of "synth" effect pedals.) Today's digital octave boxes are a lot better, and there are even pedals and rackmount units that can generate diatonic harmonies of single-note (non-chord) lines based on a specific key center. Some octaver boxes sound better than others, and some *track* better than others, meaning they follow the source signal's fundamental pitch more faithfully. (Octavers with poor tracking tend to glitch and produce unstable gurgling sounds, particularly in certain pitch registers.)

Octave dividers are great for beefing up sounds that might otherwise be too thin. For instance, putting a bit of octave underneath a guitar solo—even an amount so small you can't hear distinct octave notes—can do wonders to fatten up the tone. Piling on a more noticeable amount of octave can give a guitar a distinctive quality that sets it apart from most lead tones. Octaver is great on bass guitar, too (especially fretless), lending a quality that brings to mind Stevie Wonder's great synth-bass tones of the '70s. But you'll probably want to play the bass line an octave higher than normal; otherwise the unit might track poorly, and the octave note may be too low to be useful (or even audible). If you don't want to commit to how much of the octave you're blending in, either split your signal and record your dry and octave sounds to separate tracks, record the signal dry first and print the octave to another track afterward, or apply the octave during mixdown. Regardless, keeping the octave sound separate gives you more options, and it also allows you to pan the source and octave sounds away from each other if you want.

Digital pitch shift. An extension of the octaver idea is an effect that allows you to shift an incoming signal's pitch anywhere within a ±1- or 2-octave range, often with a precision down to one cent (a cent is 1/100th of a semitone). These devices work with any sound: single-note lines, chords, and even drums and cymbals. Employed in a pedal, the effect allows you to swoop the pitch up or down just by rocking your foot. Also, many pitch shifters can generate two independent shifts at once, with separate pan positions and perhaps also a delay parameter for each shift. The sound isn't always great (particularly when performing large shifts), but tracking isn't an issue. This effect can be heard on news programs and documentary films where it's necessary to disguise an interviewee's voice.

The ability to digitally pitch-shift a source with precision is extremely useful. Chorusing effects (see page 115) sound a lot more authentic if, instead of using a modulated delay, you shift the source both up and down by a few cents. Where a delay chorus results in a pitch that's oscillating up and down (and crossing with the source pitch), a pitch-shift chorus produces two sounds that remain parallel with the source pitch, resulting in a more uniform, solid texture. I think pitch-shift chorusing just sounds better.

 GUERRILLA TACTIC *Party Of Five*

Reach for pitch shifting when you want to make crowd noises or perform any kind of non-pitch-specific layering. For instance, if you want a song to depict the sound of a party with people shouting a word or phrase, here's a great solution: Run your mic signal through a pitch shifter set to two semitones up and two semitones down. (If your hardware device or plug-in won't do two shifts at once, use two plug-ins on the same track.) Then blend the dry signal and the two shifted signals at about the same level. When you shout the word or phrase, it will kind of sound kind of like three different people shouting. Do this on several more tracks, each time shouting at a different pitch; then bounce the tracks together. If you record five tracks this way, the result will sound quite convincingly like 15 different people in a room shouting—and as far as I'm concerned, that's a party!

You can also get cool special effects by performing a small pitch shift with a little delay and adding feedback (i.e., adding some of the effected signal back into the input). For instance, applying a 20-cent downward pitch shift and a 20ms delay to a snare drum, with some feedback, will give the snare a hard reverb (see page 114) that pitch-bends downward, kind of like an early electronic drum-machine sound. Similar downward or upward shifts applied to a vocal can produce futuristic or bizarre "alien" effects. Try it with a longer delay and a shift of a whole-step—notes will climb up or down the whole-tone scale as they fade out, a very distinctive sound. Doing the same with a minor-3rd shift will send notes cascading up or down the diminished scale, and using a major-3rd shift will do the same over the augmented scale.

Auto-tune. Auto-tuning, typically performed with a plug-in, tracks the pitch of a signal and applies a constantly changing pitch-shift in order to round off the pitch to the nearest semitone. It's kind of like a pitch version of the quantization in drum machines and MIDI recording. Depending on the parameters you set, this effect can range from subtle pitch correction to a "computerized" and artificial sound—think of Cher's mega-hit "Believe."

Sometimes, though, it's useful to apply a small, constant pitch-shift across an entire performance to improve the pitch. There are times when you may sing a few cents sharp or flat for a whole song. To correct this, process the entire track with a pitch-shift plug-in, set to shift down by a fraction of a semitone. The results sound fine—there's no audible difference, except that the performance is more in tune overall. If you do pitch-correct something, why tell anyone? What your listeners don't know won't hurt them. Keep it your little secret!

Compression As An Effect

This one is slightly different, because effects are generally audible, and in most cases you don't want anyone to actually hear compression being applied. But in recent years, extreme compression—on just about any instrument—has been showing up on the radio. Particularly in hard rock, producers have been using reverb less and less, trading it in for heavy compression instead. This creates a bold, in-your-face sound, particularly on vocals—with the added benefit of enhanced intelligibility in the words. On drums, heavy compression can result in a unique "sucking" sound (in a good way), where a drum hit seems to slam and then suddenly drops back in volume.

One thing about compression is that like distortion, it can sound better when applied gradually, in stages. You could run a lead vocal through a hardware compressor on tracking, and then you could put a compressor plug-in (perhaps even followed by a limiter plug-in) on the vocal's virtual-console channel. Each stage will operate in a different area of the dynamic range, and taken together, the result will be a smoother, more pleasing overall compression than what you might get if you applied one very heavy-handed stage. If you do apply compression in stages, your best bet is to apply your mildest compression first and your wildest compression last. This is because gentle compression may do nothing to a sound that's already been heavily compressed (depending on the settings). But if the gentle compression goes first and the heavy compression (or limiting) goes last, both stages will be able to do what you need them to do.

Enhancer Effects

These barely qualify as effects; in the recording-as-cooking analogy, they're more like the flavor enhancer MSG than a kind of spice. Enhancers come in the form of rack-mount devices, and they're also available as plug-ins or even built into instrument amplifiers. In terms of physics and electronics, there are numerous approaches, but they all aim to enhance certain areas of the frequency spectrum in an EQ-like way, but without actually using equalization. In other words, frequencies are rendered more audible without actually being boosted in level. Most of these circuits work on the high end of the spectrum; the Aphex Aural Exciter and BBE Sonic Maximizer are two examples. The Aphex Big Bottom and Waves MaxxBass enhance the low end—amazingly without eating up power or headroom, as normally happens when boosting the bass.

Enhancers are cool, especially when you first encounter them; they seem to work like magic. Everything can sound shinier and more alive, and vocals can sound more crisp and intelligible. But after you work with them for a while, they can strike you as artificial-sounding. In the end, there's only so much enhancing, exciting, and maxxing you can do before the music's natural qualities get stripped away and replaced with something that may be big, bold, and bright but just overly synthetic. I recommend getting your highs shiny and your lows big and tight naturally; that way, if you choose to enhance them a little, they'll be even better. Just don't rely on enhancers too much or consider them a cure-all for lazy recording technique. It won't work as well.

Other Effects

Tremolo and vibrato. *Tremolo*, a regular up/down fluctuation in volume, is an effect built into some vintage guitar amps (it's best identified with the "surf guitar" sound). Tremolo is often confused with *vibrato*, which is a regular fluctuation in pitch. Fast, subtle tremolo adds a shimmering quality to a track. A deeper tremolo (meaning one with more of a level fluctuation) is a specialized, ear-catching effect; it's most effectively applied when the fluctuations are in tempo with the song. (Think of the Smiths' "How Soon Is Now?") Vibrato, on the other hand, is rarely applied as an effect—usually it's just a feature of the performance itself—but if need be, you can get vibrato by using a short delay with a medium-fast modulation and no dry signal in the mix. Adding vibrato to an instrument that doesn't "do" vibrato, such as piano, can give it a curious quality. A more obscure variant on these effects, *filtrato*, is a rapid fluctuation in upper-frequency filtering; say "wow-wow-wow-wow" and you'll get an idea of what filtrato sounds like. Filtrato is easy to get on a programmable synth, but adding it as an effect requires a specific type of auto-wah (see below).

Auto-pan. This is one of my favorite effects, particularly with keyboards. If you have a sound that seems static and boring or "stuck" somehow, it might benefit from the life and movement as well as stereo-image width of auto-pan. This effect automatically varies a sound's position in the stereo field, usually back and forth around its original pan position. A width or depth parameter controls how far the sound moves from the original pan position. Some auto-pans allow you to specify the wave shape that drives the effect. A sine wave makes the sound move in a pendulum-like fashion; a triangle wave makes it shuttle back and forth at a constant rate without stopping; and a square wave makes the sound stutter between two pan positions.

There's also a "triggering" type of auto-pan that causes individual sounds to move from one starting pan position to another, but this can be difficult to set up and get to work properly. You're better off achieving this sound with automation (see page 197).

Leslie. Named after the classic Leslie rotating speaker, which is traditionally used with Hammond organs, Leslie effects (sometimes generically called "rotary" effects) combine elements of tremolo, vibrato, and auto-pan. A real Leslie speaker spins like a washing machine at a rate controlled by the player, throwing the sound around the room; rotary effects simulate this sound electronically. Naturally, they're great on organ sounds, but they can be used on just about any instrument, including vocals, guitar, and piano. When artfully applied, it's a memorable, instantly recognizable sound.

Auto-wah. A *wah-wah pedal* is a guitar effect that's essentially a semi-parametric equalizer with a sharp boost and a pedal-controlled frequency sweep. An auto-wah automates the process of moving the pedal; either it moves in a fixed, tremolo-like back-and-forth fashion (creating filtrato), or more commonly, it's triggered by changes in the signal's amplitude. The latter type of auto-wah is commonly called an *envelope follower* or *envelope filter*, because the filter "follows" the sound's *envelope*, or its shape (in terms of level) over time. You might put an auto-wah on a guitar track, for example, and set it to be fully open at the start of the note and gradually close as the note decays. This would give each note a "yowwwww" sound, with the filter boosting progressively lower frequencies over each note's duration. Most auto-wahs allow you to specify either a downward or upward filter direction; a downward auto-wah can simulate vintage synth sounds, and an upward one can produce "quacking" sounds. Auto-wah is a fairly extreme, wacky effect. Funk-bass icon Bootsy Collins of P-Funk, who has made a career out of auto-wah, is most commonly associated with this sound.

Ring modulation. Talk about strange effects—this is a really weird one. Invented by synthesizer pioneers, ring modulation works a kind of frequency-multiplying electronic magic on a signal, giving it non-harmonic characteristics and an extremely offbeat sound. Ring mod is great when you just need to make something sound truly bizarre or mess it up beyond recognition. It's a good choice for "alien" vocal sounds. I once used it on a guitar solo that just wasn't happening; the solo was too polite, too conventional, for the whacked-out feel I wanted the song to have. I tried a bunch of effects with no luck. Then I hit on ring mod, and it was perfect—suddenly the solo became evil and demonic, and my lame playing was disguised behind the twisted frequencies. No other effect could have created this monster of a sound, and it was perfect for the song.

A Final Word On Effects

I can't stress enough the importance of trying to use effects with good taste. Strive to add an effect only where the song truly benefits from it. Effects are useful for several things: to provide an element where something seems missing, movement in places that seem static, prettiness in places that are plain, or ugliness in places that are banal. You get the idea: each effect should serve an artistic function. Don't use it as sonic ketchup.

CHAPTER 7

How To Record Almost Everything

It's time to get specific about recording sounds. I've offered a lot of general observations, but now let's look closer at the tracking process, sound by sound. By the end of this chapter, you should have all the information you need to record great-sounding tracks for all of the instruments in a typical popular-music mix. Let's get to it!

Sampled Drums

As I explained in Chapter 1, the preferred Guerrilla Home Recording approach to putting drums on a song is to use sampled drums. Given limited resources and experience, it's just much easier to achieve a really good drum sound this way. And since the drum sound is arguably the most important sonic element of a mix—rarely does a song sound good if the drums don't—I believe this is the best way for home recordists to go. (Recording live drums is covered in the next section.)

This method can mean using a drum machine with samples of real drums, a sampling keyboard/rackmount device, a groove-building software program, or a sample-player card or plug-in. As long as you do it well, you can get good results with any of these methods. But bear in mind that "doing it well" means more than just duplicating a one-bar drum pattern and pressing "play." It means spending some time constructing the drum part, including building lots of the expressive, non-metronomic human element into it. This is best done by a real drummer—but non-drummers can learn to program real-sounding sampled drums as well. I'll cover techniques for creating superior drum tracks in this chapter as well as in Chapter 8.

If you're doing drums with a sampler (as opposed to an electronic kit or drum machine), have one to three standard "drum kits"—preassembled and matched banks of drum samples—at the ready so that when you have a musical idea, you can start working on it right away. Even if you intend to change some of the sounds later, having a rough-and-ready kit available will at least get you going. If step one always involves looking for a kick-drum sound, recording becomes a tiresome chore, and you'll likely get bogged down in the tedium of it all. Certainly, your creativity will suffer.

The Truth About Drum Dynamics

Most instruments, including drums, sound very different when played loudly as opposed to softly. It isn't only a matter of volume (although that's certainly a factor)—the frequency content of a crash cymbal, for example, is vastly different when you slam it as opposed to when you tap it. And even the most casual listener will be able to tell the difference. You can't just turn down, or even EQ, a hard-hit drum and make it sound like it was hit softly—you need a sample of a drum that was actually struck that way. Nor can you turn up a *pianissimo* drum sample to make it sound *fortissimo*; it'll just sound loud-*pianissimo*. Therefore, it's useful for your collection to include not only a variety of drum sounds, but also a variety of dynamics for each. And it's important that you choose drum sounds with the appropriate dynamics for what you're looking for. Otherwise they will just sound wrong.

The sounds. Assuming you aren't starting with poor drum samples (there are plenty of places to get good ones), you have an immediate advantage over a live-drum recordist: the drums have been professionally miked and sound good right away, before you've lifted a finger. Still, some drum samples sound a lot better than others, and of course, a snare or kick-drum sound that's perfect for one song may be totally wrong for another. But guess what? As long as you're recording your drums via MIDI, using samples allows you to completely change the sounds right up to mixdown.

The following are some guidelines for choosing drum samples in order to create the sound of a live drum kit. Of course, if your music is in a more electronic genre, these guidelines don't necessarily apply.

Dry Samples Are Better

Good drum samples often sound even better with a little reverb added—which is why you'll find reverb actually *on* many drum samples. Often, though, these are samples to avoid. The reverb may have been added just to boost the pre-sale "wow factor," even if it makes the sounds less useful in the real world. Most of the time, the reverb prerecorded onto a sample is not going to be appropriate—let alone perfect—for the song you want to use it on. Worse, pre-sampled reverb often gives drum tracks a prefab, right-out-of-the-box sound, one that typically lays on the reverb too heavily. Even though it's a bit more work, you're better off making a custom reverb sound tailored to the tune you're using it on. While building your own custom reverb into a sample (see page 111, Sampling Gated Reverb sidebar) can be useful sometimes, you can't really go wrong by starting with dry drum samples and then applying reverb to taste (or applying none at all). You can add whatever effects you want to a drum sample at any point in the recording process—but if it's plastered on there from the beginning, it's not coming off.

GUERRILLA TACTIC *Layering Drum Samples*

You can build new drum sounds, and make drum sounds bigger, by layering samples of individual drums. For instance, years ago when I did most of my drums with an Alesis HR-16 drum machine, I learned that I could increase the "crack" of a snare sound by layering every snare event with the machine's brush-snare sound. Even though that sample was of a snare drum being hit with a brush—which sounded mild by itself—it had a sharp-enough attack that it could give other snare sounds more impact. I also found that I could make a kick drum broader by duplicating a kick sample, panning the two versions left and right somewhat, and detuning one of them by a semitone. The kick overall ended up sounding more or less the same, but the subtle tuning difference between the two sides gave it a wide stereo image—particularly if I added a little gated reverb. These days, I use an electronic drum kit, but I still often supplement the kick and snare sounds by doubling their MIDI events and triggering additional kick or snare sounds. (Tip: If you give two layered sounds slightly different velocity-sensitivity values, the blend between them will vary depending on the velocity of the MIDI event. This can help create more sonic variation as a particular drum sound occurs again and again.)

If you use these techniques, make sure the attacks of the various samples are exactly simultaneous and not fighting each other, and also listen to the combined drum sound in mono to ensure that frequencies in the various samples aren't canceling each other and thinning out the blend.

Kick drum. A good kick-drum sample has lots of deep *thud*, plus the crisp attack of the beater hitting the head. One of the best kick samples ever recorded was built into the world's first digital drum machine, the LinnDrum. I once heard someone say that the LinnDrum kick sounds like it could blow out a candle placed in front of the speaker. That's a good thing for a kick sound—but at the same time, the low-end aspects are balanced by that sharp *snap* at the beginning. The attack defines the kick drum's timing and punch, and the *thud* imbues the sound with power. (The *snap* also tends to make the kick more audible in a busy mix.) There are so many kick samples available it's overwhelming, but whatever your situation, keep in mind both the *snap* and the *thud* when you're choosing a kick sample. In some musical styles you may not need much *snap*, but it's still something to consider.

Snare drum. Snare sounds are more diverse than kicks, and trickier to choose. You might not worry about using the same kick sound on every song on a CD, because the kick drum is kind of under most listeners' radar—but the snare is a more audible, characteristic element of a song. Choose wisely with snare samples; you probably wouldn't want to use a slamming thrash-rock snare on a ballad, or a big dance snare on an acoustic country tune. Like a good effect, your snare must be appropriate for the song. I can't tell you how many demos I've heard that were otherwise well produced but were ruined by a horrible, inappropriate snare sound.

Of course, you don't have to choose your final snare sound right away. You may want to start with a generic dry snare and then replace it with something more customized once you have the entire drum part and at least one other instrument down. (You can do that with all of your drum sounds, but among all of them, you'll be most likely to replace the snare.)

A few of the characteristics that determine a snare sound: The drum's tuning (loose vs. tight), how hard it was hit, what it's made of (maple snares have a fuller sound than metal ones), how much of a "crack" it has at the attack, and where it's hit (center, off-center, or rimshot). On a ballad you'd probably want to go with a looser snare that's hit somewhat softly and without a lot of "crack." On a hard-rocking number you might want to go with a tighter snare that's hit harder, with a lot of "crack." And on a fast punk-rock song, you'd probably want a snare that just slams. Think about songs that are similar to the one you're making, and check out the snare sounds that were used. If you want a song to have a Ramones vibe, actually put on a couple of Ramones songs and listen to the snare sounds. This should give you ideas for what direction to head in.

Hi-hat. The hi-hat is a crucial element in a drum part, and one that's often neglected. Great sampled hi-hat sounds are bright and noisy (in a good way): they have tons of high end, but with a clear attack. Even though there are millions of hi-hat sounds out there, you don't need many to cover just about any recording need. If you want to create the impression of real drums, stay away from hi-hats that sound the least bit electronic, or which sound dark; the hi-hat is there to provide pretty much only a high-end pulse, and any darkness in the sound will just detract from that. A closed hi-hat sound should have a tiny bit of duration; an instantaneous "tick" tends to sound more artificial in the context of a full drum program. A good hi-hat sample sounds like the cymbals are bright, shiny, thin discs of polished metal—not an engine part, a whistle, or a three-ring binder being snapped shut.

Naturally, if you use closed and open hi-hat sounds together, they should sound like they're from the same hi-hat (even if they aren't). Their apparent levels and pan positions should be the same, and you should make it so the closed hi-hat immediately cuts off any open hi-hat that may be sounding. (Drum machines and electronic drum kits do this automatically, which is helpful.) If you have two closed hi-hat sounds that are almost identical—preferably, two samples of the same hi-hat being struck—by all means use both, and have your pattern alternate between them. Even if you can't distinctly tell them apart, this can have an amazing effect on making the pattern sound more natural and less "drum-machine-like." Human ears, like eyes, are incredibly good at discerning patterns of repetition (such as the exact same sound being triggered again and again), so anything you can do to break up repetition will help your cause. This is especially true of the hi-hat, which occurs more frequently and steadily than any other drum sound.

In many songs, however, merely having open and closed hat sounds won't cut it—particularly on louder, rocking numbers. There's just no way to convey the sound of a high-energy drum kit on a song's shout chorus with a closed hat sound—and replacing it with all open hat can sound ridiculous. This is where a "half-open" or "loose" hi-hat sample comes in handy. Some half-open hats are struck too gently for this application, though (a problem that isn't cured simply by making it louder), so if you're doing that Ramones-type tune, choose a half-open hi-hat that sounds like it was hit appropriately hard.

Toms & cymbals. Tom-toms should sound natural and acoustic (not electronic, unless that's the sound you want), and their attack should have a strong, punchy impact. High toms should have good "pop," and low toms and floor toms should have lots of what I call "dooge": plenty of low-mid *oomph*, but with a biting attack.

Ride and crash cymbals are the toughest challenge in sampled drums—but they're also an opportunity to make your drums sound *really* real. Cymbals are by far the longest drum samples, and since long samples eat up memory and disk space, this is where the makers of drum machines and sample collections usually cut corners. Crashes (particularly on old drum machines) are sometimes cut miserably short. On real recordings, of course, crashes and rides decay into silence over many seconds, and this is one of the elements that subliminally tell the listener, "These are real drums."

When I need a good, long crash, I reach for a CD-ROM collection of drum sounds only, all very well recorded. The durations of the crashes and rides are all in the seven-second range, which is plenty. (A vintage drum machine's crash might last for two seconds or less.) Along with a sample player and enough memory to handle several of these cymbals, believe me, it makes a difference. There's nothing like a crash decaying over the course of half a verse to make people say, "You mean those *aren't* real drums? No way!"

The panning. Traditionally, a recorded drum kit is panned to represent what listeners might hear if the drums were positioned in front of them. For a right-handed drummer, the kick is usually straight up (12:00 noon on a pan pot), and the snare may be straight up or a bit to the right (perhaps 1:00). The hi-hat is quite a bit to the right (maybe 3:30), and the toms are panned differently by pitch, from the highest tom far to the right (maybe 4:00) to the lowest tom on the left (about 8:00). Crash cymbals might be panned to 10:00 and 3:00, with a ride cymbal around 9:00. Fig. 1 shows a typical (right-handed) arrangement of drum sounds within the stereo image.

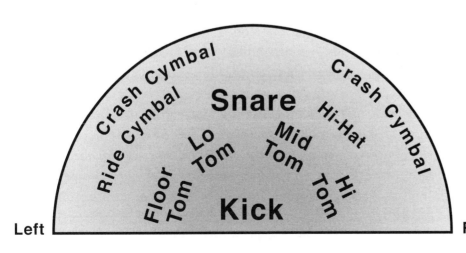

Fig. 1 Typically, drum sounds are panned to simulate the way a live drum kit sounds. For a right-handed drummer, that means high toms on the right and low toms on the left, and the kick and snare more or less straight up center.

You'll notice that in this example, with the exception of the kick and a straight-up snare, no two drums share the same exact pan position. This takes advantage of the pan-position element of separation (see Chapter 5): each individual drum tends to be more audible when it has its own pan position in the mix. Also, if the drums occupy the entire stereo field from left to right, they won't sound like they're bunched into only a few clumps, which tends to make them sound more drum-machine-like.

The guidelines above are not set in stone. You could put the snare hard-left and the kick hard-right if you wanted to—hey, in the right song, it might be bitchin'. Or you could pan all of the drums off to one side, to sound like an early stereo recording from the '60s. But if you want your drums to sound like conventionally recorded live drums, this is the way to go.

Levels & dynamics. The kick often needs to be the loudest of the drum samples, because the ear is less sensitive to its low frequencies. So, set a kick level and base everything off that. There's no strict formula, because different musical styles call for different drum mixes—but I often find myself giving the snare around 80 percent of the kick's level, the hi-hat around 55, and the cymbals around 60. I tend to set toms pretty loud—90 percent or more. They don't occur as often as the kick, snare, and hi-hat, and they're not as long as cymbals, so you can afford to crank them up a little for maximum impact.

The elements of a drum track have different individual dynamic ranges—the difference in level between their softest and loudest hits. In the language of MIDI, this is expressed in *velocity*, which represents the relative speed of a finger coming down on a keyboard, or of a drumstick striking a MIDI drum pad. If you're hitting hard, the MIDI velocity values are high (maximum: 127 units); if you're barely hitting it, velocity will be low (minimum: 1). Snare events on the *two* and *four* backbeats typically end up being within only a few velocity units of each other. Other snare events, like lighter-hit ghost-notes, can go down below the velocity halfway point (64). The same is true of the kick drum: the strong beats (like *one* and *three*) tend to be high-velocity, with other events going down to about halfway or less. Hi-hat events can vary in a more fluid fashion, from high-velocity to about two-thirds; hi-hat events on downbeats tend to be stronger than those on the subdivisions, and in 16th-note patterns, the events that fall on the eighth-notes tend to be slightly stronger than those on the off-16ths. Toms should be fairly high-velocity throughout (although some tom fills may dictate exceptions). Crashes, because they happen only occasionally and usually one at a time, are usually all around the same velocity; ride patterns vary dynamically similar to the way hi-hat patterns do.

Programming all of a sound's events at the same dynamic/velocity level will sound robotic and unreal. This is especially true with a hi-hat part: even if you give the pattern a great rhythmic feel, if all of the events are at the same velocity, the result will tend to sound mechanical. You'll get the best results by allowing both human timing variations *and* human dynamic variations to be part of your drum programs. More about this in Chapter 8.

Live hi-hat and ride. If you're a drummer or you know one, by all means try putting a live hi-hat track on some of your songs. More than any other component of a drum part, the hi-hat is responsible for the human feel element. There are also a million things you can do on a hi-hat with regard to tightness, playing location, little rolls, etc., that breathe life into a part—many of which just can't be reproduced with sampled drums. The trickiest aspect is getting the live hi-hat to mesh well with the sampled drums, in terms of playing feel, timing, and sound. Be extra-critical about whether the hi-hat and the other drums are sounding detached from each other, sonically or rhythmically, and do whatever you can to get them to fuse into a more unified whole that sounds like a real drummer playing a full kit.

Here's how to record a live hi-hat: Set up a click track and program in some kick and snare (you can polish the pattern later). Point a condenser mic straight down at the hi-hat's edge. You might want to roll off all of the lows to keep the track as clean as possible. Then, start recording and do your thing! But beware: Resist the urge to overplay. Since you're playing only the hi-hat, you may be tempted to play every roll, fill, and rudiment in your repertoire. (What am I saying . . . drummers *never* overplay, right?)

Programming is everything. If you've spent some time with a recording program or drum machine, you're probably familiar with the term *quantizing*—it's the process of rounding off the timing of notes to a grid in order to make them rhythmically exact. You know what, though? If you want to sound like real drums, *quantizing is evil!* Sure, it's easy to throw together a kick, snare, and hi-hat, and then "select all" and quantize everything to the nearest 16th-note. Home recordists do this all the time—but it might be the worst mistake you can make with your music. Not only does the result sound brutally robotic, quantizing just sucks out any human timing nuances that may have been there originally. My advice is simply to play the part in, in real time (unless it's too fast for you to do so). Perform the part in sections, and if you screw up, just go back and re-do it. You may want to do the kick and snare together first (while a click track plays), or do the hi-hat first, to a click, followed by the kick and snare with the click turned off. Another approach is to lay down a scratch vocal or guitar part first; this may inspire you to do more interesting and appropriate things with the drum program.

Programming drums is such a crucial element of recording, I'm devoting all of Chapter 8 to it—that's where I'll go into more detail about humanizing your drum programs and MIDI sequences.

Live Drums

If you're up for the challenge of recording live drums at home, keep the setup as simple as possible. The more mics you put up, the more complex things get. Adding a couple more mics does not mean the sound will be that much better—in fact, it may be worse. Unless you have considerable experience miking and mixing drums, don't try to get it done with more than four mics.

The first thing to do is decide how many mics you will use: one, two, three, or four. Let's look at each approach.

One mic. It might sound strange, but you can get a very useful drum sound out of just a single microphone. Back in the '60s, sometimes that's all engineers used on the drums—so if you're going for a '60s sound, or a low-fi sound, this may be the way to go. If possible, use a large-diaphragm condenser mic; this will give you a warmer sound with more lows than a small-diaphragm condenser, which produces a crispier, more high-endy sound. Position the mic somewhere over the middle of the kit, pointing downward. This is called *overhead* miking. You may want to position the mic a little out into the room, pointed toward the kit, to get more kick drum into the mic.

Two mics. This is similar to the one-mic approach, except that it can produce a stereo sound if you use two overhead mics. (Anytime you use a pair of mics in stereo like this, they should be the exact same model of microphone; otherwise the channels won't match and you won't get a true stereo image.) Separate them by three or four feet and pan them hard-left and hard-right. As an alternative, you can use one condenser mic as an overhead (in this case you can use a small-diaphragm condenser), and a dynamic mic on the kick. More on miking the kick and snare below.

Three mics. Probably the best way to use three mics is to use two small-diaphragm condensers as overheads, plus a dynamic mic on the kick. If you're lucky enough to be recording in a good-sounding room, you could instead use one overhead and one kick, supplemented by one room mic, or two overheads and a room mic on the floor. More on room-miking below.

Four mics. The typical four-mic configuration involves two overheads in stereo, a mic on the kick, and a mic on the snare. This is a fairly standard setup and can yield a very good drum sound if you spend some time setting up and adjusting the mics.

Miking the kick drum. First of all, it really helps if you have (or can borrow) a large-diaphragm dynamic mic for the kick drum. Two classics are the Electro-Voice RE-20 and the AKG D 112. Don't try to use a condenser mic on the kick (or the snare, unless the drummer is playing with brushes)—the high sound pressure levels could destroy its delicate internal components. Place the mic just inside the kick-drum shell, somewhat off-center, pointing toward the head at the point where the beater hits it (on the other side). If the drum has a front head without a hole in it, you

 Go Drum In A Corner

You might be able to improve your overall drum sound by moving the drums into a corner of the room, actually facing the corner. Low frequencies tend to pile up in the edges and corners of a room, and if your drums are sounding thin or wimpy when you record them, this may be just the thing to get a meatier, heavier sound, especially on the kick and toms.

might want to remove it for recording. It's common to deaden the playing head with a pillow or blanket, which will reduce its resonance and make the kick drum sound punchier. However, even with a deadened head, you can still get a low-frequency "ringing" or resonance in the room. If the sound in the mic seems to continue after the head has stopped vibrating, move the mic and/or the entire kit to try to eliminate this acoustical phenomenon, as it can seriously muddy up the overall sound (and you'll never be able to remove it with EQ).

Miking the snare. The all-around favorite mic for a snare drum is the Shure SM57. This is also one of the most popular mics for guitar amps, and since SM57s cost only around $100, you should have one anyway—it's one of the few cases where a Guerrilla recordist can use the exact same mic that the world's best engineers use. The idea with snare miking is to keep as much hi-hat out of the mic as possible. So, find a safe place for the mic underneath the hi-hat, and try to angle it so it's pointing at the middle of the snare head *and* directly away from the hi-hat. In other words, the snare should be on-axis with the mic, and the hi-hat should be close to 180 degrees off-axis. You want to isolate the snare from the hi-hat because the overheads will already pick up plenty of hi-hat, and this will allow you to EQ the snare without the hi-hat's sizzling highs getting in the way.

Miking the room. Putting up a room mic really makes sense only if the room itself sounds good. The best rooms in which to record drums are large, with high ceilings and hardwood floors. Wall-to-wall carpeting can kill the sound of a room; if there's carpeting that can be removed easily, do so. If there are heavy drapes or upholstered furniture, you might move them out, too. You don't need to turn the room into an empty echo chamber, but for recording drums, a live room sound is much more useful than a dead one.

It's tough to find a spot for a room mic and play drums at the same time. If you're the drummer, get someone else to play a basic beat, and then walk around the room slowly to find out if there's a place where the drum sound is especially good. Don't be afraid to crawl around on the floor and get up on a chair. Check out corners of the room and areas near walls; the reflections and buildup of sound waves at these areas can do interesting things. One technique is to put a room mic near the floor, six or eight feet away from the kick drum. This gives the kick's low frequencies some room to develop, which can result in a bigger or deeper kick sound.

Signal routing & soundcheck. Your best bet is probably to record each mic straight in, without any EQ or other signal processing. Just make sure the loudest drum hits come close to 0dB on your meters (within 2dB is fine) but not over. Keep in mind that drummers *almost always* hit harder when actually playing a song than they do while soundchecking individual drums. If you are technically unable to record each mic to its own track, you have a decision to make: you'll need to either submix your drums to two tracks in stereo (which will require a mixing board), or change your miking plan.

Don't Be Stuck On Stereo Drums

In several places in this book I discuss the stereo placement of drum sounds. But if you're recording live drums with a limited number of available tracks, consider giving up stereo and opting for isolation and flexibility instead. For example, if you can record only two tracks, use one overhead and one kick mic rather than two overheads, or in the case of three, a kick, snare, and an overhead rather than two overheads and a kick. It's unlikely that the listener will miss the drums being in stereo, but in the final mix the drum sound could be much better if you're able to treat the kick and/or snare by themselves—even if that necessitates all of the drums being mixed in mono. (Some busy mixes can be cleaned up by centering the drums in mono regardless, something to keep in mind even if recording them in full stereo isn't a problem.)

Before you record a take in earnest, record a few test takes and listen back to the sound you're getting. (Without a soundproofed and isolated control room, listening back is the only way to check your sound—it's tedious but necessary.) The kick drum should sound deep and full, and you should be able to clearly hear the beater hitting the head. The snare should have nice "crack" as well as solid "body," and the overheads should sound crispy. (If there's too much crash cymbal, try pointing the overheads a bit away from the cymbals.) Try to achieve an overall sound that's balanced across the frequency spectrum; you should be hearing deep lows, punchy mids, and crispy highs in equal proportion. If all of this is new territory for you, put on a couple of CDs with drum sounds close to what you're looking for. You're better off trying to emulate the sound on an indie, alternative CD than a commercial, big-budget drum sound that used 800 mics and a million-dollar drum room.

Make one-shots. Once you've got a good drum sound set up, take the opportunity to make "one-shot" recordings of each drum—five or so hits of each, at different dynamic levels. By themselves and uncontaminated by other drum sounds, these can really come in handy if you need to replace a mis-hit somewhere in the song. It's also nice to have a sample library of your own sounds, which you can use months from now to build your own sampled drum parts.

After you record. After your drum tracks are recorded, go to work EQing them. You'll probably need to EQ each mic track; concentrate on subtractive EQ, where you're removing frequencies rather than trying to boost them. On a kick mic, you can clean up the sound by heavily pulling down the mids—everything between about 200Hz and 1.5kHz, as well as everything over 4kHz. The snap of the beater hitting the head lives around 2kHz, so leave that alone. On a snare mic, roll off everything below about 300Hz (unless the drummer uses a really big, deep snare; if so, try 200Hz).

Uncompressed drums are difficult or impossible to get to sit in a mix with any consistency. The best way to solve this problem digitally is with a limiter plug-in on a submix of the drums. In your virtual console, set up a stereo bus (see page 70) and route all of the drum tracks to this bus. (Use a mono bus if the drums will be mixed in mono.) This will allow you to put a single plug-in on all of the drums, while still keeping the tracks separate. It's a matter of taste regarding how much limiting to apply (lower threshold settings with higher output-gain settings equal heavier limiting); very heavy limiting can result in a kind of messed-up, even subtly distorted, sound that can be very cool in certain contexts. For a more natural sound, have the limiter tame hits only in the louder end of the dynamic range, but apply enough limiting so you're able to boost the overall drum mix by at least 6dB without going over.

If your drum tracks sound too dry, add a bit of reverb. Assuming your computer can handle it, you could put separate reverbs (with different parameters) on the kick and snare tracks—heavy limiting can really bring out this reverb and give each drum hit more apparent sustain. If you aren't going for a special effect, with reverb you're best off erring on the side of subtlety. Try to get the reverb simply to enhance the way the drums blend into the overall mix; you don't really have to be able to hear reverb for it to be effective. If you can't hear distinct reverb on the drums in the final mix, but muting the reverb makes the drums sound too dry and/or detached from everything else, you're on the right track.

Fixes for a bad-sounding kit. You may find yourself in the position of having to record a cheap or otherwise bad-sounding drum kit. There are a couple of remedies for this (short of buying or renting a better kit). For one thing, new heads will sound much better than old, battered ones. Another likely culprit is simple: faulty tuning. Many drummers, particularly inexperienced ones, have no idea how to tune their drums and have never tried it. Drum heads that are uneven or flop around like pieces of paper almost always sound bad. So, a crash course is in order: go online and look for a drum-tuning tutorial. Keep in mind that with cheap drums, a lot of times you'll get a better sound by opting for fairly tight tunings all around.

Get educated. If you're serious about recording live drums, don't try to reinvent the wheel—actually learn how it's done, from people who do it professionally. One way to do this is to intern at a commercial studio. As an intern you won't get paid, but you'll be able to observe and get involved with setting up and positioning mics (that is, when you aren't fetching coffee for the second engineer). Watching how several different people approach the task might be the best possible way to get schooled on the art and science of recording live drums.

Drum Loops

An alternative to using sampled or live drums (aside from using no drums at all) is to use *drum loops*. First popularized by disco producers in the '70s and refined by hip-hop artists, this technique involves repeating a short segment of a prerecorded live-drum performance, resulting in a seamless, never-ending drum track over which other instruments are added. Originally this was done with a piece of analog tape, spliced together end-to-end to create a loop. (The famous sound-effect loop that begins Pink

Making Loops With A Groove Program

Groove-building software programs, such as Ableton Live and Propellerhead Reason, are excellent tools for creating and customizing drum and instrumental loops. Most of these can be used right inside your recording program as plug-ins (at the expense of CPU power), but they also have a function that allows you to select a loop and export it as an audio file, which you can then bring into a sampler or sample player or import directly into your recording session. When I do this, I like to create several variations on the groove and export them separately, and I save the master file so I can go back and tweak the loops if necessary. (Tip: When you export a loop, include the tempo in the filename, such as: **bitchindrums.144.aif**.)

Many of these programs also allow you to record MIDI information and even audio directly into them—so more and more people are using them as their primary recording tool.

Floyd's "Money" is a good example.) In the mid '80s, samplers became the primary tool for creating drum loops; today, there are software programs and plug-ins devoted entirely to playing, chopping up, and reassembling loops. So many hit songs have been made with drum loops, there's a whole industry devoted to producing them. Some of these loops are taken from old vinyl records (presumably with all copyrights cleared); others are made from original performances. Loop collections can come in the form of audio CDs that must be sampled, edited, and looped by the user. There are also CD-ROMs and download packages made for particular brands of samplers and their software equivalents. These are obviously more convenient, as they typically come pre-edited and looped and ready to load. Frequently, the loops include not only drums but other instrumental parts (with matching tempos) in a "construction kit" format that you can mix and match at will.

Usually, drum loops made from live drum performances not only sound great, they feel great, too. The downsides are that they're obviously repetitive (which can be good or bad), and if you're making your own drum loop from an old record, you have to secure permission from the copyright holder in order to use the sample legally.

Making your own loops. If you want to live dangerously and make your own loops (without permission) from other artists' music, use them on songs you don't intend to release, such as demos for more polished productions. Dig out your old turntable and the record you want to sample. Vinyl turntables produce an extremely weak signal and must be grounded to reduce hum, so wire it up to a stereo receiver that has "phono" inputs and a grounding screw for a turntable. Listen to the space between two songs to ensure that the sound you're getting is decent and hum-free. Whenever I need a line from a turntable, in true Guerrilla fashion, I just take it from the receiver's headphone jack rather than mess around with the dusty, crowded RCA jacks in back. Hey, it's quick and it works—that's all that matters. Plug a ¼" "Y" adapter into the headphone jack, and then plug a regular RCA stereo cable into the adapter's male RCA jacks. What you do with this signal depends on your studio. When I was using a sampling keyboard, I had cables permanently wired up to the sampler so I could grab a sample from the receiver anytime; this allowed me to sample off not only vinyl records but CDs, cassettes, videotapes—anything that could feed sound into the receiver. Since I do all of my sampling within the computer now, I run the line into two input channels of my mixer, using two more adapters and the line-input option. I control the level going to the mixer with the receiver's volume knob. (Remember, to minimize added noise in the sample, get plenty of signal to the sampler/mixer—but not so much as to light overload LEDs. If you're using a sampler, check the owner's manual to learn how to monitor the levels of incoming signals.)

Next, sample (record) the segment you want. You don't need to be exact—you'll need to edit the sample later, anyway. If you recorded the sample on your computer for use in a program or plug-in that only plays samples, now is the time to load it into that program. Listen to the sample on headphones to make sure you've got both channels and that the sound is good. Still using headphones, find the *exact* starting point of your loop, which is normally the first downbeat of a bar. By moving the sample's starting point ahead in time, slice off piece after piece of the sample, retriggering it each time, until you hear the downbeat's attack soften—that's when you know you've gone too far. Back off the start point just enough until all of the downbeat's attack is there, but no further. When you then trigger the sample, it will start *immediately*.

Most samplers allow you to edit a sample's end point so that it loops within the sampler (i.e., when you hold down a key, the loop repeats indefinitely). But you probably don't want to set up your loop this way, unless you're recording to tape with no synchronization. This is because if you allow a sample to cycle freely on its own, it won't stay aligned to your recording program's time grid for long. If you do choose this "free run" looping method, listen on headphones to ensure that the loop point—where it ends and then begins again—is smooth, with no clicks. (A click occurs if the position of the wave is different at the beginning and end of the sample.) You want the end of the wave shape to flow smoothly back into the beginning, like one continuous wave (see Fig. 2). Also make sure the timing is the way you want it. A popular, funky hip-hop technique involves having a drum loop's rhythm "hiccup" a bit at the loop point, but if you don't want this feel, make sure the rhythm is solid and steady through the loop-point transition. If it isn't, or if there's a click, move the loop point until the problem is gone.

A better way to loop is to get the sample to trigger exactly on the downbeat of each bar (see Fig. 3), or for two-bar loops, on every other bar's downbeat. This is because as the loop repeats again and again, its timing will drift in relation to your recording program's grid (and any tracks that may be already laid down), so it will probably start to fall out of sync within 15 to 30 seconds. Tell the sampler *not* to loop the sample (some samplers call this "one-shot" mode). Then, set up your MIDI track so that the

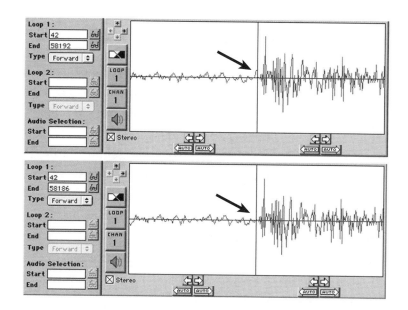

Fig. 2 In a drum loop, if the wave shape is not smooth across the loop point (top), there will be a click in the audio. Moving the loop's end-point so that the wave shape is continuous (bottom) eliminates the click, for a seamless-sounding transition between loops.

sample is triggered exactly on the downbeats. This way, no matter how long the song is, the loop will *always* start exactly at the beginning of each bar.

This technique invites a problem, though: there might be a small audible gap at the transitions between loop points, because the recording program is sending a MIDI note-off message to the sampler before it sends the next note-on message. There are two ways to get around this problem: You can increase the sample's release value slightly on the sampler, which will prevent it from cutting off abruptly at the end of the bar; with any luck, there will be enough data at the end of the sample that the sound will continue across the bar line for a bit, smoothing over the gap. Alternatively, you can turn off the sampler's key tracking, so that the sampler will play the sample

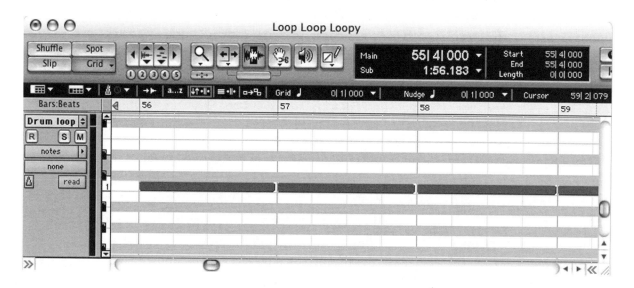

Fig. 3 Triggering a "one-shot" drum-loop sample at the beginning of each bar.

at the same speed and pitch regardless of which MIDI note it receives. Then, in your recording program, stagger the sample-triggering events so that as the sample is ending on one note, it's beginning on another note. Once you've done this, lengthen each note slightly so they overlap just a bit (see Fig. 4). Tweak these end points (also try adjusting the sample's release value) until the loop transitions are perfect.

Adding fills. As I mentioned, drum loops are by their nature endlessly repetitive. But that doesn't mean you can't incorporate fills and variations into the drum pattern—you just have to do a little extra work. Some software loop players make it very easy to chop up and rebuild loops, as well as to play loops at different tempos without changing the speed/pitch. Here's how to make a fill from a loop on a conventional sampler: Duplicate the loop sample, and edit the copies to create samples of the individual drum sounds. Then, add them over the main loop (or have them replace the main loop) to form a kind of fill. For example, you can make individual kick and snare samples from your loop and, every eighth bar, introduce a syncopated fill made up of the shorter samples. One advantage here is that the fill's sounds will be the same as the loop's sounds, so the drum track won't suddenly change sonic textures at the fill. Alternatively, you can use samples—either your own or from collections—of actual drum fills. The fill will likely sound very different, but that can be a cool way to add variation and interest to a static drum track.

Layering & changing loops. Sometimes, using one stock drum loop for a whole song not only sounds boring, it's cookie-cutter. There's nothing worse than playing a song for someone and hearing, "I used that same drum loop on a song yesterday!" It's a lot more creative and interesting to *build* a drum loop from several parts and customize it to the song you're doing. It could be a matter of simply changing the playback speed by altering the sample's tuning; this immediately makes the loop less

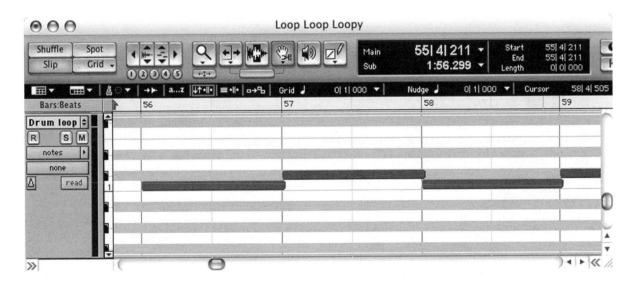

Fig. 4 Staggering a drum loop between two MIDI notes. Turn off key tracking so the sample plays at the same speed on both notes.

recognizable. Or, you could find two loops that sound different but share the same tempo and feel (one's playback may need to be adjusted so their tempos match). To give them some separation, pan one loop slightly to the left and the other slightly to the right; if they're stereo samples, pan one sample's channels hard-left and about 2:00, and the other sample about 10:00 and hard-right. You can get some exciting, extremely funky drum loops this way.

If you have the patience, you can also layer and build drum fills in the same fashion. Have the fill start with one sample panned to 3:00, and then finish it with another sample panned to 9:00. Or, create variations of a fill with the sampler's filter parameters. The possibilities with drum loops are endless (no pun intended); get your hands in there and just start having fun with them!

Electric Bass

The drum track represents one-half of a mix's foundation, and the bass represents the other half. It's often said that if the drum track doesn't sound good, nothing sounds good—and in many ways this goes for the bass track as well. Fortunately, it's pretty easy to get a good electric bass sound. You need: (1) a bass that produces a good-sounding signal, and (2) a decent direct box. That's about it—there are plenty of other toys you can put into the signal chain, but as long as you have a good-sounding bass and a decent DI, you can record a good-sounding bass track.

So what defines a good-sounding bass? That's highly subjective; every player has a different idea of the perfect sound. I personally like a bass with a strong, muscular tone, a smooth low end, lots of grind and growl in the mids, and a nice top end that sounds natural, not hyped. Here are some things to listen for in a bass, either when the bass is amplified or taken direct: Is there plenty of low end or "booty"? You can't create low end with EQ; pumping up the lows from a thin-sounding bass will just sound artificial and cardboardy, and the bass will tend to "woof," making the dynamics of those low

---

 ### *Beware Of Bass & Guitar Buzz*

Many basses (and guitars)—even those with electronics that are thoroughly shielded by foil or graphite paint—electronically "buzz" depending on the instrument's physical orientation. This is especially true if there are fluorescent lights nearby, or if you're recording near a CRT computer monitor. My own bass buzzes in this way—*unless* I point the neck in one particular direction, or 180 degrees from that direction. So, before I record, I sit in my chair, put on the headphones, and play a note while I slowly rotate my position. At the position where there's minimum buzz, I make a mental note of where in the room the bass's headstock is pointing. Then, when I'm actually recording, I try to keep the instrument pointing in that direction for the whole performance. This minimizes the buzz that creeps into the recording, keeping the bass track cleaner overall.

frequencies unpredictable and hard to control. Second, listen to the notes' definition. Can you clearly hear all of the pitch centers down to the lowest note, or are they all blurry variations on a *woooo* sound? Next, do the mids and upper-mids sound nasal and honky, or are they a natural part of the whole sound? Finally, do the highs sound sweet, or are they inappropriately bright, full of clacky string noise and electronic hiss?

If you get a chance, compare a few different instruments and just use your ears. I've heard $400 basses that sounded fantastic, and $1,500 basses that sounded terrible. You're usually safe with long-established favorites like the Fender Precision, Fender Jazz, and Ernie Ball/Music Man StingRay.

Just because a bass has onboard electronics, that doesn't mean it's better than a passive bass (i.e., one that doesn't require a battery to operate). In fact, some studio vets prefer basses that are not only passive but don't even have volume or tone knobs. This is because onboard controls can slightly "choke" the sound, even when they're turned all the way up; some people like the slightly more open sound of a bass with few or no onboard controls.

Tracking bass direct. The basic signal chain is simple: just plug the bass into your direct box, and connect the direct box to an input channel on your mixing board or digital audio interface with a balanced XLR cable. I always run bass through a compressor/expander/EQ insert sub-chain (see Chapter 3) before recording it, although I usually bypass the EQ part. You may try mildly boosting the low end to beef up the sound, although this isn't always necessary. It just depends on how much low end you envision the bass tone having in the final mix.

The Case Of The Canceling Bass Tracks

Anytime you combine signals representing two sonic versions of the same performance—such as a direct signal and a miked-amp signal—you run the risk of phase cancellation. This is especially true with bass, because the frequencies are lower and it's more obvious (and detrimental) when it's happening. Phase cancellation results when the waveforms of both signals aren't synchronized exactly; one is lagging a tiny bit behind the other in time. (Usually the miked-amp signal is the one that's behind, because the sound has to encounter a speaker, the air, and a microphone, and the direct line doesn't.) When you combine two signals like this, instead of

reinforcing each other the way they should, they can partially cancel each other out. The result is a thinner sound—not good on bass.

To combat this problem, as you're searching for up your miked-amp sound, be sure to pan both the direct and mic sides together and listen to the blend in mono. Compare that blend with the direct-only sound by muting and unmuting the mic signal. What you want is a combined tone that's better than either signal by itself. If the blended tone is thinner than the direct, frequencies are canceling. You can usually fix this problem by positioning the mic a little closer to or farther from the speaker. If your mixing board has phase-reversing buttons, flipping the button for one of the channels can get you a lot closer to a "phase-coherent" sound.

If you're adding compression during tracking, start with about a 3:1 ratio. The compressor's threshold setting is important. Watch the compressor-active LED as you play notes with different dynamics. See if you can get the light to blink on with notes that are about halfway between the quietest notes and the loudest notes you plan to play. Listen closely for "squash"—if you can hear the compressor kicking in and audibly squeezing the note, and you can hear the compression ease up as the note decays, you might be using too much compression. (You can get away with heavier compression on a loud, rocking song with a full mix than on a quieter, more sparsely orchestrated song.) If need be, slowly back off the ratio setting, and/or raise the threshold setting, until the compressed bass sounds more natural.

If you want, you can get an idea of how tightly you're locking in with the drums by putting both tracks in one window, one on top of the other (see Fig. 5). Zoom in and see how they line up with each other in time. Keep in mind that it's absolutely normal for bass notes to fall somewhere other than directly on the beats; consistency and feel are more important than metronomic accuracy. If the bass and drums sound good together, that's all that matters—just let them be. Don't become a victim of "Pro Tools-itis," where you can't resist making every performance digitally perfect. Over-tweaking can really sap the life out of your music.

Getting gritty. If you want to add a little more grunge or dirt to your bass track, you have a couple of options: you can mic a cranked-up amp, or you can get distortion direct—either from an amp-modeling device or some other distortion box. Keep

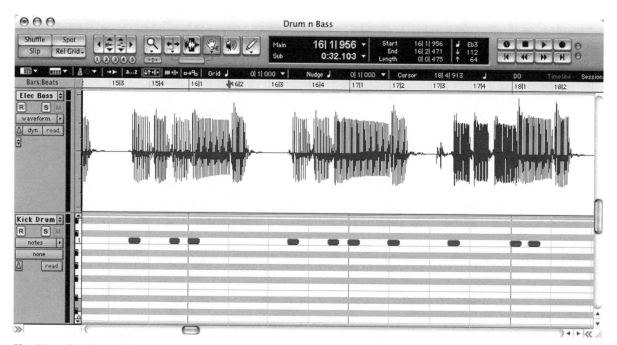

Fig. 5 In a digital recording program, putting a bass track on top of a MIDI drum track gives you an idea of how tight a bass performance is with the drums—but it's only a visual check. Sound is what matters most.

in mind, though, that a distortion stage (especially if the device isn't manufactured for bass) can thin out the bottom end. When pro engineers record distorted bass, they often split the signal into a clean side and a dirty side, so that the bottom end is there in the clean side no matter what happens to the dirty side. So if you want dirt on your bass track but your tone is thinning out, find a way to split the signal—for example, by using an effect send to deliver some of the signal to a modeling device. You could then blend in the distorted signal using an effect return. Even better, if possible, record the clean and dirty sides on separate tracks. That way, not only will you be able to pan them apart a little for a broader bass sound, you'll be able to alter their blend right up until mixdown—and you'll be able to EQ them separately, which can really come in handy for getting the bass sound to "sit" just right in the final mix.

If you're miking an amp, use a dynamic microphone. If you have a large-diaphragm type like an AKG D 112, all the better. Miking an amp is tricky, though; you may need to spend some time trying out different mic positions to find one that captures the distortion you're looking for. Often in a multi-speaker cabinet like a 4×10, one speaker sounds better than the others, so try different mic positions on different speakers to see if one combination gets you a better tone. And of course, all of this is a serious challenge if your bass amp isn't acoustically isolated. If the sound of the amp itself is an issue while you're trying to monitor your miked tone, the only way you may be able to get it done is through trial and error, recording and playing back the miked tone again and again.

Another alternative to miking a live bass amp: simply record a clean signal only, and "re-amp" it later (i.e., send the *recorded* clean signal to an amplifier, and mic and record that amplified tone). This is often an excellent solution, as it allows you to get the distorted sound just right at a time when you're not also dealing with playing the instrument. Re-amping is discussed in Chapter 9.

Technique tones: slap & pickstyle. Slap (or thumbstyle) bass isn't as popular now as it once was, but it's still a great sound. Slap bass is more difficult to record direct than fingerstyle, because of the intense attack of the thumb hitting the strings and the resulting blast of harmonics from the string bouncing off the frets. At the front of every note, there's a sharp dynamic spike that can try the response of a compressor as well as the fidelity of all the signal chain's gain stages. Also, getting the proper balance of bottom, mids, and top can be tricky. Set up your signal-chain EQ to "scoop" the sound. Gently but broadly pull down the mid frequencies, from roughly 300Hz to 2kHz, so that the thump on the bottom comes through as well as the metallic upper-mids and the brilliant, zingy highs. A graphic EQ, placed in the insert sub-chain after a compressor/limiter, works well for this. Use a smooth "smiley-face" curve for the most natural sound. Certain basses produce a much better slap tone than others; the Ernie Ball/Music Man StingRay is one of the best ever, but there are many other good ones. New strings, or at least strings that aren't old, are practically a must for slap bass.

If you're having trouble getting a slap sound with your DI box, consider miking a bright-sounding amp and blending it with your direct line.

Playing bass with a pick can really accentuate the attack of each note, and it tends to emphasize the "grind" aspect of an instrument's sound, so it works well on harder-rocking tunes. You may need to compensate for the stronger upper-frequency content, though, or else the bottom can be weakened. Besides EQ, one popular solution is to mute the strings slightly with the heel of your picking hand. The pick's attack still comes through and gives the bass lots of presence and pitch focus, but the palm-muting tames the more harsh, metallic aspects of pick tone, while the lows—which are less affected by your muting technique—power through. This underappreciated sound works well in pop, R&B, alternative, and country styles, to name only a few. I personally find myself using palm-muting more and more on my recorded tracks; sometimes it can be like a magic fix for getting the perfect bass tone.

Clean Electric Guitar

Clean (undistorted) guitar can be recorded using almost the same signal chain you use for electric bass: guitar into direct box, which feeds an input channel, preferably with a compressor/EQ sub-chain inserted into the channel. You can ease up on the compression, though; instead of putting the threshold at the halfway dynamic point (as with bass), you can make it more like two-thirds or three-quarters.

Naturally, compared to bass, clean guitar sits much higher in the frequency spectrum. Its function is high-endy, not foundational. Therefore, getting the highs to come through on the track is important. New guitar strings can go a long way toward this goal, as can using a guitar with single-coil pickups rather than humbuckers, which tend to sound darker.

Sometimes a direct-box guitar tone is just too flat and sterile, however. If you need to jazz up your clean tone, consider putting it through an amp-modeling unit. These usually offer a combination of clean and dirty tones, and they let you specify all sorts of simulated guitar-amp parameters as well as speaker types—tons of options to choose from. Doing this is easy enough: Run your guitar cable into the modeling device, and connect the modeler to an input channel using another guitar cable. (A direct box isn't necessary here.) A well-chosen modeler setting can add considerable bite and personality to a clean tone. Alternatively, you can do it the old-fashioned way, by miking a real amp. The fact that the guitar signal is going through an acoustic stage between the speaker and the mic, exciting the air and interacting with the environment, can get rid of the flat, somewhat electronic quality of a direct clean signal. Of course, it takes more time and care to mic an amp, but it's often worth it.

If you're miking an amp, listen to the amp in the room and find a setting that gets something like the sound you want. Don't be afraid to crank it up a little, as (particularly with a tube amp) this tends to make a guitar amp sound livelier—but play chords and make sure the sound is clean enough for what you want. Since we're looking for quality high frequencies here, use a condenser mic. Position it one to three feet from the speaker. Pointing a cardioid-pattern mic (see Chapter 2) directly at the speaker cone's center results in a slightly brighter tone (see Fig. 6). If possible, compress the mic signal as you would a direct clean signal. It won't require a lot of compression (amps tend to do some natural compression on their own), and don't squeeze the tone too much—a little dynamic "pop" can make a clean guitar track sparkle more than a highly compressed one.

Fattening it up. Perhaps more than any other instrument, clean guitar tends to sound thin in a mix. That's why effects like stereo chorus or flanging are popular to fatten it up. A great approach is to record an identical performance and pan it to the other side. You can get a really nice clean-guitar sound with two identical performances panned to, say, 9:00 and 3:00. For an easier fix, give the guitar track a short delay and a bit of modulation (see page 115) and pan it to the other side from the dry track.

Clean but loud. Sometimes you want a guitar tone that sounds loud but isn't really distorted—for instance, hard-strummed chords on a tune that's big and rockin' but not necessarily heavy. For this sound, try a modeling device (although the ones I've encountered tend to favor either clean or full-on crunch tones, without as much attention to this in-between tone). If you need to mic an amp, crank it up without

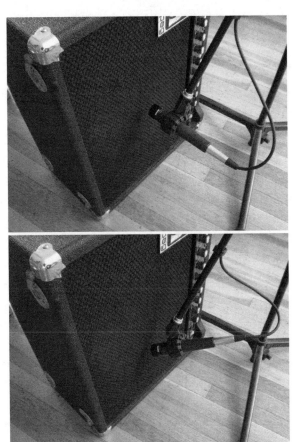

Fig. 6 Pointing a directional mic straight at the center of the speaker (top) usually produces a brighter tone than pointing it toward the wall of the cone (bottom).

Isolating A Guitar Amp

If you're miking a guitar amp, it's best to be able to acoustically isolate it in some way from the rest of your studio. Commercial studios have soundproof booths (or entire rooms) for this purpose; recording at home, you'll probably have to improvise. I put my guitar amp out in the hall, facing it toward a stairwell, and I shut the door. That's not exactly a soundproof solution, but it's better than having the amp in the same room—plus, the stairwell throws a bit of real acoustic space into the mix. Recording in the same room with an amp, you really have no idea what sound you're capturing until you play it back. While this is workable, it takes more time, and you're more likely to settle for a just-okay sound because getting a really good one is too much of a hassle.

letting it actually distort, and play *hard*. Your goal here is to create the sound of the speaker being pushed. Record a few seconds of playing—if the guitar sounds "loud" on a medium-volume playback, that's a good sign. If it sounds thin, wimpy, or weak, try again. Look for a tone that's muscular; for this job, you need a sound with broader frequencies, meaning more mids and perhaps even low-mids, than the tinkly jangle of a straight clean guitar. You may want to turn up the amp's midrange or bass knob; if the sound is too jangly, turn down its treble (or high) knob. This kind of tone really needs to be created at the amp. Don't settle for a weaker sound in hopes of making it heavier in the mix; this won't work as well.

Distorted Rhythm Guitar

Perhaps no sound is more fun to record—or play back—than a great distorted electric guitar. It's been keeping rock & roll alive for decades, and it'll make your music rock, too. I discussed distortion as an effect in Chapter 6; here are some tips for actually putting together a good "crunch" tone.

Good crunch guitar sounds big, loud, and complex. One way to get that is to play into three $2,000 guitar amps at once, each double-miked in its own separate isolation room, with the six mics recorded to six different tracks. But that's not feasible for us Guerrilla recordists—so we have to improvise. You can get a decent sound with just one guitar performance, one amp, and one mic—but if you want a tone that's bigger and more powerful, try layering sounds and spreading them around the stereo field a bit.

A great way to layer crunch guitar is to put down slightly different tones with each pass, playing the parts as tightly with each other as possible. An amp-modeler can really come in handy here. I usually start by recording two passes of direct guitar through one amp-model setting, but I use a different speaker-cabinet model for each (perhaps a 4×12 and a 1×12), and I pan these tracks apart—say, 10:00 and 2:00. I might also change the guitar's pickup-selector switch or the pickup-blend knob's setting between passes. When I'm finished with the direct passes, I record two miked-amp passes.

Since my guitar amp doesn't have that great a crunch sound (one of these days I'll get myself a real amp!), I again use the modeling device, but this time I bypass the cabinet models and dial in a loud but fairly clean setting on the (actual) amp. This way I get the sound of real output tubes and a speaker being pushed hard, without relying only on the amp for the distortion. As before, I record a slightly different sound with each of these passes, perhaps by changing the guitar's pickup settings/blend *and* changing the amp's settings slightly *and* moving the mic an inch or two. I pan these tracks apart as well, but not to the same positions as the direct tracks—perhaps 8:30 and 3:30. With some luck, this process results in an enormous, powerful sound, and if you do a good job in the playing department, it'll sound like one massive performance.

Before I got into modeling devices, I used an approach similar to the one above, only I ran my guitar into a distortion pedal before the amp, I relied more on the amp's distortion, and all four passes were miked-amp. (Without using amp-modeling technology, pretty much any direct distorted tone sounds flat and electronic.) I've gotten much better sounds since adding the modeling device to the chain.

Don't forget the chunk. In most applications, distorted guitar needs to be *heavy* and *chunky*. That means you should make sure you're capturing plenty of low end—or at least low mids—in your recording. Don't rely too much on EQ after the microphone or modeler; turn up the bass and mid settings on the amp or modeler itself to get a really beefy sound, and then record that. You might even need to tame the highs, as excessive high end on a crunch tone can be buzzy and annoying, undermining the sound's power. Focus on capturing the sonic equivalent of a brick house. If you go overboard, you can always bring down the guitar's lows with EQ later.

Lead Guitar

It's not very practical to record lead guitar using the same layering techniques as with crunch rhythm guitar—in most cases there are too many articulation and phrasing subtleties for the part to sound good layered, and if the part is improvised, layering is out of the question. So, you'll probably have to get the sound down in just one performance. Lead guitar, usually consisting of single notes played high, is more prone to sounding thin than chords played low on the neck. The key to fattening it up is to mess with the signal quite a bit—both before the guitar amp/modeler and after. Try putting effects such as mild distortion, a tone booster, or a phaser in line just after the guitar to give the tone more complexity and sustain, and feed the resulting signal into a close-miked guitar amp or modeler with the power stage cranked up. If possible, compress/expand the signal to clean it up and smooth it out before recording.

To thicken up a lead tone further, try a bit of octave divider—either before the distortion stages or after (they will likely sound very different). If you mix the octave-down sound fairly low, it won't really be audible, but it will give the lead tone considerably more balls. Turned up higher, it's more of an effect with a distinctive sound. Octaver is a great secret weapon for thick lead tones.

After your solo is down, perhaps add a widening effect such as light chorus, pitch-shift chorus, or mild flange. Spread out the returning effect signal somewhat in the stereo field, so that it "surrounds" the dry tone. With some careful EQ, not to mention patience tweaking the controls on all of the stages, you'll get a very usable lead guitar tone. If applicable, on mixdown add some reverb that's similar to the lead-vocal reverb; this will put the lead vocal and lead guitar in the same space in the final mix.

Acoustic Guitar

Compared to distorted or even clean electric guitar, acoustic guitar is pretty easy to record: Just put up a condenser microphone one to two feet away from the instrument. If you want a bigger, more mix-filling sound, position the mic more toward the guitar's soundhole—this is where the body of the sound comes from. If the guitar is there just to provide texture and rhythm to a denser arrangement, position the mic more toward the neck; this will tighten its frequency profile and make the guitar less likely to muddy up the mix.

Strummed acoustic guitar (particularly a hard-strummed part in a busy arrangement) can benefit from compression, which makes it more punchy and present in the mix. Fingerpicked parts, particularly a delicate one in a sparse arrangement, call for gentler compression. As for EQ, you could gently boost the upper mids and highs if the sound needs a bit more sparkle.

Many acoustic guitars come with a built-in pickup, typically of the piezoelectric variety. These are great for live performances, but many people aren't crazy about using them in recording; piezos are notorious for sounding "scratchy" in the highs and somewhat artificial. But a piezo signal can often be blended with a mic signal to give the sound more dimension. If you're able to record them on separate tracks, you can pan the two signals apart a little to broaden the sound. Or, for an even wider sound, pan one of the signals to center, pan the other off to one side, and then pan a very-short-delayed version of the second source to the opposite side (see Fig. 7). Magnetic acoustic-guitar pickups—the kind that you fasten inside the soundhole—tend to give a more muscular, electric-guitar-like sound that's great for modern country and harder folk-rock. Again, try blending in a magnetic signal with a mic signal and see what you get. But remember, anytime you blend two different kinds of signals from one performance (as with a mic signal and a direct signal), pan them together and listen on headphones, comparing the blended sound with its individual components, to make sure low frequencies aren't being cancelled and thinning out the sound. If you notice trouble, get the mic either closer or farther away from the guitar and try again—and once you find a good distance, keep it steady while you record. Otherwise the tone will change as you move closer to or away from the mic.

Of course, you can double-track acoustic guitar with two identical performances and pan them differently. The result is a broader sound that fills more space, and the subtle differences between the two performances add excitement and movement in

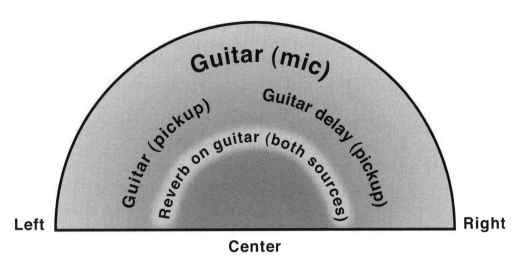

Fig. 7 Giving a single guitar performance a wider sound by using two sources and a short delay.

the stereo field. But if the mix is dense and a lot of instruments are competing for space, double-tracking may not be necessary; it may only clutter things up. Double-track only when you think doing so will help the recording, not just because you have an extra track open.

Sampled Non-Drum Sounds

Having a sampling keyboard or sample player in your arsenal opens up all sorts of possibilities for sounds. Not only can you get good facsimiles of keyboard sounds—piano, organ, vintage keys like the Wurlitzer and Fender Rhodes, and vintage synths—you can also add fairly decent sounds for strings, brass, woodwinds, and much more. How convincing these sounds are in the end depends on three things: the quality of the sounds themselves, the way you play or program them when recording, and how prominent the sound is in your mix. The quality of a sampled instrument—and by that I mean its likelihood to sound like the real thing, regardless of how you play or record it—depends on how well it was recorded, as well as the total amount of data that makes up each sound (i.e., the duration, the number of individual samples that make up the instrument, number of dynamic levels that were sampled, sampling rate, and bit resolution). But remember, if an instrument is sampled poorly, its data specs are meaningless. The only way to gauge the true quality of a sampled sound is to listen to it, or better, actually use it in a recording.

It's one thing to have a sampled brass-section riff in a dense mix—but if you put in a sampled-trumpet solo, particularly if the arrangement is sparse, you probably won't fool anyone (especially if your performance unwisely uses keyboard-specific things like pitch bend). If realism is your goal, don't play anything a real player of that instrument wouldn't—or couldn't—play. A few rules of thumb: The more expression aspects the instrument offers, such as vibrato on a violin or tonguing on a horn, the harder it is to reproduce with sampling. For example, a piano is easier to reproduce than a tenor saxophone. Also, the more that dynamics factor into the instrument's sound, the harder it is to reproduce. This makes a harpsichord (which has only one dynamic level—you cannot play it harder or softer) easier to reproduce than a piano. Finally, solo instruments are much harder to reproduce than ensembles. You *can* record sampled solo instruments well; it's just more challenging. Therefore, if you want to do a song featuring 15 harpsichords, you're all set! Bust out that sampler. (And when you're done, you might want to lie down with a cold compress.)

Guitar, both electric and acoustic, tends not to come across well sampled, either. Because of the way it's played, the only thing that really sounds like a guitar is a real guitar. An exception is if you create custom samples yourself, tailored for a particular task. For example, if you're doing something experimental with a riff that isn't actually playable (at least by you), a good option would be to play segments of the riff through your actual recording signal chain, sample them, and then put them together afterward via MIDI. In contrast, building the same riff out of canned power-chord samples played by someone else would probably just sound like a lame attempt by a keyboardist to "play guitar."

If you're doing your sampled sounds with real-time MIDI (where the sampler or sample player is generating sound each time you run your recording program), you aren't actually recording them until mixdown. But there may be times when you'll need to "print" the audio for your sampler parts, for instance when you're running a sample-player plug-in and it's bogging down the recording program. By now you probably know all you need to do this well. Just make sure you're gain-staging properly (see Chapter 2) so that your tracks are clean and quiet. You probably won't need to add any compression, as MIDI-generated sounds are usually much more dynamically consistent than acoustic sounds. Make sure to mute all other sounds when you record your sampler track, so that non-sampler sounds don't get accidentally blended in.

Synth Bass & Other Synth Sounds

Synthesizer sounds, produced by either hardware synths or "virtual" software synths, are a mainstay of many genres. Regardless of the type of synth you're using, it helps to be able to tweak its factory sounds or even create your own sounds from scratch; rarely is a stock preset perfect for what you need on a specific song. Plus, someone might recognize that you took the easy route and used Program 1A from last year's best-selling virtual synth. Synth programming is beyond the scope of this book; for an overview, I recommend Jim Aikin's *Power Tools for Synthesizer Programming* [Backbeat Books]. It will give you plenty of background as well as specific information on synth programming, regardless of the gear you're using.

Getting a synth signal into your recording gear is straightforward: Just connect the output(s) to one or two input channels using a standard shielded cable with

¼" jacks. As with any electronic device that outputs sound, make sure the synth's master volume is turned up; otherwise you'll need to boost the signal downstream, which will compromise your signal-to-noise ratio. Compression shouldn't be necessary, but expansion can be useful to clean up the silence between passages, particularly from noisier synths and/or with sounds that cut off quickly rather than fade out.

Naturally, if you're able to use MIDI rather than printing the synth parts, do so. It's much easier to tweak a sound on the synth itself than to try fixing an already-recorded track, or to tweak the synth program and re-record the track. Just don't forget to store your sounds before you power down your gear!

Non-Drum Loops & Grooves

Groove programs like Propellerhead Reason and Ableton Live have made it incredibly easy to build complex grooves, either imported into a recording program (as you would drum loops) or built right inside the recording program (with the groove generator working as a plug-in). I don't have much to say about "recording" these sounds; as long as they aren't generating their own distortion, such grooves almost automatically sound fantastic and can give a "pro" vibe to a song with little work (or even skill—don't get me started!). Treat them the same way you'd treat any drum loop or synth sound.

Vocoder

You don't hear vocoder all that often on songs these days, but it's a cool, retro sound. A vocoder is a device that dynamically filters a sound based on the frequency characteristics of a second input's signal. The typical setup involves running a synth through the vocoder, with a mic plugged into the vocoder's modulator (secondary) input. When you play the synth, you hear nothing—but if you also speak into the microphone, the synth comes through with speech-like characteristics, creating a "robot" sound. (Think "Mr. Roboto" by Styx.) More creative applications involve using different modulation sources—for example, you can create catchy, rhythmic synth patterns by modulating a synth's sound with a drum or percussion track rather than a mic.

A vocoder can be difficult to record because it tends to be "peaky"—you set up your gain staging, only to find that on certain notes or vowels the signal level goes through the roof, causing wild distortion. The solution to tame those peaks is heavy compression. Use a high compression ratio, such as 10:1, and listen to make sure the rest of the vocoder part isn't getting squashed by the compressor. (If it is, raise the compressor's threshold or lower the ratio.) If you need to EQ the vocoder sound—and you probably will—put the EQ in line *before* the compressor. This will allow you to tame the vocoder's most resonant frequencies somewhat, which should reduce the amount of compression you need overall to get a smooth, even sound.

Lead Vocals

As with drum tracks, the sound quality of a recording's lead vocal is extremely important. Drums (and bass) provide a foundational role, meaning that inadequacies in these areas weaken a recording the way a poor foundation weakens a building. But lead vocals are a song's emotional focal point and most obvious feature to most listeners, like the paint and windows on the outside of a building. Weak drums and bass will make a song sound bad to many listeners even if they can't put their finger on why—but if the lead vocals are bad, everyone will know why the song is hurting.

You may think the first requirement of a great lead-vocal track is that it be performed by someone who can sing really well. But there are many examples in rock & roll of distinctive, memorable vocalists who don't exactly have operatic voices; Bob Dylan and Lou Reed are two names that come to mind. Usually, a sense of conviction and a unique style are what get these singers by—even if they aren't Freddy Mercury, they put their heart and soul into the performance and they mean every word and inflection, and that's what connects with listeners. So, vocal technique aside, let's just get you to make the best recordings of the vocals you or your musical collaborators have to offer, whatever they may be.

Lead vocals are usually recorded with a condenser mic, as this type offers superior top-end detail and clarity, but some singers prefer their sound through a dynamic mic. The classic studio vocal mic that you see in music videos is the Neumann U87 tube condenser—but if you're reading this book, you probably don't have a grand or two (or five) to spend on a single microphone, and that's okay. For years I've done well with an affordable AKG C 414 (another perennial studio favorite), and in recent years several companies have introduced vintage-style condensers that sound great and cost considerably less.

Condenser mics often come with a slide-on windscreen, and there are also third-party pop filters that connect to mic stands; these protect the mic from bursts of breath resulting from plosive consonants like P's and B's. Aside from using one of these, avoiding "P-pops" is largely just a matter of technique. As long as you avoid singing directly into the mic at close range, you should be able to keep P-pops to a minimum. Angle the mic about 45 degrees away from your line of breath, and sing slightly *past* or over the mic. The mic will still "hear" you perfectly well—but it will be out of the direct line of fire of unsavory wind-related noises. As a side benefit, singing slightly off-axis in this way will soften sibilance, the excessive high frequencies that can accompany "s" sounds. I don't know why so many people haven't figured this out, but when you hear a vocal filled with P-pops and sibilance blasts, you know the singer was aiming straight for the mic. Even worse is when an amateur recordist tries to correct the track afterward by rolling off all the lows (to tame the P-pops) and highs (to reduce the sibilance)—the result is a dull, muted vocal with no bottom-end support. There's no reason to do this. Angle the mic properly and you'll get a more natural sound that doesn't have to be wrestled into submission afterward.

I touched on another aspect of vocal mic technique in Chapter 4: adding "manual compression" to a vocal. When you're singing, be mindful of how your distance from the mic relates to your performance's dynamics. If you're singing along and you know a loud phrase is coming up, back off from the mic a bit just before you deliver the phrase. If you know you'll need to move forward and back to do this during a vocal performance, stand with your feet staggered somewhat; this makes it easier to lean into the mic or pull back. You can also turn your head a little more away from the mic, but don't do it so much that your tone disappears. Experiment and learn what works best for you on any particular performance.

The signal chain. If any instrument can benefit from pre-recording compression, it's vocals. Vocals are so dynamic and important, rarely does a totally uncompressed vocal work well in a recording. And it really helps to clean up the track if there's an expander in line as well. That's why I recommend putting all vocals through an insert sub-chain with a compressor/expander and EQ (see Chapter 3).

To set the compressor's parameters, get into your intended position in front of the mic and vocalize (you don't need to sing yet) at different dynamic levels while you watch the compressor-active LED. I like to see the LED come on about one-third of the way between the quietest passage I'm about to sing and the loudest. A suitable compression ratio should be somewhere between 2:1 and 4:1—the louder the song and the more dynamic the vocal, the higher you can set the ratio. Still, unless you're going for a particular effect, you don't want to hear the lead vocal get "squashed" when the

---

GUERRILLA TACTIC

What If Your Voice Just Sucks?

Sometimes we Guerrilla recordists just have to make do with sub-par vocal talent, whether it's ourselves or a guest singer in our studio. Or, regardless of talent, maybe you're just morbidly insecure about hearing yourself sing. In these cases, your best friend is layering: double-tracking, triple-tracking, or quadruple-tracking identical (or at least similar) performances. Not only does this cause individual inaccuracies to disappear into the blend, a layered vocal sounds richer and more supported.

At the very least, make sure you're singing in key. (If you can't do that, nothing may be able to help you—consider becoming a rapper.) Then build up a second and third layer. Each time you

add a performance, monitor the previous ones at about 50 percent the level of the current performance. Pan previously recorded tracks to the left or right somewhat, with the current performance panned center. This will help your ear to distinguish between what's been recorded and what's being recorded. When you're done, blend the tracks at roughly the same level; if one performance is significantly stronger than the others, bring that one up a bit. Pan the tracks together, or almost together. If you'll need more tracks for background vocals or other instruments, bounce the vocals together (see Chapter 1).

Other techniques that can help the vocally challenged are track compositing, pitch correction, and open-air recording; all are covered in Chapter 9.

compression kicks in; it should sound as natural as possible. Whispers should still sound like whispers and screams like screams, only their actual level on the recording should be much closer to each other than they would be in a live, uncompressed performance.

As when recording any instrument through an expander, make sure the expander isn't cutting off the ends of words or phrases at all. The slightest noise you make vocally should open up the expander, but it shouldn't stay open or flutter open and closed due to background noise. If it does, adjust the expander settings and/or try to reduce the background noise.

As for EQ, you may not need to add any during the tracking stage. Sometimes it helps to give lead vocals a little "bump," or slight boost, at around 2kHz—but if you're unsure, you might as well wait until afterward to think about EQ. You may want to cut frequencies below about 40Hz, however, as this will reduce wind noise as well as any rumble that happens to be transmitted from the floor to the mic by way of the mic stand. (Using a rubber shock-mount to hold the mic helps in this regard, too.) Alternatively, the low-cut switch on many mixing boards' input channels is perfect for doing this—just don't forget to defeat this switch before you use the same channel to record bass guitar or kick drum.

Performing. The time to be watching meters and LEDs is *before* you're recording a performance—not during. (This applies to any kind of recorded performance, not just vocals.) Make sure everything is set up properly, and when it's time to record, concentrate on the performance only, not the gear. If you find out afterward that something went technically wrong, such as clipping on a loud note, tweak your settings and go again. If the vocal performance was perfect except for that one note, though, you can punch in just that portion or attempt to de-clip the note through digital editing (see Chapter 9).

My vocal performances generally get stronger after a few takes, so I record and keep each take until I've filled up four tracks. If I then determine that my first track is worthless compared to my last, I erase track 1 and record a fifth take over it. I've also noticed that when I compare four lead-vocal takes, usually one stands out as being the best for almost its entire duration—it's as if I were particularly "in the zone" for that performance. Still, a vocal track can often benefit from the technique of *comping* or compositing—building one performance out of bits and pieces of several takes. I discuss comping in Chapter 9.

Naked or supported vocal? If you aren't a particularly strong singer, or just can't stand to hear your own voice, you may not like the "naked" sound of a single vocal track leading a song. This is where layering a vocal can help. But you might not want to hear four layers of yourself singing the lead vocals at equal volume—your song may benefit from the focus a single lead-vocal track provides. If so, as long as you have enough available tracks, augment one lead-vocal track with two support tracks, mixed 3dB to 6dB below the main track. Choose the best take as your main track, and then turn down the levels of the others (perhaps eliminating the worst of four takes altogether); then blend them in at the same pan position, or have them "surround" the main vocal slightly. Aim to achieve an effect where you can't quite hear the support tracks distinctly, but the lead vocals sound different—specifically, thinner and weaker—when the support tracks are taken out.

There's a lot more you can do to improve lead vocal tracks after you've recorded them. I'll cover these techniques in Chapter 9.

Background Vocals

Well-done background vocals, or BVs, can do a lot to make your recordings sound fantastic. Few sounds are as pleasing as good vocal harmonies, and if you're making music by yourself, you have the advantage of instant perfect vocal blending—after all, whose voice could blend better with yours than your own? Still, plenty can go wrong when recording BVs, causing them to detract from a song rather than do what they're supposed to do: support the lead vocal and add power, shimmer, or sophistication to the mix.

Background vocals can consist of several voices coming in to support the lead vocal, all in unison with the lead, at certain spots. Or, they can be in unison with each other but different from the lead vocal, for example to provide a counterpoint or a call-and-response role. They can also provide a unison harmony to the lead vocal, or they can be split into full-on three- or four-part harmonies (or more). The type of BVs you create depends on the artistic needs of the song, as well as your comfort level with arranging vocal harmonies. (If you're interested in learning to arrange more ambitious BVs, spend some time teaching yourself about the theory of musical harmony, or take a harmony class. It can really come in handy.)

Charting a course. If you're planning on doing harmonies but you don't have much experience singing harmony, arrange and chart out your BVs before you start

---

 Making BVs Bigger

If you're laying down background vocals and don't have many tracks to work with—or if you want your BVs to be exceptionally full and massive—electronically thicken up each performance before you record it. A good way to do this is to add a pitch-shift effect that can create two or more simultaneous small shifts (in the five-cent range, both up and down). If you don't have this capability, a delay set up with chorusing parameters (see Chapter 6) may suffice. Take an effect-send from the mic's input channel and send it to the pitch-shifter or delay, bring back the delay line with an effect return or another one or two input channels, and blend them together at roughly the same level. Then record this blend. Do this with each BV track, and your final blend will be significantly bigger and richer than it would if you recorded each track dry.

recording them. The best way to do that is on a musical staff with notation—but if you can't read music, you can improvise a system by drawing lines on a piece of paper to represent notes (see Fig. 8). You'll have an easier time with this if you're familiar with smaller intervals like semitones, whole-steps, and major and minor 3rds; if you aren't, reading this kind of chart can be a great crash course.

Sitting down with a keyboard, and playing bass notes with the left hand and chords with the right, may be the best way to figure out which notes work with the melody and which don't. Keep in mind that sometimes, the best BV parts are not those that harmonize directly with the lead vocal but rather provide harmony counterpoint. The Beatles and Beach Boys were masters of this kind of arrangement. Dig out some of your favorite recordings and listen to the way the BVs augment the melody and create tension, release, and complexity in the arrangements.

How many parts? The term "three-part harmony" gets thrown around a lot, but don't feel you *have* to arrange elaborate harmonies for a song. In a lot of cases, just two parts—perhaps a double of the melody and one harmony a 3rd above—can do wonders. (In fact, this is probably the most common vocal-harmony arrangement.) In any case, you'll get a thicker, more luxurious BV sound if you double-track or even triple-track each individual line. So, your BV arrangement may consist of two tracks of melody support and two tracks of harmony. Three tracks of each, if available, will create a sound that's thicker still. Alternatively, coming up with a third part and only double-tracking each part will yield a "taller," more choral harmony sound. It's an artistic decision whether to go for a sound that's thicker or has more harmonic complexity.

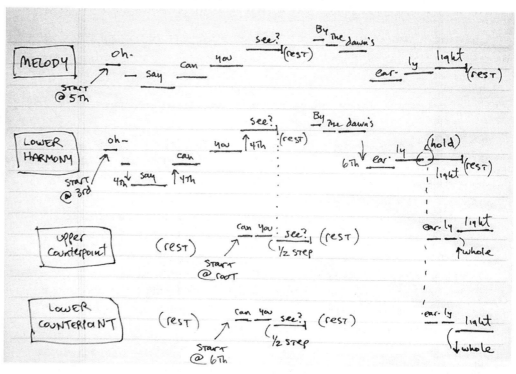

Fig. 8 Non-music-readers can use an improvised "notation" system to chart out background vocal parts, indicating approximately when and in what intervals the various parts move. This chart shows a four-part arrangement of "The Star-Spangled Banner" with the melody, one harmony, and two counterpoint lines.

The signal chain. It's convenient to record BVs right after finishing the lead vocals (or vice-versa), because you can use the same signal chain: mic, set up the same way, with a compressor/expander plus EQ insert sub-chain. BVs tend to sound better when you crank up the compression a little. The ratio can be somewhere between 3:1 and 6:1, and the threshold can come down a little compared to where it was for lead vocals. You'll probably want to EQ differently, too. While lead vocals need a certain amount of low-mids to give the sound "body," BVs function higher, and more narrowly, in the frequency spectrum. Also, as you add more and more layers to your BVs, the tracks will tend to muddy each other up. If you gently roll off a bit of the lows and low mids from each BV track before you record, a blend of four or six voices will still sound crisp and clear enough to sit in the mix with little or no additional EQ.

Performing. The manner in which you address the mic for a BV performance depends on the part itself. Is it a worded part with sibilant and plosive consonants? If so, then angle the mic and sing past it the same way you would with a lead-vocal part. But if all you're singing is vowel sounds ("ahhhhh") or a worded part without any troublesome consonants, try getting close and singing right at (or at least next to) the microphone. Doing so will create a more intimate tone with more breath noise, which sounds great in BVs. For this reason it's nice to sing BVs with a bright, airy vocal sound using lots of extra breath—this helps to create a glossy sheen that really flatters the rest of the song.

If you sing very close to the mic, you'll want to roll off the lows more heavily. This is because of something called the "proximity effect," which is the tendency of low frequencies to be accentuated when a sound source is close to a cardioid-pattern mic. The closer you are to the mic, the stronger the proximity effect. If you're building up six tracks, each sung two inches from the mic, you'll almost certainly need to roll off some lows to prevent your BVs from being weighed down by mud.

Naturally, your BV performances should be as tight with each other as possible, both rhythm-wise and pitch-wise. So, once you get going, it helps to have some of the already-recorded BVs in your headphones for reference. But your ears can be easily confused as to which are the previous (recorded) parts and which is the current (live) part, which may cause you to drift off pitch. For this reason, while recording BVs, it helps to turn down the BV tracks you've already recorded by several decibels and to pan them off to one side (say, 9:00 or 3:00), while your current performance is louder and panned straight-up. This way you'll be able to monitor yourself effectively while still hearing the tracks you need to lock in with, on the side. Your ears will have no problem telling the difference between already-recorded performances and the current one, which is critical to performing the part well.

Evaluating your work. If you're going for a slick BV sound, carefully scrutinize the tracks you've laid down before you move on to something else. Listen to the tracks together at roughly the same level. (Bringing down higher harmonies by a couple of decibels may help them blend better with lower harmonies.) If it sounds like one or more tracks aren't working for some reason, solo the tracks one at a time to find the offending track, and re-do it.

When you're satisfied with the performances, try to find panning positions for the BVs that you think will work well in the final mix. Sometimes it works better to pan BVs around the stereo field; sometimes they need to be bunched together. If you're spreading them out, you'll get a fuller, more lush sound if you balance doubled tracks on each side—for instance, putting the two lower harmonies at 10:00 and 2:00 and the higher harmonies at 11:00 and 1:00. Alternatively, panning the lower harmonies together on one side and the higher harmonies on the other will result in a more "live" sound, because each harmony will appear to come from a single point in the stereo field, as opposed to being part of a broad mass of BVs. The choice is up to you.

Percussion & Other Miked Sounds

By now you should have a pretty good handle on how to mic up anything—from a guitar amp to a human voice—and set up a signal chain for it. For big, loud sounds use a dynamic mic, which is less likely to distort at high sound pressure levels, and experiment to find a mic position that produces the sound you want. For woodwinds and miscellaneous acoustic sounds, like percussion instruments, use a condenser mic. Rule of thumb: The more "rock & roll" a sound is, the more likely you should use a dynamic mic. For example, for a folksy, natural-sounding harmonica sound, use a condenser mic. But for a screaming blues-harp sound, pump that harmonica into a cranked-up amp, and capture the amp's sound with a dynamic mic.

Adding a real shaker or maraca track can really liven up a sampled drum track or loop. Even better, record two acoustic percussion instruments and pan them left and right. But be careful, as things like shakers and tambourines can be extremely dynamic. Even if you think you've set up your signal chain with plenty of headroom, one hard shake could send your signal well above 0dB—which, of course, can mean distortion.

Sound Effects

In some musical styles it's common to have voice-overs, pop-culture sound bites, and other sound effects in songs. In the case of sounds that already exist on a CD (such as in a sound-effect collection), you can just play the CD and take a feed from your stereo receiver's headphone output, as described on page 138. Or, you can put the CD into your computer and extract the file digitally with iTunes or an equivalent program. To get sounds from a DVR or DVD player, first disconnect any TV-signal cable that may be coming into it, either from a cable box or straight from the wall. (If you don't, the sound may be rendered unusable due to ground-loop noise—see Chapter 2.) Then take a feed from the device's RCA audio-out jacks and run them straight into one (for mono) or two (for stereo) of your input channels. Signals transmitted for TV and radio tend to be heavily compressed, but you may want to compress the sound some more to improve intelligibility, and/or add expansion to clean up its dynamic range's lower end. If a spoken-word track doesn't need a natural, full-range sound, EQ out the hissy highs and muddy, rumbly lows. They'll just clutter up your mix; besides, all of the information needed to get the words across is contained in the middle of the frequency spectrum, around 1kHz. The track will pop out even more if you create a niche in the mix for this band through frequency slotting (see Chapter 5), or if you process it with a limiter plug-in (see Chapter 9). If it's some other sound effect, like crowd noise or a train passing by, spend a little time thinking about where the sound's signature frequencies exist, and consider attenuating frequencies that don't fall in these areas. If you don't need them, removing them will make your mix that much cleaner.

Recording A Live Band

So far I've discussed recording only one instrument or voice at a time. But maybe you and a friend want to record two parts at once—or perhaps you want to record an entire band performance. While this is more challenging than recording one instrument at a time, it can certainly be done. You'll need a mixing board or two, with at least as many available mixing busses as the number of tracks you'll be recording. This will allow you to assign each audio source to one output bus, with each bus feeding

---

GUERRILLA TACTIC *Track-Expanding Options For Live Recording*

As wonderful as it is to record using a computer, you just can't record that many tracks at once with one, unless you have a really expensive pro-audio setup. If four or eight tracks just isn't enough, consider using another recording medium for the task. Perhaps you know someone who has a couple of old (and working) ADAT-type machines, or a stand-alone hard-disk recorder that will accept 12 or 16 inputs. Once you've done your live session, you can digitally transfer the recorded tracks to the computer and work with them there.

Actually, there *is* a Guerrilla way to get more tracks out of computer recording: Use two entirely separate digital audio workstations, and record eight tracks to one system and eight to another,

for example. It sounds like it wouldn't work unless the machines were synchronized with each other. But actually, they kind of are. Unlike the mechanical motor of an analog machine, a digital clock is what drives a computer recording system's timing, and that clock is as accurate as any digital clock—meaning very accurate. Here's what to do: Record one percussive sound, from the same mic or direct source, to both systems at once before the song starts. (This is equivalent to the "slate" they use in film when shooting a scene.) This will provide a synchronization reference. When you're done recording, import all of the audio tracks from one DAW into the other, and line them up so the percussive "slate" sound happens at exactly the same time. All of the tracks will then remain synchronized, all the way to the end of the song.

one input on your digital audio interface. Then, in your recording program, you'll have one track recording each of those input signals (a stereo signal can be recorded on a single stereo track).

The first thing you need to do is decide how you are going to configure the signals and the tracks. The limiting factor will likely be the number of tracks you can record at once. A typical digital audio interface has only eight inputs, limiting you to eight tracks (some interfaces have only four inputs). So, depending on your band's instrumentation, you'll have to make some compromises. Start by deciding whether you want to record drums to two tracks (a stereo mix) or four (say, kick, snare, and overheads). If you're a three-piece band with bass and guitar and a singer, you can probably devote four tracks to drums. If your instrumentation is more complex, the drums may have to go onto two tracks. Alternatively, you can agree that one or more instrument (such as lead guitar) won't be recorded until afterward; that will free up inputs for the live tracking session.

When recording multiple instruments, a major concern is separation—not the kind I discussed in Chapter 5, but rather, preventing the sounds from contaminating each other, as this can make mixing more difficult. Some "bleed" is inevitable, but the less you allow, the better. This may require, say, recording the bass direct only and putting the guitar amp in another room. If you can't isolate a loud amp in another room, try at least putting up homemade "baffles"—mattresses, pillows, or anything else that can keep the sound from getting into the other mics. (Another option for the guitar is to record a clean direct track and later "re-amp," discussed in Chapter 9. But that may not sit too well with the guitarist.)

You may not be able to record good live vocals using this setup, unless the singer can be acoustically isolated somehow. (Vocals require much more isolation than a guitar amp.) But even in commercial recording sessions, "scratch" vocal tracks are often the only vocals recorded during full-band performances. This means they're guide tracks only, meant to be replaced later, under more controlled conditions. It's difficult if not impossible, though, to replace only part of a live vocal track. There will probably be a lot of drums and who knows what else bleeding into the mic, and the vocal will sound weird if that bleed suddenly isn't there for one verse or one phrase.

Monitoring is another issue. The easiest solution is to monitor yourselves as you would onstage—put vocals and direct instruments through PA monitors. However, then you have the problem of amplified vocals getting into the other mics, and if you want to replace the vocals later, you may also have to replace tracks that were contaminated by the old vocals. So, there's monitoring through headphones. But now you have to figure out how everyone will get a headphone mix that inspires them to perform well, which is an art and science in itself. And it can quickly become a signal-routing nightmare.

If all of that sounds like a headache, perhaps the best Guerrilla compromise is to record only drums (to four tracks), one track of direct bass (with the bass also feeding an amp in the room), and one or two more instruments during the live session, plus any MIDI instruments (they can be recorded without taking up an audio input). Either perform the song with no vocals, or don't sing into mics. You can then lay down vocals and any missing instruments individually afterward. Fig. 9 shows a sample setup for this method of live-band recording.

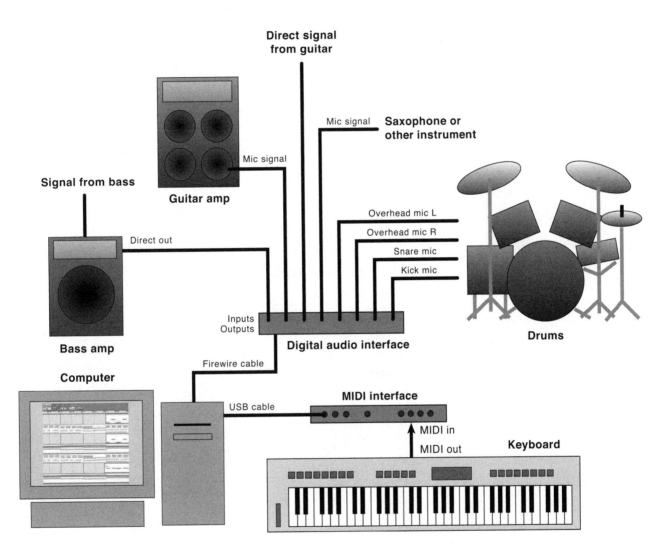

Fig. 9 One approach to recording a live band: drums to four tracks, direct bass (from a live amp), two channels of guitar, and a mic. A keyboard is recorded via MIDI.

CHAPTER 8

Humanizing Drum Patterns & MIDI Parts

This chapter is for non-drummers who want to get natural-sounding drum parts in their music, and non-keyboardists who need to lay down tricky keyboard parts. It's also for drummers who are open to recording MIDI drums instead of live drums, but who have never recorded this way before and don't have an electronic drum kit. Many home recordists use short-cuts like quantizing and step programming to get MIDI parts down. If you do this and you're unsatisfied with the results, or if you resent it when people say your drum tracks "sound like a drum machine," read on.

Much of the popular music from the 1980s—particularly music made between 1982 and 1986 or so—has a particular sound that's easy to recognize. From the Human League's "Don't You Want Me" to Prince's "Kiss," the era was known for mechanized dance beats and pulsating, metronomic synthesizers. It's no coincidence that 1982 was also the year that the first programmable digital drum machine, the LinnDrum, was released. By the time Peter Gabriel had a hit that year with "Shock the Monkey," the world was hooked on the new sound of programmed drum machines spitting out samples of real drums in perfect time. And the following year, manufacturers began mass-producing the first MIDI-equipped musical instruments, which allowed drum machines, synthesizers, and digital sequencers to be hooked together and churn out rhythms in perfect lockstep.

Today, dance music and other electronic styles still incorporate the perfect rhythms that result from sequencing the musical parts—i.e., recording their MIDI information—and quantizing (time-correcting) them strictly to an eighth-note or 16th-note grid. However, in a lot of musical styles, that '80s sound can be dated and out of place. If you're making rootsy rock & roll, punk-rock, or country music, you probably don't want a computerized feel; you want it to sound like music played by human beings. Even hip-hop can be livened up by a real drummer playing the drums and a real keyboardist playing the keys. Can we take advantage of this in the Guerrilla studio? You bet we can—that's what this chapter is about.

It is possible to reap the benefits of computers, samplers, and drum machines *and* make them sound real and human. Once you know how, it's actually quite simple.

I believe this is the real secret to Guerrilla Home Recording, because without it, no matter how well you've recorded your sounds, your music may still sound like "one-man-band" drum-machine or computer music.

Lesson No. 1: Play It!

Naturally, people have different skill levels on various instruments, and different levels of rhythmic sensitivity. If you're a guitarist making your own music, for instance, the most you might feel comfortable doing with a drum machine is choosing a stock factory pattern and hitting the play button. But if you want to broaden your musical horizons and improve your music's feel (and ultimately its sound), I urge you to start trying a little harder and stretching yourself in musical ways that may fall outside your primary instrument or your comfort zone. If you're aiming only to create a karaoke-like backing track for your guitaristic genius, then that's what your music will sound like: a guitarist playing over a lackluster, stock backing track. Let's aspire to achieve something better than that.

To begin, if you aren't doing it already, play programmed (MIDI) parts into your recording program (or drum machine) in real time, or at least "slow real time" (see the next section). In other words, don't step-program them, and don't choose stock patterns—*play* your patterns instead! Even if you're comfortable on only one non-MIDI instrument, like guitar, it doesn't matter. Just dive in—you can benefit from these techniques almost immediately, and they'll get easier with time as you continue using them. As a side benefit, your overall musicianship and rhythmic sensitivity will improve, which can only help your playing on your primary instrument. With any luck, before long, nobody will know that a live drummer didn't play on your songs.

Laying down drums with a keyboard. Let's say you're using a MIDI keyboard to enter a drum part into a recording program, and that the drum part will be "played" by a sampler loaded with drum sounds. This isn't ideal, but it's a lot better than

 GUERRILLA TACTIC *The One-Key Undo*

My deepest, darkest musical secret is that sometimes I labor for hours trying to get a MIDI part just right. I've never counted, but I'm sure there are some short sections that I played, undid, and re-recorded 50 or more times. The three-step process of stopping the recording program, getting it to undo, and then recording again is both tedious and annoying (especially when things aren't going well). I was able to make this less painful by putting a macro utility to work. This is a small computer application that runs in the background, allowing you to assign a single keystroke to perform a more complex string of actions. My "one-key undo" is the "0" key on the computer's numeric keypad. Whenever I'm recording and I hit that "0" key, the program stops, performs an undo, and starts recording again, almost without missing a beat. This takes some of the tedium and frustration out of recording a tough section over and over.

trying to play drums with the little pads on a drum machine. (If you are using a drum machine, you can still use this method—just consider the drum machine your sampler.) First, set things up so that the keyboard is sending MIDI data to both the program and the sampler. You can do this in various ways: with a MIDI splitter or MIDI interface, by enabling the program's MIDI Thru option (so that the program passes all incoming MIDI data back out to the sampler), or by sending the MIDI into

---

GUERRILLA TACTIC *MIDI Drums: The Interface Matters*

If you've ever tried to play a drum machine in real time using its small pads, you know it's difficult. It's even hard playing drum parts on a keyboard—a set of keys, let alone a bunch of tiny pads, just don't physically say "drums" like something you can hit with a stick. So, for programming drum parts, a MIDI drum controller is a valuable tool to have. Years ago I bought a first-generation Roland Octapad on eBay for this purpose, for $100 or something, and it was one of the best studio purchases I've ever made. The Octapad allowed me to play kick and snare, or hi-hat and cymbals, or all of the toms, at once. (With a little practice, you can play *all* of the drum parts in real time on such a controller.) Of course, there are much more sophisticated drum controllers on the market nowadays. Hitting one of these devices isn't exactly like hitting real drums, but at least you're hitting *something* with *something*, and that makes a difference.

I've since moved on to an electronic drum kit, and that upgrade proved to be yet another quantum leap. In addition to just being more drum-like—which tends to make your drum patterns simply *sound* more drum-like—the electronic kit allows me to work on my drumming skills (without bothering the neighbors). An electronic kit is just a blast to play, even if you're only messing around or playing along with a CD. Electronic drums are the best of all worlds: They play very much like real drums, but you never have to mic them, they offer a lot of sounds, and they offer all the post-performance tweakability as any other MIDI instrument.

Using an electronic drum kit, such as Roland's V-Drums (right), is a great way to get sampled drums into your recordings. But even the most obsolete MIDI drum controller, such as Roland's 1980s-era Octapad (left), can make it easy to lay down a good MIDI drum performance—at least compared to trying to play drums on a keyboard.

the sampler first and then out its MIDI thru jack to the computer. In any case, when you play a note on the keyboard, it should trigger the drum sound associated with that note, causing the event to be recorded onscreen, all at once. Assign one key to the kick sound and another to the snare. I've found it's easier to do kick and snare when the keys you assign are an octave or two apart rather than next to each other; you can get into the performance a little better when your fingers aren't crammed together in a two-square-inch area.

Next, you'll need to be able to hear a click track so you can play in time with the recording program. You can set it up so that the click track is a closed hi-hat—but this may be problematic when it's time to lay down the actual hi-hat part, so you may want to select another sound. Make sure it's a short one; a crash cymbal makes a terrible click-track sound! A woodblock or cross-stick sound works much better. Set the tempo and give yourself one or two bars of countoff time before the part begins, or set up the program to count off a similar time period before it begins recording.

Now you're ready to lay down a kick and snare. Hit record, listen to the click and settle into its tempo, and start playing. If you aren't used to playing a rhythm instrument, try to get your body to move with the groove as you play—it really makes a difference.

The trickiest thing about playing a drum part by itself is keeping track of where you are in the song. Sometimes you can hear the as-yet-unrecorded parts in your head, and sometimes you can't. If you're having trouble, one solution is to pause your efforts for a moment and lay down a scratch track to the click. A quick guitar-and-vocal track, recorded together in real time (they don't have to actually sound good), can make it much easier to keep track of your place in the song, and it will help you play things in the drums that are appropriate for the moment. Then again, if you haven't yet figured out the chords, song structure, etc., maybe it would be best simply to lay down a kick/snare backbeat, or something similar that captures the song's overall feel, for a few bars. You can then duplicate that segment of the pattern again and again until you have enough rough drums for the whole song. You can always lay down a more refined drum part after the other parts are down.

Let's assume you've laid down a kick and snare for the whole song. Next up is the hi-hat. If you haven't switched the click sound over to something other than hi-hat, now would be the time. When laying down a hi-hat part, it also helps for the click sound to be panned to the side across from where the hi-hat is panned. That way, it will be easier for you to hear if your timing starts to drift off.

Unless the hi-hat part consists only of quarter-notes or slow eighth-notes, assign two keys to the sound. That way you'll be able to play the part with two fingers. For this task, I suggest using adjacent black keys, such as C♯ and D♯, because it makes things physically easier and less prone to mistakes. I'm right-handed, so I play stronger beats on the higher key and weaker ones on the lower key. Hey—a drummer tends to play downbeats with the dominant hand and offbeats with the weaker hand, which may explain why this method gives programmed hi-hat a more natural feel.

In some situations, particularly if you're trying to throw together a quick song sketch, it can be pointless (and tedious) to lay down a hi-hat part for the whole song. Instead, lay down just four or eight bars. Once you're certain that it feels good and solid, duplicate the segment again and again for the entire song's length, or at least for parts of the entire song. If need be, fill in parts that require a different pattern. Remember, you can always tweak things later.

Finally, with the kick, snare, and hi-hat done, finish the drum programming by adding tom fills, crashes, or whatever else is needed. To do this, it really helps to be able to play a little "real" drums, or at least to be familiar with what drummers do on drum kits. There are certain things that aren't physically possible for most drummers to do, such as hit the snare, hi-hat, and a tom at once, or two crashes and a hi-hat at once. It's not a serious problem if you leave such "impossibilities" in your drum program, but if you edit them out (or don't play them in the first place), your program will sound more authentic. For example, when a tom fill happens, drop out the hi-hat completely (perhaps replacing it with a pedal-hi-hat sound playing eighth-notes). You've heard this kind of thing on countless recordings, even if you don't know it. Subliminal details like these will make your drum programs rise to a new level of authenticity.

If you've never played drums and don't really understand how drum parts work, spend some time listening closely to some great drum performances on record, and consider even transcribing them, or learn to "play along" (even if it's just air drums). The exercise called "re-production," described in Appendix C, is a great—and fun—way to learn about real drum parts.

Slow "Real Time"

You say that at least on some instruments, you're a bad musician with little or no technique? No problem! One of the greatest things about MIDI is that you can *slow it down*. If you're unable to play an instrumental part at full tempo, why kill yourself trying? Just insert a temporary tempo change that makes performing the part easier. Do it at half speed, if need be. There's no shame in this! Nobody needs to know.

Now, if you've already recorded audio, you'll need to mute those tracks—they won't be in sync anymore. (That is, unless your program automatically corrects for this; check to see if it has a "half-speed recording" function.) If you recorded a scratch guide track at full tempo, it will be useless for this task. One solution is to re-record a new guide track at the slower tempo. Or, if your program allows you to time-scale an audio track—change its playback speed without altering its pitch—time-scale the existing guide track so that it plays back, in key, at the slower tempo. (Be sure to keep the original guide recording so you'll be able to use it again once you return the song to full tempo.)

If you've recorded audio that's in segments or has edits, even if they're muted, the pieces will smoosh together and overlap when you lower the tempo. I don't know about you, but after making a bunch of careful edits, that's not what I like to see. To avert the Humpty Dumpty possibility of not being able to get those pieces back together exactly

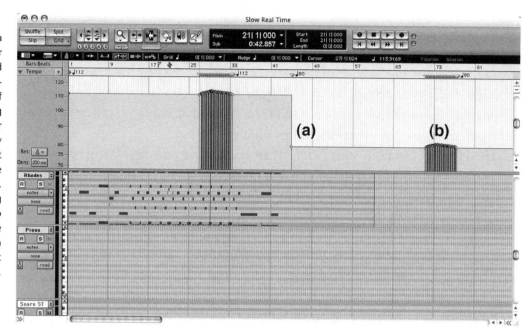

Fig. 1 To record a MIDI part at a lower tempo, first copy and paste all tempo information after the end of the song (a); then drag everything to a lower tempo, including any tempo changes that happen during the course of the song (b). Paste all pre-existing MIDI information into the beginning of the slowed-down version of the song, and start recording.

the way they were, record your MIDI somewhere else, where there isn't any audio—such as after the end of the song. If there are tempo changes, copy and paste them to the new location, along with any MIDI parts you've already recorded (but no audio). Then, select all of the tempo values after the end of the song and bring them down together (see Fig. 1). Now you can record the part in "slow real time." When you're done, you should be able to simply copy the notes you just played back into the song (see Fig. 2). As long as you didn't also accidentally paste in the slower tempo changes, your part should be there—up to tempo, played well, super-tight, and sounding great. You're brilliant!

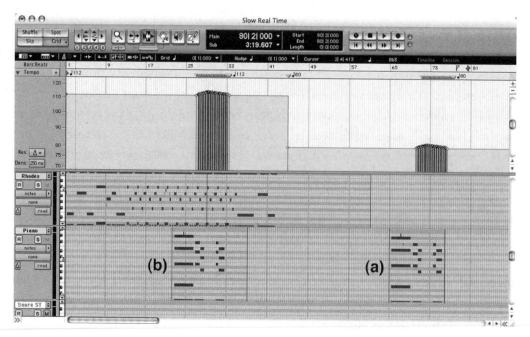

Fig. 2 After recording your part in "slow real time" (a), paste it into the corresponding location in the full-tempo version of the song (b).

Other Ways For Non-Keyboardists To Cheat

Nothing says you have to play the left-hand and right-hand components of a keyboard part at the same time; trying to do so can be frustrating and pointless for an unskilled keyboardist. Instead, make a few passes to record the left-hand part (it's okay to use both hands!), and then overdub the right-hand part on top (again, you have two hands, so use 'em if you need to). If you do it right, you'll sound just like Elton John. Nobody needs to know that you cheated!

If you find that getting your fingers where they need to be is compromising your rhythmic feel, here's an idea—*don't worry about the notes*. Just pick one chord, and record yourself playing that one chord with a great feel; afterward, drag the notes vertically to where they need to be. You can even play just *one note* and then vertically copy the notes to their proper places (see Fig. 3). You'll probably want to temporarily mute any pitched tracks that you've recorded previously, as they'll clash with what you're playing. Alternatively, if the previous tracks are important to the feel of your performance, you can keep them un-muted and instead mute the sound of your current (minimal) part. Use whichever method eventually helps you get the full part down with the best feel possible.

Of course, these "cheating" methods are no substitute for playing something the right way. But if you can't do that, don't kill yourself trying. Fake it instead! You may fall asleep each night convinced that someday you'll be revealed as a fraud—but in the meantime, people will be impressed and your music will sound good. What more could you ask?

The Beauty That Is Partial Quantization

In Chapter 7, I said that quantization is evil. Actually, that's only half true—I was just trying to get a point across. More specifically, when you're trying to create a human feel, *full* or *total* quantization is evil, because locking everything to a rigid time grid

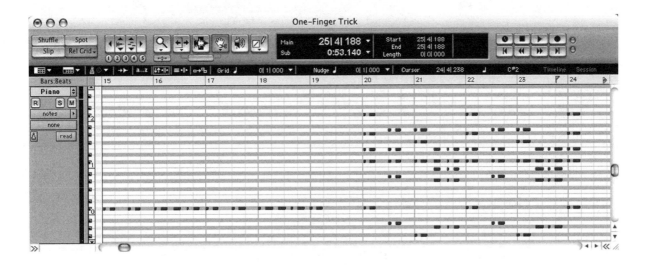

Fig. 3 One way to fake a rudimentary keyboard part is to play one note in rhythm (left), and then drag copies of the notes wherever they need to go (right).

Use Your Ears, Not Your Eyes

When you're looking at a part onscreen that you just laid down, it's extremely tempting to judge the performance visually, based on how all of the little MIDI events line up with the time grid. Even when a part is sounding perfectly fine, if you see a kick-drum event go by that's much farther away from a grid line than all of the others, sometimes every cell in your body wants to stop the playback and get that kick closer to that line. Don't! If it sounds fine, then it *is* fine. Only work on a part some more if it *sounds* wrong to your ears—preferably, before you've had a chance to see what it looks like onscreen. If you laid some of the world's greatest drum grooves onto a metronomic time grid, probably nothing would be visually "locked in." So give your eyes a break and just listen—then decide how to proceed.

(which is what full quantization does) sucks the life right out of the part. However, there's something called *partial quantization* that can be very useful, and it's a feature of many recording programs. When you partially quantize a performance, each MIDI event is moved earlier or later in time—but only part of the way, not all the way, to the nearest value on the time grid. In other words, partial quantization makes a performance rhythmically tighter, but it doesn't force that rigid, metronomic feel where everything is exactly on the beat (see Fig. 4). This is especially useful for people who are rhythmically sloppier with their MIDI performances than they'd like to be.

Partial quantization is usually expressed as a percentage. If you record a MIDI event that falls ten time units after the downbeat, fully quantizing the event would

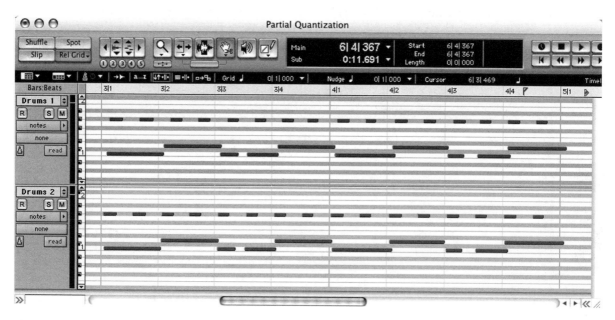

Fig. 4 At top, a sloppy MIDI drum pattern. At bottom, the same drum pattern after partial quantization. The hi-hat (the uppermost part) was quantized at 75 percent, and the kick and snare at 50 percent.

move it earlier by ten units, making it occur exactly on the beat. But if you partially quantize by 50 percent (in the quantization window my program refers to this parameter as "strength"), the event will be moved earlier by only five units. If your quantization strength were 30 percent, it would be moved earlier by only three units. So the MIDI event still isn't exactly lined up with the time grid—but it's closer, and assuming that the other parts are rhythmically tight with the grid, the MIDI part will sound tighter than it did when you originally played it.

For someone like me with okay but not rock-solid time, partial quantization is a godsend. If I lay down a kick/snare pattern and it sounds a little sloppy, I'll partially quantize it by perhaps 40 percent. Actually, drum parts tend to feel tighter when the kick drum is quantized stronger than the snare, so I might quantize the kick by 60 percent but the snare by only 30 percent. Once I'm happy with the kick and snare, I might lay down a hi-hat part and quantize that by 50 percent. If it still feels weak, I may quantize it again by 50 percent, which will move each event half again closer to the time grid.

Some programs offer other quantization parameters. Exclude and include quantization (your program may call them something else, like sensitivity) are especially useful. These apply quantization to some MIDI events but not others, depending on how close they already are to the grid. If you set the exclude parameter to zero percent, all of the events are affected equally. But if you raise that value to 15 percent, the quantization function will ignore (exclude) any events that are already within 15 percent of the way to the closest point on the grid (see Fig. 5). This comes in handy when most of your performance feels great and doesn't require any quantization, but

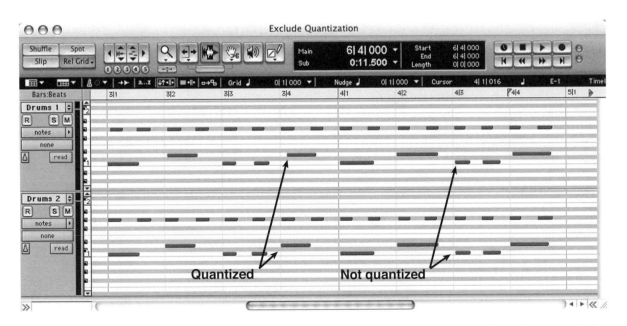

Fig. 5 When you apply exclude quantization to a loose MIDI drum pattern (top), the events farthest off the grid get quantized, but the tighter ones do not.

there are a few loose events that need help. Include quantization does the opposite: At 100 percent, all events are affected equally, but at a lower value, only the tighter events are quantized, while the less-accurate ones are ignored (see Fig. 6). This can be useful if you want to gently quantize an entire performance except for tuplets, rubato passages, or other places where you deliberately strayed from the grid. However, I tend not to trust include's selectivity, so if there are events I know should not be quantized, I usually take a few extra moments to deselect them instead before I click the quantize button. That way I know they're safe from being moved.

Your quantization window may also include a "randomize" or "smear" function. This applies a random shift, either forward or back (you may be able to specify which), to all of the notes being quantized, and it may be applied at the same time as the tightening aspect of quantization. You can think of randomizing as *un*-quantizing (see Fig. 7). I found this function extremely useful when I was recording a project that began as a notation score. The composer gave me all the parts via MIDI files, but since they were exported out of his notation program, the events were all hard-quantized to the grid. In order to make them sound a bit more realistic, I started off by randomizing them by a few percent—not enough to sound sloppy, but enough to sound more like a group of people playing together. My program also allowed me to randomize the events' durations, as well as their velocities (which I'll get to in a bit), so I was able to roughly approximate a lot of real human performances very quickly, without having to re-play all of the parts myself. Re-playing them would have gotten much better results, but it was a 75-minute opera arranged for full orchestra, and I wasn't getting paid . . . you get the idea.

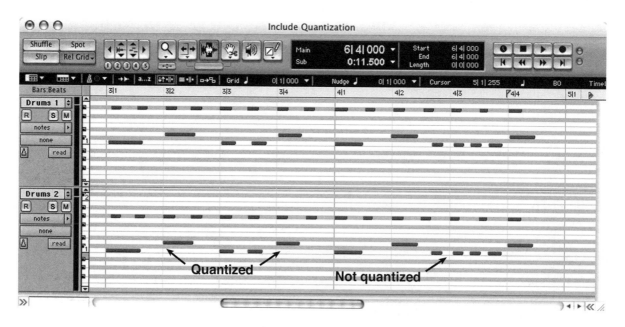

Fig. 6 With include quantization, all events are affected except for a loose tuplet (at right), which remains untouched.

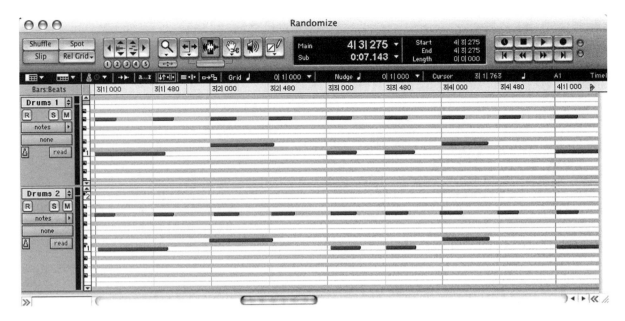

Fig. 7 A fully quantized pattern (top) can be randomized to loosen it up a bit and make it slightly more human-feeling (bottom). This example is exaggerated for illustration purposes.

Getting the most out of partial quantization involves applying some or all of these functions, in combination or separately, and in a particular order, depending on what each part needs. For example, you may decide to quantize an entire part just a bit, and then go back and do an exclude partial quantize to help out only the loosest stragglers. With practice, you can become quite good at this skill. Laying down drum tracks is the perfect way to practice the art of quantizing, because with drums, it's easy to hear when something is sounding loose and weird, or tight and groovy.

Swing Factor

Most drum machines and recording programs offer swing factor as part of their quantizing functions. Like partial quantization, it's expressed as a percentage. Swing factor determines whether subdivisions are to be played with a straight (evenly spaced) feel, a triplet feel, or somewhere in between. The concept of swing factor recognizes that there aren't only two ways to play a series of notes; rather, there's a continuum between the straight feel and the triplet feel, and this varies from groove to groove. In other words, some grooves are straighter than others. My favorite example to demonstrate this is the Beatles' "Hey Jude." A minute-and-a-half into the song, the tambourine starts playing 16th-notes, and even though the melody and everything else essentially feels straight, the tambourine is subtly swinging—not playing with a strict triplet or shuffle feel, but not straight, either. Later, when the tambourine comes back, it's swinging even harder. On a MIDI part that's quantized, swing factor determines exactly how straight or how shuffled the subdivisions are to be played.

I've seen the percentage parameter used in different ways from program to program, but here's how it works in Pro Tools: Say you have a MIDI performance of

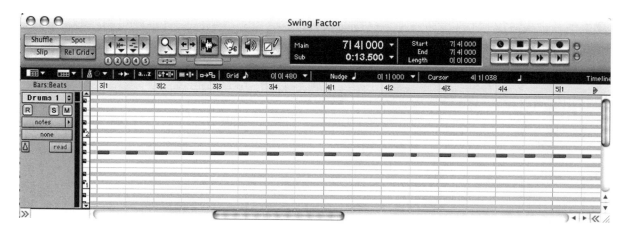

Fig. 8 Quantizing eighth-notes with swing factor set to zero percent yields a very straight eighth-note feel.

eighth-notes. If swing factor is set to zero percent and you fully quantize everything to the nearest eighth-note, the upbeat eighth-notes will fall exactly halfway between the downbeat eighth-notes (see Fig. 8). Those are very straight eighths—straighter, in fact, than real drummers typically play. In live drum feels, upbeat eighth-notes tend to drag a little compared to the downbeats, so they have a slight delay—this is what swing factor aims to emulate. So, if you then set swing factor to 30 percent and re-quantize, the upbeat notes will be moved a bit later in time; they'll fall 30 percent of the way between strictly straight eighth-notes and triplet eighths (see Fig. 9). If you set swing factor to 100 percent and quantize once more, the upbeats will produce an exact triplet feel (see Fig. 10). Some people refer to this as "swing feel," but understand that real human feels (swing or otherwise) may fall anywhere between 0 and 100 percent, and even beyond—crank that number past 100 percent (if your program allows it) and see what you get. If you'd like an exercise for using swing factor, try to reproduce those tambourine grooves from "Hey Jude" starting with straight and fully

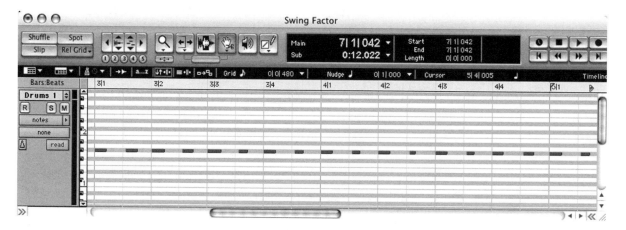

Fig. 9 With swing factor set to 30 percent, the offbeats fall slightly after the halfway point between the downbeats, for a looser straight-eighth feel.

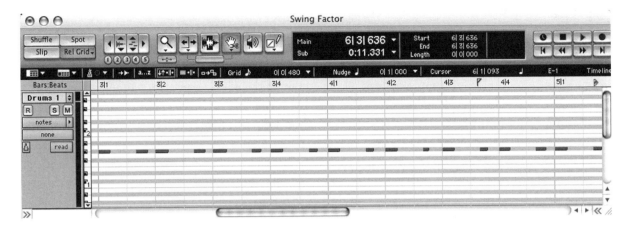

Fig. 10 With swing factor set to 100 percent, the offbeats end up at the two-thirds point between the downbeats, for a strict triplet feel.

quantized 16th-notes. You'll notice that if given a dash of swing, a strictly quantized part can come to life a little.

I'm actually not a big fan of swing factor, because it seems lazy. It's intended as a quick fix to give a hard-quantized part a "human" feel—but I say, you *are* a human, right? Then don't fake it, just play it! Swing factor is great, though, if you're roughing something together and/or don't have time to actually play a part in. (And if your song happens to be an ironic commentary about machines replacing humans, it might be perfect.)

Swing factor + partial quantize. One way to put swing factor to work is to combine it with partial quantizing. If you lay down a MIDI hi-hat part on a straight-eighths song, and partially quantizing all of them to eighth-notes doesn't thrill you, try adding a bit of swing. Maybe you weren't jazzed by the part because you just played it too stiffly; in this case, swing factor can loosen things up a little. It's such an easy function to perform, there's no reason not to try it. You can always undo it if the results aren't happening.

The Importance Of Dynamics

The timing of each MIDI event is critical to a part's feel or groove, but also important are dynamics. For example, only a machine could spit out a hi-hat part in which every event is at the exact same volume. No human can do this, because human muscles don't contract the exact same way each time. The ear is incredibly good at recognizing regular, repeating patterns (such as a quantized, non-dynamic hi-hat part), so this is an area we can exploit. The goal is to include some variation and subtle dynamic "inaccuracies"—not enough to sound bad, but enough to break up the monotony and help trick the listener's ear into thinking it's a live, not programmed, part.

In MIDI, dynamics are specified by velocity values; the higher the value, the harder the note was played, and the louder the resulting sound will be (unless velocity sensitivity is turned off). If you step-program a hi-hat part, or create one event and

Editing Dynamics Onscreen

If you're recording MIDI drum events on a keyboard or drum pads, and the part is a consistent series of stronger and weaker beats (such as steady 16ths on the hi-hat), set it up so that you're playing the stronger beats with one drum pad or key, and the weaker beats with another drum pad or key. This should result in the stronger beats being recorded on one MIDI note and the weaker beats on another MIDI note. That way, if you need to separately adjust the dynamics of either the stronger or the weaker beats, you'll be able to select one set but not the other. You can then scale that set's dynamics up or down by whatever amount you need, set a maximum velocity (effectively compressing the sound's dynamics), etc. You can also adjust timing in this same way. For example, if you want the weaker beats to have a more laid-back or swinging feel, just select all of the weaker beats and move them later in time by a small amount, leaving the stronger beats where they were.

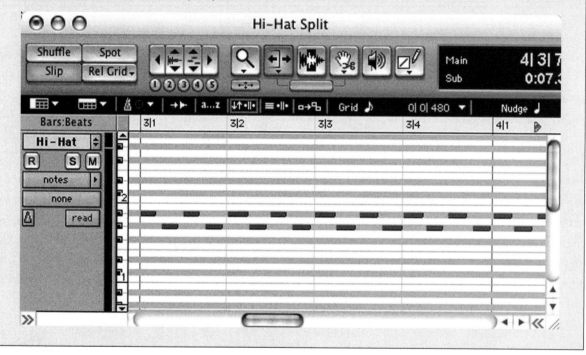

copy it a zillion times, each event will have the same velocity—so it won't sound very human. If you play it in, though, the velocities will all be different. This is a good thing, to an extent. Programmed drum parts, hi-hat in particular, benefit from a lot of dynamic variation.

As an exercise, program a simple series of eighth-notes on the hi-hat, using a keyboard or whatever MIDI controller you have. Then check out the velocity values. If you have some rhythmic feel, the stronger beats will have higher velocities than the weaker beats, as in Fig. 11. If the offbeat velocities are close to the downbeats' values, you may be playing the part too stiffly. Also, you shouldn't be frequently hitting the dynamic ceiling of 127, at least on a hi-hat part (kick and snare get up there sometimes); if you are, give yourself some MIDI headroom by turning down the

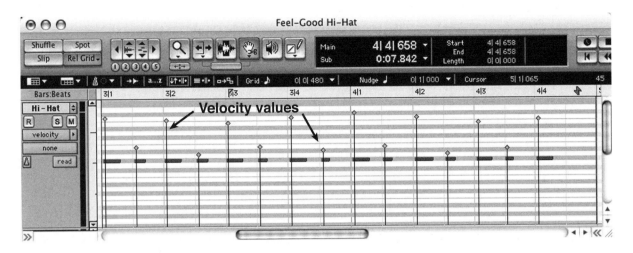

Fig. 11 The velocity display of this hi-hat pattern indicates how hard each event was played. The performance incorporates plenty of dynamic variation for a looser, more human feel.

velocity sensitivity of your controller. If your dynamics are all over the place, check the manual to see if you can adjust your controller's velocity curve to one that's more "compressed."

After you've laid down a MIDI part for a song, it's perfectly fine to go back and raise the velocities of some of your weakest events, which may end up being inaudible, and/or lower those that may pop out of the mix too much. If you're lucky, your recording program will allow you to quickly select only those events with the highest or lowest velocities. This makes the task less of a note-by-note chore.

When programming drums, people tend to underestimate the amount of dynamic variation that needs to go into creating a human feel. Consider the simple kick-and-snare part shown in Fig. 12. That pickup 16th-note on the kick is close to the velocity of the downbeat that follows; this isn't how a real drummer would play that pattern,

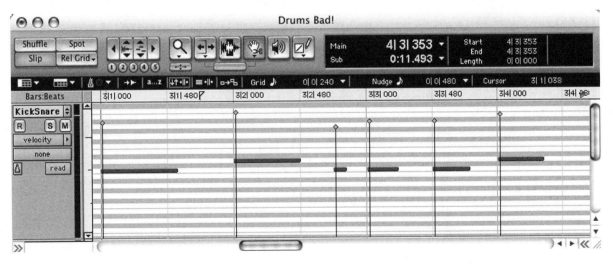

Fig. 12 A drum pattern with a syncopated kick (the lower part), but the kick has a very non-human feel—the velocities are too even for something this syncopated, and the events are too tightly quantized.

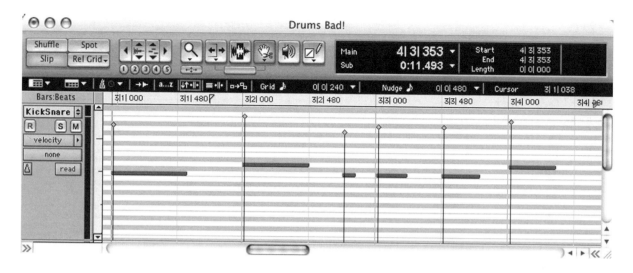

Fig. 13 The same pattern can sound much more human with a few adjustments. The pickup note on the kick drum has a lower velocity to emphasize the strong beat after it, and it's also moved a bit later, for a more swinging feel. Other velocities are varied slightly as well.

so it's not going to sound like a real drummer (or at least like a good drummer). The velocities shown in Fig. 13 will produce a much more realistic feel for this part. In general, if a kick-drum pattern is syncopated at all, try not to make the velocities too consistent. A real drummer will hit certain beats stronger than others; if your pattern doesn't, it will sound like a monotonous drum machine.

Flams

A technique that drummers use all the time is the *flam*—two hits on the same drum, a split-second apart. Flams are easy to work into a drum program, provided you're

Fig. 14 In a flam, two drum events occur very close together in time, often with an increasing velocity. This mimics the way a drummer plays the first stroke with the weaker hand, followed by the second stroke with the dominant hand. Since they're typically used as accents, they often reach a higher velocity than surrounding snares (like the note two beats earlier in this pattern).

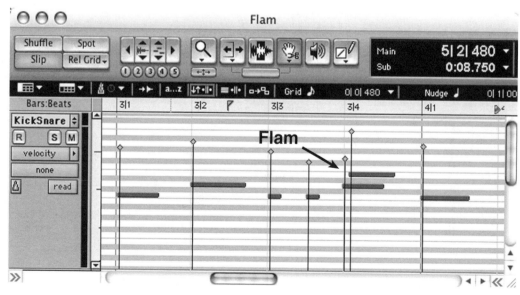

playing the part in, not step-programming. In a good flam, the two events kind of surround the beat they fall near, and the second hit, played with the dominant hand, is typically a bit stronger than the first (see Fig. 14). The flam is one of those nuances that people rarely program into drum patterns—but it's too bad, because flams make drum patterns more expressive and realistic-sounding.

Tempo Changes & Rubato Passages

Who says a song has to stay at the same tempo? Subtle tempo changes can really humanize a drum pattern, and when done well, they can make the entire song feel much more "organic." For example, songs often speed up a bit as they head into the chorus. To reproduce this effect with tempo changes, it really helps to be able to graphically draw in tempo changes with a pencil tool on the tempo track, or whatever your program calls the place where tempo changes are stored. Start ramping up the tempo in the last bar or two before the chorus begins, and have it reach its peak right at or shortly after the start of the chorus. You may then want to bring the tempo back down when the chorus is over. (See Fig. 15.) When you're going for a subtle tempo change, don't increase the tempo more than two or three BPM (beats per minute). The tempo change should only add a bit of intangible excitement; you shouldn't necessarily hear the song speed up.

Some songs call for passages that are *rubato*, or played freely without a specific tempo. Where a song has a rubato section, perform the passage in real time, or at least

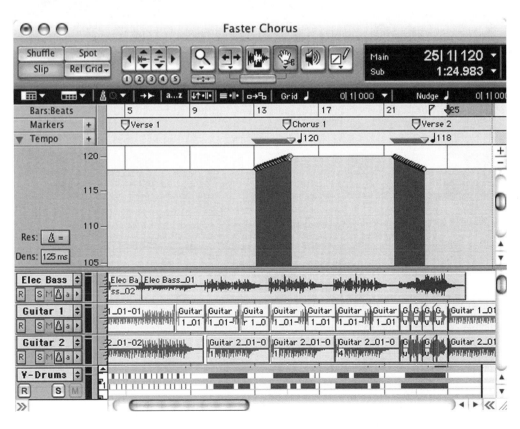

Fig. 15 A ramping-up tempo change—in this case from 118 to 120 BPM—can add excitement going into a song's chorus. Here, the tempo ramps back down as the chorus ends.

close to real time. Turn off the click sound; it can only be distracting to have it in your headphones when you're trying to play expressively out of tempo, and when you're recording audio, you certainly don't want the click bleeding onto your track there.

There's a slight complication with doing a rubato passage: When it ends and the song returns to tempo, unless you're very lucky, the downbeat won't fall on the start of a measure on your recording program's time grid. It'll likely be somewhere in the middle of a measure, because you've been playing out of tempo. To solve this, first record the rubato passage in real time, but stop after playing the first note where the song returns to tempo. When you're done, drag that first at-tempo note so it starts exactly on the closest bar line. Now your job is to mess with the tempo at the very end of the rubato section so that there's a musically satisfactory transition from the rubato section to the at-tempo section. Do this by programming a tempo change that lasts from just after the start of the last rubato note to the start of the first at-tempo note (see Fig. 16). It doesn't matter how extreme this tempo change is; it's not something the listener will hear. The goal is merely to get the song's downbeats to coincide again with the tempo track's downbeats. If a tempo change isn't enough to make this happen, insert a meter change, such as a single bar of 1/4 time, at the end of the rubato section (see Fig. 17).

Fig. 16 Inserting a sudden but brief tempo change—here from 118 to 48 BPM—is a way to get back into tempo following an out-of-time passage. In order for this to work, the tempo change can't start until the attack of the out-of-time passage's last note.

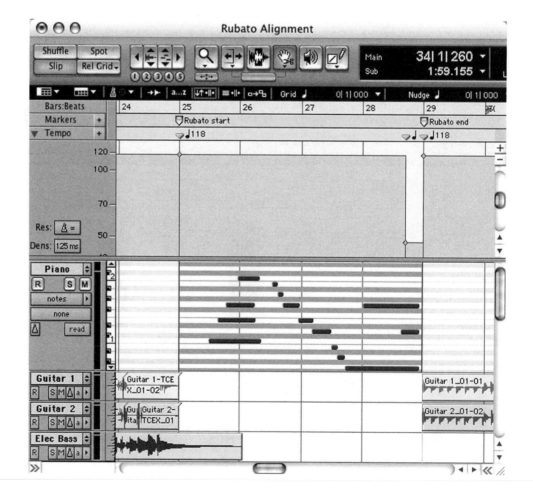

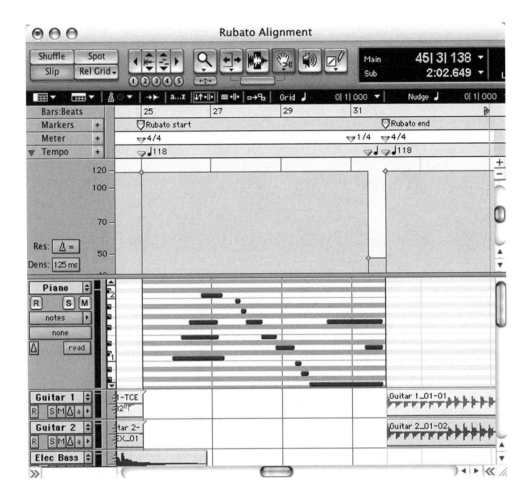

Fig. 17 Inserting a bar of 1/4, as well as a tempo change, may be necessary to get back into tempo.

By the way, you can also apply this technique where you want to interrupt your song with something that isn't a whole number of measures in length (a TV audio clip, for example). If the song stays at tempo, there will be a gap at the end before the next measure begins. To fix this, just put in a tempo change that starts and ends while the audio clip is playing, and adjust this change until the song comes back at just the right moment.

Great-Feeling MIDI Parts All Around

Most of what I've said about programming real-sounding drums applies to recording any MIDI part. Whenever possible, record MIDI parts by playing in real time, and don't fully quantize anything unless you want it to have that rigid feel. Utilize partial quantization if you need to tighten up your performances, and if it's a velocity-sensitive sound (such as piano or Wurlitzer keyboard), build dynamic variations into the part in a way that's appropriate and that enhances the part's human feel.

CHAPTER 9

Miscellaneous Techniques

Guerrilla Home Recording is all about creating the illusion of live musicians playing solidly together, as if they had been recorded in a professional studio by a skilled engineer/producer. As you've already seen, this can involve all sorts of tricks and devious acts of deception. But there's more you can do to stretch what you can get, in terms of sound and apparent performance skill, out of your studio. Many of the techniques in this chapter aren't really Guerrilla tricks—they're used by the pros, too, to help achieve that slick and seamless studio sound. Why not use the same tools to get the most out of your home studio?

Punching In & Out

Aside from multitracking itself, this is perhaps the most basic studio "trick." Punching in is the technique of switching a recording system from playback mode to record mode on the fly, without stopping—even while you're playing or singing. Punching out switches the system back to play mode and the recording stops, even though the song keeps playing. My old Tascam 38 8-track had a ¼" jack on the back for a footswitch, and hitting the footswitch while the machine was playing toggled it into record mode; hitting the footswitch again toggled it back into play mode. Modern digital systems (standalone systems as well as digital audio workstations) make punching in and out much easier, because they allow you to automate punch points. The program or machine will be playing along, and when it gets to a particular point in the song, it will switch over to record mode, or back to play. Check the manual to learn how to set points for punching in and out.

see page 228

In case you've never used this essential home-recording technique (which the pros use all the time, by the way), punching in is a way to fix mistakes or finish an uncompleted track. It allows you to start recording in the middle of a song; you can hear (and play along) with the song for a while, taking a moment to settle into the groove, before the recording actually begins—which happens just before the point of the mistake or where you stopped playing. If done properly, the result is a seamless edit that sounds like you played the performance straight through the first time. Dastardly studio trickery!

Actually, when you're recording digitally, punching isn't even necessary. An alternative to punching is to simply mute the older performance, record the new performance to a new track, and edit the two tracks together (see Fig. 1). However, this requires a couple of extra steps, so most people recording digitally punch simply for convenience. (I'll cover how to make a seamless digital edit in a bit.)

In the old-school analog world, punching in is kind of scary—it actually *erases* part of the previous performance, so if you are punching in, you have to be certain you aren't erasing anything that you might want later. With digital, that isn't a problem. Digital punching falls under the category of "non-destructive editing," meaning you aren't destroying or erasing any data by performing the function. For example, Fig. 2 shows a few seconds of a new part being punched in over an older part, and then portions of the older performance being recovered again. Try doing that on analog tape!

This brings me to a tip: Since punching in is non-destructive, always set your punch-in point to be a little earlier than the point where you expect the edit eventually

Fig. 1 In a digital recording program, recording a segment on a second track (top) and then splicing it in (bottom) is basically the same as punching in.

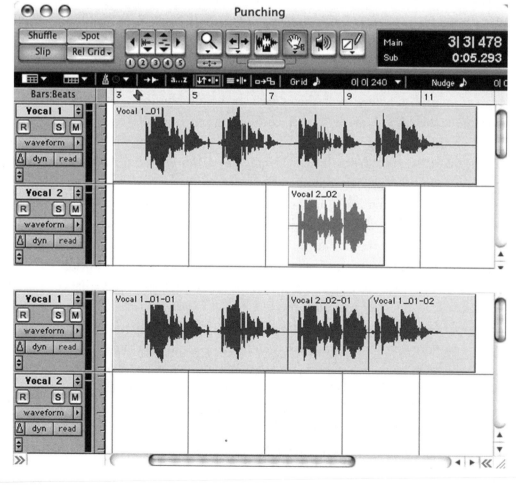

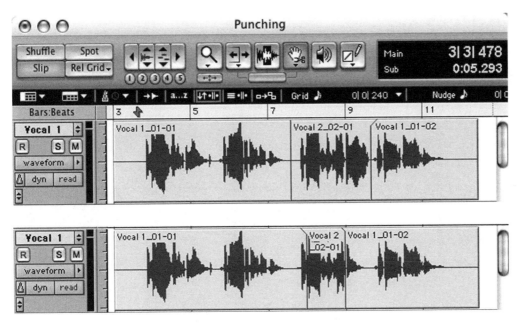

Fig. 2 Even after punching in or splicing in another take (top), the original audio can be recovered where needed (bottom).

to be, and likewise, set your punch out point to be a little late. This way you'll have a bit more sound to work with when you're cleaning up your edit points, and there will be less chance of cutting off the beginning or end of your new take. In other words, since on a digital system there's virtually no downside to punching in early and punching out late, you might as well play it safe and do it. Someday, it will save a perfect take of yours that otherwise would have been ruined—I promise.

Making Digital Edits

This is one of those areas that makes home-recording veterans like myself wonder how we ever got along recording to tape. In a digital recording program, with one move of the mouse, you can slide a track (or a piece of a track) to the left to make it play earlier, or to the right to make it play later—*and* you can also slide it up or down,

---

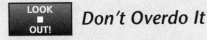 *Don't Overdo It*

In some circles, digital recording has gotten a bad reputation because it makes editing so easy to abuse. Some perfectionist types just will not rest until they've edited every last note into submission. But in many musical styles, rock & roll among them, this is a bad idea. As with absolute quantization, you can suck the life and energy out of something by performing numerous time and pitch corrections. Real music is never perfect; the mild inaccuracies are what make it human and (we hope) interesting and exciting. So perform your edits judiciously, know when to say when, and always use your ears—not your eyes—when deciding what to keep and what to change.

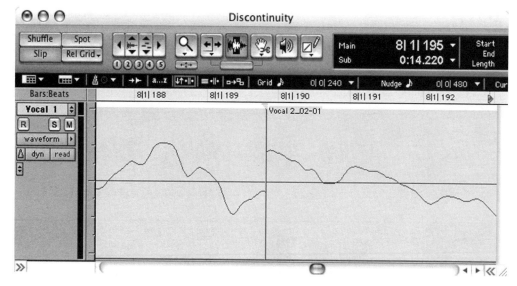

Fig. 3 If the ends of the waves don't meet up at the splice point, the result will be an unpleasant click and a painfully audible edit.

transferring it to a different track. On many occasions, I've gone looking for a small piece of an old, long-forgotten take and spliced it into a newer take, resulting in what sounded like one continuous performance. But it does take a little skill in order to make the transitions between takes seamless.

Here's why: If you randomly splice together two different pieces of audio, there will likely be a discontinuity in the wave shape as it crosses from one piece to the other (see Fig. 3). When this happens, the result is an unpleasant click at the transition point. There are three ways to fix this: First, you can slide one of the pieces ahead or back by a tiny bit on the program's timeline, until the ends of the waveforms meet up exactly (see Fig. 4). Or, if you don't want to alter the performances' timing at all, you can lengthen or shorten one piece by a tiny amount until you get a match (see Fig. 5). But sometimes the waveforms don't cooperate; in this case—assuming your program

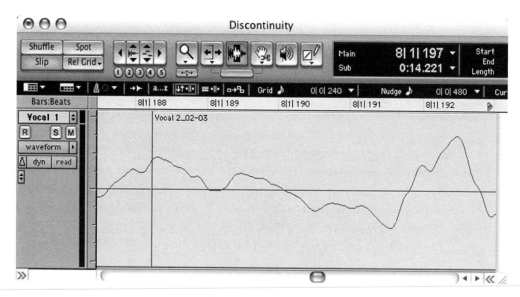

Fig. 4 One solution is to slide one segment earlier or later until the wave ends meet in a smooth, continuous way. In this case, the segment on the right was moved to the left.

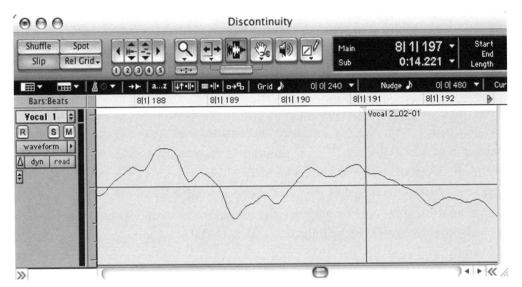

Fig. 5 Or, you can change the splice point without moving the audio, by lengthening one of the segments. Here, the splice point was moved to the right.

offers this function—you can create a digital crossfade between the two pieces (see Fig. 6). If you've chosen the crossfade option, make it a *short* crossfade so that the listener can't hear one part transition into the other; there's no need to make the crossfade longer than a few milliseconds. And whatever method you use, when you're done, solo the track (i.e., play it by itself) and listen to the transition on headphones. It should sound completely smooth. If it doesn't, tweak your edit point some more.

There's one catch to making digital edits: Wherever there is one, your hard drive needs to jump to a different location on the disk to find the file you're transitioning to. When a lot of edits are happening on a lot of tracks, this can bog down your drive and possibly cause playback errors. If "edit density" (as it's called) is causing you problems, one solution is to bounce some of the more highly edited tracks into

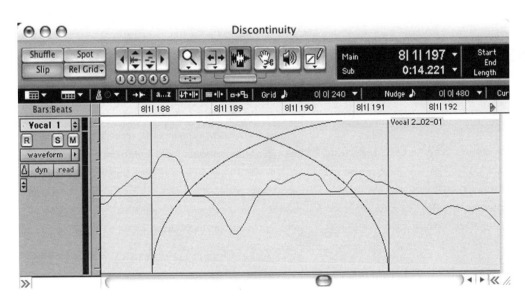

Fig. 6 Adding a cross-fade, which blends the waves together on either side of the splice point, is another option.

single, continuous files (see page 14). But if you've made only a few edits (i.e., you don't have a raging case of "Pro-Tools-itis"), you'll probably be okay.

Some recording programs allow you to redraw wave shapes with a pencil tool. This can be a godsend for getting rid of momentary anomalies in the wave. Sometimes you hear an unexplained glitch or click on a track, and when you zoom way in on the wave shape, you realize why: There's a sudden discontinuity or jagged spike in the wave, perhaps due to a digital error. If your program gives you a pencil tool, you can just draw the glitch out of the wave—zoom in really close, and draw a smooth and flowing curve at the error point, just like the wave shape around it. If you don't have a pencil tool, one solution is just to remove the offending portion of the wave and splice in a "clean" segment from nearby. As long as the wave shape is smooth across the cuts, the edit should sound perfectly fine.

Compositing A Track

see page 229

Compositing, or *comping*, refers to building a track by piecing together parts of other tracks. This technique—which is powerful but can be a little tedious—is most often used on lead vocals to build a perfect "take" out of several less-than-perfect takes.

Let's say you're recording a lead vocal and have four vocal tracks set up. The first step is to get a solid take on each of the first three tracks. Next, listen back to each vocal track, one at a time, and decide if any one of them is significantly better than the others. If so, mark this as your best take. (You may need to do this verse by verse or chorus by chorus.) Then, listen to *each phrase* of each take and decide which take has the best performance of that phrase. If the best performance of a phrase was from one of the alternate takes (i.e., not the best one overall), separate this "replacement" phrase from the rest of the track (see Fig. 7). Do this for the entire song.

GUERRILLA TACTIC	*Make A Take Report Card*

When comping a track, an alternative to judging several takes one phrase at a time is to make a "take report card." For a lead vocal, for example, write the lyrics down the page's left side, one phrase on each line. Then draw vertical lines down the page to delineate columns, one column representing each take. Next, listen to each take in its entirety, and scrutinize the quality of each phrase from that take. In the appropriate spot on your page, grade the phrase either with an A (great), B (good enough), or C (not worth using). Add plusses and minuses to the grades if you want. Do this for all of the takes you recorded, and use the report card to choose which phrases from the various takes should make it into your comp.

This technique is especially useful in analog recording, where you have to mute and crossfade manually as the tracks bounce down. The "report card" provides a visual map of what moves you need to make, and when.

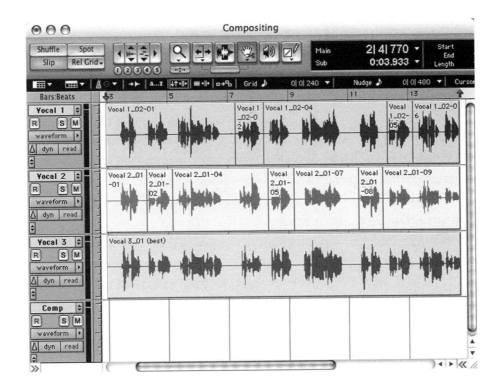

Fig. 7 To create a composite performance (comp), first record three takes, choose the best take (here, Vocal 3), and then choose and separate replacement phrases from the other takes.

Now that you've done the heavy lifting, here comes the fun part. Start by copying the entire best take to your fourth track, the comp track. Then drag the "replacement" phrases from the original tracks to the comp track, one at a time (see Fig. 8). You may

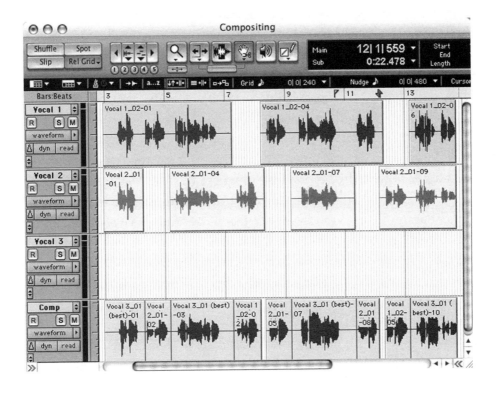

Fig. 8 To complete the comp, drag the best take to a fourth track, and then drag the replacement phrases into place. Make sure none of the audio segments move earlier or later on the time grid when you do these moves.

find, even after cleaning up the edits so they're smooth, that some of the transitions aren't quite working for one reason or another. If so, adjust the transition points or try using other takes.

Comping isn't only good for replacing phrases or even individual words—you can bring in just a single *consonant* (such as a "t" sound at the end of a word) from another take, perhaps because it wasn't audible on the otherwise best take. And comping isn't just for lead vocals. Many of rock & roll's most famous guitar solos were pieced together from several improvised takes, one phrase at a time. If a track needs to be as good as it possibly can be—and lead vocals and guitar solos certainly qualify—it makes sense to put this technique to work.

As you might imagine, comping can get incredibly nit-picky, but the goal is to create the sound of a single, unified performance that just *kills*. If done well, you can put together a performance that's better than anything you could actually perform in one piece—and for the Guerrilla recordist (or the pro producer, for that matter), that's a very powerful tool.

Manual Pitch Correction

I mentioned auto-tune plug-ins in my Chapter 6 roundup of effects. But if you (a) don't have an auto-tune plug-in, (b) only need to correct a few notes, or (c) have a moral objection to auto-tuning an entire track, you can combine a standard pitch-change plug-in (or other signal-processing option) with digital editing. (See Fig. 9.)

First, find the offending note or passage, and select it. (You may need to separate it into its own region as well—check the manual on how to do that.) Extend the selection a little beyond the part that actually needs to be corrected. The idea here is the same as with punching in and out: Since you're editing non-destructively, there's no reason not to give yourself a little wiggle room for later editing. Then, using your recording program's pitch-change plug-in or digital signal processing, process the selected audio, shifting it up or down by five or ten cents. (Make sure to use settings that preserve the segment's duration.) Without going any further, listen through the offending portion several times to determine if it's better, was pitch-shifted too much, or needs to be shifted more. (Try to ignore the bad edits for now.) If it needs a bigger shift, undo the previous shift, change the fine-tuning parameter, and process the segment again. Don't do successive shifts on the same piece of audio, as that will unnecessarily degrade the sound quality. When you're happy with the shift you've chosen, bring in the edit points closer to where they should be, and use the techniques described above in Making Digital Edits to give the whole thing a seamless, pitch-correct sound.

At times you may find yourself shifting entire phrases up or down by 20 or 30 cents, or words by as much as a semitone. I've found that the shorter the audio segment, the more shifting you can get away with; if you're shifting only a quick syllable, a semitone

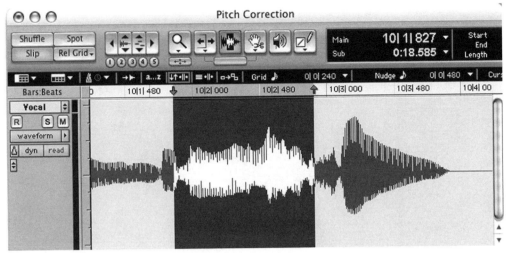

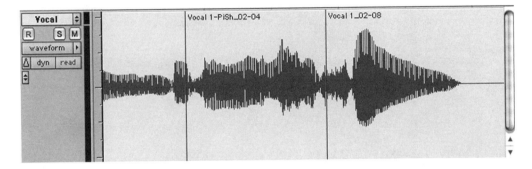

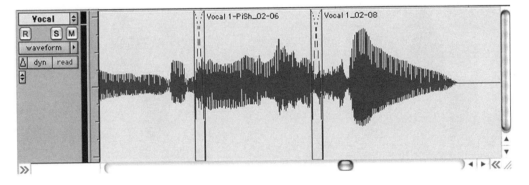

Fig. 9 Correcting a single note's pitch: First, select the note slightly beyond its beginning and end (top). Adjust the pitch with a plug-in or your program's DSP. Then, bring in the ends of the pitch-changed segment appropriately, and give each splice a crossfade (bottom).

probably won't be noticeable. Longer segments with large shifts end up sounding weird, though. If your performance is off by that much, it's probably better just to re-record it.

De-Clipping A Track

Few recording experiences are as tragic as nailing the perfect take, and then learning that you went over 0dB, causing the track to distort at the peak moment. But provided you otherwise did a good job of gain-staging, such moments of wave clipping can be very brief, even if they sound absolutely horrible. If you want to try to save the take, here's a technique that works surprisingly well: Zoom way in on the waveform's

Fig. 10 An emergency method of de-clipping a brief moment of digital distortion: Select only the clipped portion (top), and then remove all of its highs with an EQ plug-in or your program's DSP, and clean up or crossfade the splice points. The bottom two waveforms show the clipped portion, zoomed in: High-frequency details in the wave shape have been rounded off (bottom), including the clipped peaks.

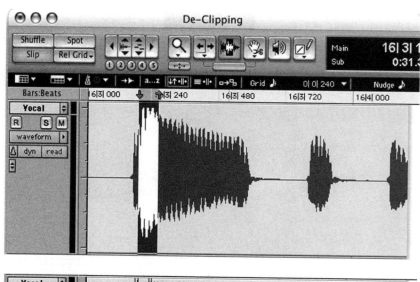

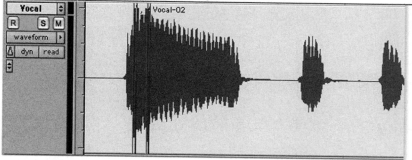

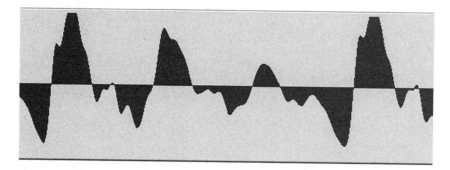

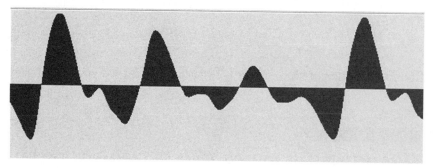

clipped moment to see how many wave peaks are affected. If only a few peaks have been clipped off, you're in luck. Select the clipped waves, and then with an EQ plug-in (or your recording program's digital signal processing), process the segment by rolling off all of the highs—i.e., cut everything over about 2kHz. This should filter out most of the frequencies that clipping artificially added. (See Fig. 10.) If doing this creates a discontinuity in one of the wave endpoints, perform a crossfade or otherwise get the endpoints to match up smoothly again (see Making Digital Edits, above). Then listen to what you did. The formerly clipped moment may now go by without anything sounding wrong at all. (If you still hear distortion, undo and try rolling off at a lower frequency, like 1kHz.) As long as the segment is very short, it will just fly past, and your ear won't detect that frequencies were massively removed.

If the distorted moment is longer than a few wave cycles and the above method has an audible result (meaning you can hear the tone "dip" or cut out for a moment), there are other options. You can separate the word or phrase, attempt to excise the distorted portion, and edit the phrase back together again, hoping it doesn't sound weird or out of time. Or, you can try duplicating a clean segment from before or after the distortion point, paste it over the distortion, and edit until the endpoints match up. If necessary, try a combination of these techniques.

Non-Real-Time Dynamics Processing

Inspired by the above techniques, one thing I've discovered in recent years is using plug-ins on multiple tracks to process audio for dynamics. I've found this especially useful for applying limiting to vocal and guitar tracks, in order to make those sounds really up-front, in your face, and intelligible—enough to cut through practically any mix. Of course, you could achieve the same goal merely by putting a limiter plug-in on the tracks and letting them do their thing in real time, but that would eat up processing power. Plus, after a while you can get a feel for how heavily a track has been limited just by comparing the waveforms onscreen (see Fig. 11). So, this has become

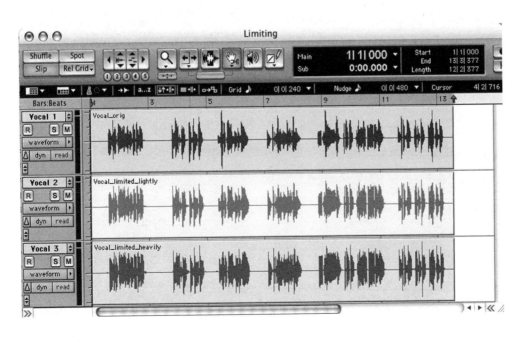

Fig. 11 A raw vocal track (top), and the same track after processing lightly with a limiter plug-in (middle) and with heavy limiting (bottom). The heavier the limiting, the more that loud peaks are brought down while quieter moments are brought up.

my preferred method for limiting vocals: I just select a block of audio, call up a limiter plug-in, set some parameters, and click the "process" button. If those parameters didn't quite get the job done, I undo and try again.

Even though this is a non-destructive editing function, the processed tracks will cover up or replace the non-processed tracks onscreen, which isn't always a good thing. Sometimes you want to go back and change the processing, or apply a slightly different processing to the choruses compared to the verses, etc.—and even though the original track exists somewhere on your hard drive, it can be a pain finding it and re-syncing it. So, before you process a track, first duplicate it, and then mute one of the duplicates. This way, if you need to go back to the unprocessed track, it'll be right there. Just unmute it and throw out the processed track, and you'll be back to where you need to be.

If you don't want to (or can't) duplicate all the tracks you're processing, there are a couple of workarounds. One option is to copy all of the audio segments you'll be processing and paste them after the end of the song, where they will remain as unprocessed "safety" copies. If you use this method, copy all of the song's tempo changes to the new location as well; otherwise you'll mess up any edits that you've done. (I described how to do this in the section on "slow real time" recording on page 169.) A second option is to leave an unprocessed "tag" at one end of every distinct audio segment you're processing; that way, you can always get the original audio back by just deleting the processed portion and dragging the end of the tag so the unprocessed segment returns to its original duration (see Fig. 12). This becomes unpractical once you've made a lot of edits on the audio, however.

Fig. 12 One way to keep a raw audio track easily recoverable is to leave a "tag" at one end. Most of the vocal track at the top is processed (second track down), except for a short segment of silence at left. If you need to recover the raw vocal, just delete the processed portion (third track down), and drag the end of the raw vocal all the way back out again (bottom).

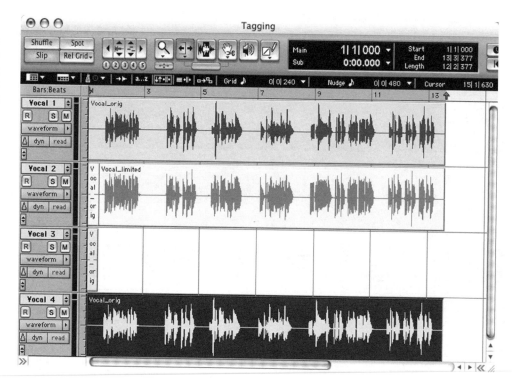

Automation

One of digital recording's most valuable functions is the ability to automate mixdown moves like level changes, pan sweeps, and even changes to EQ and other plug-in parameters. This is especially valuable for the Guerrilla recordist: For years, pro studios had to use million-dollar consoles to automate mixdowns—but with DAW recording, Guerrillas and pros alike can automate the functions right on the computer screen's virtual console.

With some programs, if you switch a track into record mode and then begin recording, any changes you make to that track's virtual-console controls will be recorded. (Other programs allow you to record console moves without necessarily being in record mode.) If you then play back the song from the same spot, you should see the controls move by themselves as you had moved them previously. Welcome to automation! It should be clear how powerful this functionality can be. In addition to getting mixdown moves *exactly* the way you want them, they're stored right in the computer file along with the song itself, so the same exact moves will still be there when you open the song a year from now.

Dragging virtual faders and knobs with the mouse can be a little awkward, so dig into your recording program's manual to find out how to program automation moves in other ways. For example, if you want a track to fade in smoothly over the course of a whole verse, you just create a straight line in the window representing the track's fader level (see Fig. 13). If you're a perfectionist, you may find yourself spending hours in these windows adjusting and readjusting automation moves, listening to portions of a song over and over, until everything is just right. It may sound obsessive, but such attention to detail can make your productions sound very slick, if that's what you're

 GUERRILLA TACTIC *Automating MIDI*

Audio tracks aren't the only things you can automate within a recording program. Things like MIDI drums and keyboards can be automated to a certain extent, too. If you draw a ramping increase in an electric piano track's MIDI volume window, for instance, the sequence will send the electric piano module not only MIDI information for notes and velocities but also for MIDI volume values—which will cause the electric piano to get gradually louder as the song plays. You can do the same thing for panning and perhaps other parameters as well. An important distinction, though: Unlike audio automation, MIDI automation depends on each MIDI instrument's ability to respond to the necessary MIDI messages. For example, my electronic drum kit doesn't respond to volume-change information, so I can't automate the volume level of the drums via MIDI. (I usually get around this by altering the drums' velocity values instead.) This isn't an issue with audio automation; whatever automation your program allows you to add to audio, you can be pretty sure the automation will actually happen.

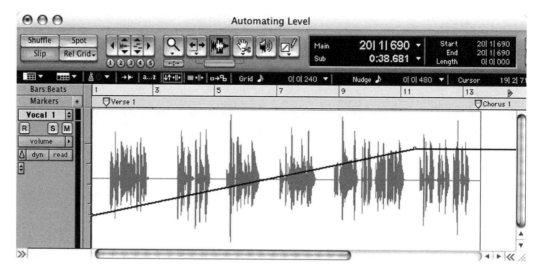

Fig. 13 Ramping up the volume of a vocal over the course of a verse.

going for. In terms of getting a "pro" sound, it can give you a huge advantage over other home recordists who spend just a few minutes setting levels and are done with it.

Automation even allows you to create effects that might otherwise be impossible. For example, in a guitar track's panning window, you could draw a triangle-wave shape that cycles once every quarter-note, perfectly synchronizing the instrument's panning with the song's tempo (see Fig. 14). By doing something similar in a level window, you can create a tremolo effect that's perfectly synchronized to the song.

In addition to setting automation moves for individual tracks, your program probably also allows you to create busses, or groups of tracks, on the virtual console—and you can automate these as well. For example, if you want eight background-vocal tracks to fade in slowly, don't program a move on each of the eight tracks; instead,

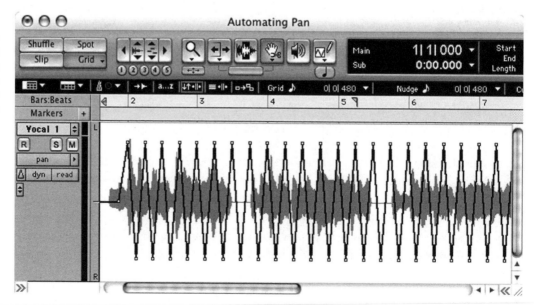

Fig. 14 Drawing in a zig-zag (or triangle) shape into the pan window can create an auto-pan perfectly timed to the tempo of your song.

LOOK OUT! ***Don't Erase The Audio!***

When you're recording automation moves into a track of existing audio, you may need to disengage the program's audio-recording capability; otherwise you may erase the audio while you're recording your automation moves. In other words, you need to set up the program so the track can record automation moves, but you aren't actually recording audio onto it; see your documentation to learn how to do this with your own program. (This caution doesn't apply to programs that allow you to write automation without being in record mode.)

create a bus that groups the BVs together, and program the move on just the single bus. In addition to making it easier to automate the fade-in now, assigning a bus will make things much easier if you need to adjust the fade later on.

Automating Hardware Effects

The virtual console allows you to automate everything, down to the parameters of effect plug-ins (in most recording programs). But what if you also use an external hardware effect, such as a reverb or delay unit? With a little ingenuity, you can at least partially automate such a device right in the virtual console.

The trick is to set up a bus and output whose only responsibility is to feed the outboard effect's input; then you can automate that bus. For example, say you have a reverb device and you want to automate how much reverb it's contributing to your mix. Start by setting up a mono reverb-send bus in your virtual console. Assign the bus to go to one of the unused outputs on your audio interface, and run that output signal straight to your reverb box—either directly through a cable, or through the effect send of a muted, pre-fader input channel on your mixing board (see page 56). Finally, in the virtual console, assign an effect send to feed the reverb-send bus you set up. Now you can either automate the levels of each effect send in the virtual console, or the overall level of the reverb bus. As the effect-send levels (or the reverb-bus level) go up or down, the reverb box will get a stronger or weaker signal, and that will result in more or less reverb coming out of the box and going into your mix. Naturally, proper gain-staging means that over the course of a song, the reverb box should never receive so much signal that it distorts—but to minimize noise, it should come close. Try to get the maximum level 3dB or less from the top (0dB) of your reverb's input-signal meter. (See Chapter 3 for more on gain-staging.)

Re-Amping

As I mentioned in Chapter 7, one way to record an amplified guitar sound is to put down a track of clean direct sound first, and then play the recorded track into a guitar amplifier (perhaps with effects placed between the playback and amp). By

Plug-In Re-Amping

If re-amping appeals to you, check out the various plug-ins that use modeling technology to simulate amplification signal chains. Rather than setting up a "real" signal chain during the re-amp phase to get your sound, you can just try running your recorded direct sound through different plug-ins with different parameters. Unlike with conventional re-amping, plug-ins allow you to quickly and easily tweak your sounds right until mixdown time. Naturally, this has a few limitations. For example, you won't be able to get real amplifier feedback. If nothing else, you can use these plug-ins to broaden and thicken your conventionally recorded or re-amped guitar sounds, resulting in complex, absolutely monstrous tones.

miking the amp at this stage rather than for the actual performance, it's easier for the do-it-yourselfer to get just the right tone. You don't have to be both a guitarist and a producer at the same time; you can concentrate on playing well first, and then you can go back and work on getting the perfect sound.

You probably won't get a good re-amped sound if you record the guitar's direct track through a direct box and later send this track straight to an amp. This is because direct boxes change the electronic properties of the signal so that it can sound crisp and clear when it becomes audio—but this isn't the kind of signal that you deliver to an amp when you plug a guitar into it. Plugging a guitar into an amp creates an electronic interaction between the two known as *loading*, which causes a significant shift in tone. When a tone is loaded, the highs get rolled off somewhat, but there are other changes as well. The loaded tone, when run through distorted circuitry, is what we recognize as a normal distorted guitar sound. In contrast, sending a crisp, broad-frequency direct line to a distorted amp can result in a nasty, brittle type of distortion.

One solution is to load your tone before you record it, by recording your direct track through a direct box that offers variable impedance. If your DI has this feature, turn down the impedance knob until you get a significantly muted or dulled tone— that's the sound you want. (Don't worry, to an amplifier input, that sounds like a nice, bright tone.) If you don't have one of these boxes for the recording phase, another solution is to load the tone before it hits the guitar amp during the re-amping phase. Several companies offer boxes built specifically for this task—they turn a direct-recorded guitar signal into a signal optimized for the amp's input. If you don't have one of these boxes, check your direct box—if it's the passive type (i.e., it doesn't require a battery to operate), you can simply use it "backwards": Run your clean, high-fidelity direct signal from your audio interface to the direct box's output jack, and then send the signal out of the box's input jack into the guitar amp's input. It should hit the amp's input properly loaded.

If neither of these methods is feasible, when you record the track initially, try plugging the guitar into a ¼" instrument- or line-input jack on one of your board's input channels or your audio interface. It might not sound pretty, but this may load the

> **GUERRILLA TACTIC** *Re-Amping As A Last Resort*
>
> I once used re-amping to save a clean guitar track that had gotten messed up at some point. The sound was just a bit gritty in an unpleasant way, suggesting that digital distortion was on the track, but I wasn't sure where it came from. Borrowing from the "de-clipping" technique described above, I put the track through an EQ plug-in to roll off some of the highs (and the distortion), and I followed that with an amp-simulator plug-in to bring some liveness and excitement back into the sound. It didn't completely solve the problem, but it was much better—and a whole lot easier than playing the whole track over.

signal sufficiently so it will sound fairly normal when amplified later. As a last resort, try rolling off the highs quite a bit during either the recording phase (right out of the guitar) or during the re-amping phase (before the amp). Although this won't sound exactly like a properly loaded tone, you should be able to reduce the amount of harsh distortion coming out of the amp.

By the way, re-amping isn't just for guitar tracks. For instance, if you want a sampled organ sound to be more "rock & roll," try running it into a guitar amp that's turned up loud (but not necessarily distorted), and mic it onto a new track. You can even do this with drums, vocals, and other sounds. Experiment and see what you come up with—if it works for the song, then it works, period.

Printing MIDI Instruments

Recording keyboards and drums via MIDI rather than audio (see Chapter 1) not only lets you get good sounds very quickly, it also gives you maximum flexibility for making last-minute changes. However, sometimes it's useful to "print" these sounds—i.e., record them as audio alongside your other audio tracks. Here are a few reasons why you might want to print a MIDI instrument:

1. No sync. This applies only if you're recording to analog tape with a MIDI sequencer or drum machine and aren't using a sync tone (see Appendix A). If so, you'll need to print the MIDI instruments' audio signals. How many tracks you use is a tradeoff: Printing them to just two tracks in stereo saves tracks, but you'll never be able to adjust the instruments' blend afterward. But using up four or five tracks may not leave you much room to work with for recording other audio.

2. Not enough MIDI instruments. If you want a MIDI organ sound *and* an electric piano on your song, but you have only one keyboard and it can't do both sounds at once, print one of them. Set up your program to play one of the sounds via MIDI—preferably the less important one—and connect the keyboard's audio out(s) to one or two of your recording inputs; then run the song while recording the keyboard's audio to a new track or tracks. (Make sure no other audio is accidentally getting onto the new track.) For the rest of the tracking process and during mixdown, you can let the other keyboard sound run via MIDI, blending the first keyboard's audio track into the rest of the mix. Naturally, if you need three instruments you can print two of them and run the third in real time. And you can always print all of your MIDI instruments if that's your preference.

3. Sound not thick enough. Assuming your system can't handle dozens and dozens of high-quality MIDI sounds being generated at once, you can also thicken up sounds by printing MIDI. For example, you could make a more complex string sound by printing several different string sounds that are playing the same notes, and blending them with a real-time MIDI string sound during mixdown. Pan the various strings differently if you want them to sound broader overall. Just make sure the sounds are sufficiently different from each other; if one sound is just a slight variation on another one (perhaps the same sound with a slower attack), it's not going to add anything, and it could potentially harm the blend through frequency cancellation.

4. Effect needs. Suppose you use a hardware reverb unit and want a cavernous reverb on a string sound, but you want to use the reverb unit on the vocals, too, with a different reverb sound. The solution: Print the string sound onto two tracks in stereo, along with the cavernous reverb. Alternatively, you could print *just* the cavernous reverb and run the dry strings in real time, which would allow you to easily alter the reverb blend whenever you need to. The tradeoff is a minor one: If you need to mute the string sound, it's a two-step process, because you have to mute the dry strings and the reverb separately.

5. Simplify mixdown. Maybe you have a MIDI track with fader, pan, or EQ moves that you can't automate for some reason. Rather than repeating these moves each time you make a pass at mixing the song down, perform them while printing the instrument to two tracks in stereo. That way, each time you run the song, the moves will be there—almost as if you had automated them. This is especially useful if the moves are an important part of the song's arrangement, as hearing them can affect your subsequent playing and/or arranging choices. Actually, this technique applies to any tracks—not just MIDI instruments. For example, if you want a lead vocal's reverb to undergo complex panning and level changes that can't be automated, print the reverb (only) to two tracks with these moves in place. Then they'll be there each time you run the song.

Whatever the case, don't delete the MIDI tracks for any instruments you print; instead, simply mute them. You never know when you'll want to go back, tweak a sound or a blend, and re-print. Keep your options open; a muted MIDI track takes up virtually no disk space or processing power, so why erase it?

Open-Air Vocals

If you are like me and have trouble singing with headphones on, there's no reason to record all of your vocal tracks that way. You may be able to eliminate the problem by singing "open air"—listening to the backing tracks over speakers rather than headphones.

There are a couple downsides to doing open-air vocals. First, the sound from speakers bleeds into the vocal mic more than it does from headphones, contaminating the tracks slightly and reducing instrument separation. But you should be able to minimize this if you use a cardioid (directional) mic, position the mic so that it's pointing directly *away* from the speakers, and keep the speakers as quiet as possible. The speaker volume should be *just* high enough so that you can accurately keep your place in the song and sing in tune with enough energy. Unfortunately, reduced monitor levels can make it hard to really rock out, but that's another compromise you have to make with this technique.

CHAPTER **10**

Mixing & Mastering

We've reached the end of the line. Mixing is your last chance to finalize all of a song's individual sounds, levels, EQs, and pannings, and mastering is your last chance to make sure the final mix sounds balanced and has the proper overall dynamics for burning onto CD.

Mixing Goals

In some recording sessions, especially in pro studios, it can take longer to mix a song than it took to record it. That's a testament to the importance of this step—it's absolutely critical. However, if you've been following the "mix as you go" concept (see Chapter 1), most of your work is already done by the time you get to mixdown. In pro studios it's common to "wipe the board" (zero out all of the mix settings) before beginning a mixing session, so the process can be done from scratch. But if you've been mixing the song all along, it becomes simply a matter of fine tuning, listening closely, and asking yourself questions about what you're hearing and what you'd like to be hearing.

see page 230

When you go into final-mix mode, the first thing to consider is: What kind of impact do you want this recording to have on the listener, and which of its ingredients contribute the most toward creating this impact? Should the song have a strong emotional pull because of its beautiful melody and poignant lyrics? Is it a party-hearty rock tune with a catchy riff that should cause impromptu fits of air-guitar? Should its infectious beat make you want to shake your booty? These are very different goals for a song. Having an objective view of the big picture is a great way to start the mixing process, as it will inform the fine-tuning (or perhaps not-so-fine tuning) decisions you'll make in your quest to build on the song's strengths.

In any song with vocals and instruments, there's always a tradeoff between the two. On one hand, you don't want the instruments to dominate to the point where they detract from the vocals' visceral impact. Plus, if the lyrics are important, you don't want the instruments to obscure them. On the other hand, way-up-front vocals can make the music behind them sound small—in effect, detracting from the instruments' impact. This isn't an exact science; there are no standard levels at which vocals and instruments are set against each other. It's always an artistic decision. But it helps at least to ask yourself questions. That way you can decide where on the continuum, from vocal-heavy to instrument-heavy, you'd like your mix to fall in order to best achieve your goals for the song.

Have A Frame Of Reference

Before you start a mixing session, play a song from a professionally mixed and mastered CD at a moderate volume through your studio monitors. Ideally, choose something in the same genre as the song you're about to mix, and/or with a sound similar to what you'd like to achieve with your song. It's hard to mix in a vacuum, so it helps to have a sonic frame of reference before you begin. It may also inspire you to try a few new things in your mix. And by all means, don't be afraid to bring up that reference song *during* your mixing session. It can be humbling (especially since the reference song has been mastered and yours hasn't yet), but putting your music up against professionally recorded music is an important part of the process. Since the beginning, you've been trying to get your song to sound as if it had been professionally recorded, right? So, why stop at this critical juncture? Do your best to get your own mix to sound as smooth and balanced as your reference mix. The extra effort will pay off.

The Importance Of Monitor-Dimming

We tend to love the music we record, and we tend to play music we love *loud*. That's fine for listening enjoyment (as long as you aren't hurting your ears), but in the studio we have a job to do—so don't combine too much pleasure with your business. Understand that most people aren't going to play your song as loudly as you'd like them to. That's why it's important to frequently "dim" your monitors, which is a fancy way of saying, *turn down the volume*. And when I say down, I mean way down—to the point where you could easily have a quiet, even whispered, conversation over the music. It may feel silly to mix a song this way, where you can't even hear some of the instruments. But it can be very revealing to *zoom way out* and take a very broad listen of the song. That's what dimming the monitors does. You'll find out what's jumping out too much, as well as what's completely inaudible. Or, you may think a vocal is totally buried and unintelligible under the cacophony of the music—but if you dim the volume way down, surprise, you might be able to hear every word. That suggests turning up the vocals is unnecessary—maybe even an outright bad idea.

When mixing, try to have the monitors dimmed about fifty percent of the time. In addition to having a more varied perspective on mixing, you'll give your ears a break from fatigue. Your neighbors may thank you, too.

Headphones vs. Speakers

Throughout this book I've mentioned that a good pair of headphones is useful during the tracking process. They're also useful for mixing. However, as with loud vs. dimmed monitoring, balance out headphone listening with speaker listening. Consider the strengths and weaknesses of each method: Headphones (good ones, anyway) offer a very "up-close" listening perspective; they let you hear every subtle detail, and if you turn your head slightly, the stereo image won't change as it will with speakers. But headphones can play weird psychoacoustic tricks on your ears and brain, and you can't get a true read of the low frequencies through headphones. Speaker monitors provide a more accurate low end—at least the good ones do. However, they're subject to acoustical interactions with their immediate surroundings as well as with the room, which can seriously affect your perception of a mix. For example, placing monitors close to a wall causes bass frequencies to build up, making the monitors (and consequently your mix) sound boomier than they really are. This effect is more pronounced if the speakers are near the corners of a room, or worst of all, near the corners *and* the ceiling or floor. Also, the louder you monitor, the worse the bass buildup. So, for more accurate mixing, it helps to put some physical space between your speakers and the wall. If possible, put something heavy—but not rigid—behind the speakers to soak up some of the lows. (I hung a chunk of an old futon behind my speakers.) And remember, frequently dim those monitors!

Triple-Check Your Mixes

In addition to listening at different levels through both your studio monitors and headphones, it's always a good idea to listen to a CD of rough mixes on at least two other stereo systems, as such variety will tell you much more than hearing a mix on just one set of speakers will. After all, you never know what kind of system people will play your CD on. Even pros do this; I read of a studio that ran a snake cable out to the owner's truck so people could go out and listen in the vehicle as the mix ran down. (In fact, the car is a great place to check out rough mixes.) Regardless, at least one of your listening systems should be something with small speakers, such as a boombox or a personal computer, as they respond differently to sound than large speakers. If one of your songs has a prominent midrange-heavy sound, such as a lead vocal EQed to sound like a telephone, you may find that on a boombox it jumps out too much—even though it sounds fine on your home stereo. In this case, you might try bringing down the vocal's level by a decibel or two; you can then dim your studio monitors and determine whether the vocal is still sufficiently present and audible in the big speakers. It probably will be.

Besides being extra work, the downside to listening on several systems is that the results can be overwhelming—kind of like a "too many cooks" effect. On one system you might be hearing too much guitar; on another, too much vocals; and on another, too much bass. The trick is to strike compromises so that your mix is optimally satisfactory on all the systems you check it through. Your mix can't please every listening system all of the time, so the best you can do is find a middle ground for everything.

The Listen-Back Checklist

People without a lot of recording experience might mix a song simply by setting a level for each instrument, and deciding the mix sounds fine like that. Unfortunately, that's not good enough. In order to get more professional-sounding mixes, push yourself to scrutinize them more carefully. Consider the dynamics, frequency content, and pan position of *every* instrument or sound, as well as the mix relationships between related sounds, such as keyboards and rhythm guitar or lead vocals and background vocals. As you gain experience, you'll find yourself becoming increasingly aware of these things.

I learned a valuable lesson years ago when I was recording a demo for a singer/songwriter who went on to join a multi-platinum band. When we were mixing his songs, he was asking me to adjust the background-vocal levels by what seemed like ridiculously small degrees—nudging the faders by just a millimeter or so. He said the vocals just weren't "sitting in the mix" exactly right. Eventually he was satisfied, and the recording turned out really well. After that experience, I found that I began scrutinizing my own mix levels more carefully, looking for that "sweet spot" for each instrument where it fit perfectly into the mix. This is what you should strive to do, because getting every single instrument "seated" just right can make an enormous difference. It's often what makes a mix sound like a real *record*, as opposed to a demo thrown together by an amateur.

To help you improve your critical listening skills, here's a checklist you can follow when listening to a rough mix. Keep in mind these are only guidelines for achieving a fairly conventional popular-music sound; your own aesthetics may be wildly different. Also, needs change depending on the style. In a punk-rock song, for example, a half-open hi-hat may be a major energy provider, so in that case you'd probably treat the hi-hat differently than you would otherwise.

Kick drum: Can you hear the attack? Does the sound's "body" provide a subtle feeling of power? Or, does the kick pop out of the mix too much, causing your meters to peak every time the kick drum sounds? The kick usually causes the meters to jump somewhat; that's normal. But if they jump too much, the kick may be robbing your other instruments of dynamic range—due to the dominating kick drum, they all need to be quieter in order to keep the overall mix from being too loud.

Snare drum: Is it providing enough of a backbeat sound to fulfill its function? Does it have enough "body" to prevent it from sounding tinny, with enough top-end "crack" to balance the rest of the sound? Or, is it (or its reverb) too loud—are you getting an '80s sound like an old INXS record, when you actually want the snare to sound more contemporary? Listen to the snare on a small-speaker system. Is the "body" causing the snare to jump out too much? Inexperienced recordists tend to mix the snare too loud, because it's such an exciting sound. Set it just loud enough that it fulfills its function and doesn't step on the other sounds.

Hi-hat: Is it bright enough? Or, is it *too* bright? The hi-hat's unique high-frequency domain means that it can usually cut through even dense mixes at low to moderate levels. Considering this, is it too loud? Hi-hat levels can be sneaky; when they're too high, it can sound like *something* is wrong, even if you can't put your finger on it. You may try pumping up everything else, eventually causing the whole mix to get too loud, when all you needed to do in the first place was bring down the hi-hat. Make sure it's there providing a pulse in the background; that's usually all the hi-hat needs to do.

Toms: Do they have enough punch? Do they attract your attention when they occur? Or, are they bombastically loud? Toms sound great when they're bold and assertive—but they shouldn't blow away the other sounds.

Crash cymbals: Are they moderately audible? Crashes often don't need to be more than just somewhat audible to be effective. Are the crashes blasting out of the mix? Nothing is more annoying or amateurish than crash cymbals that obliterate everything else when they occur. (I once read an article that said crash cymbals were a good way to hide tape hiss. Worst idea ever!)

Ride cymbal: Similar to the hi-hat, is it sufficiently bright and audible? The lower-frequency "body" of a ride is a component of its overall sound, but this is not what you should hear when a ride part comes in; you should notice only the "ping" of its attack. Also, the ride doesn't need to be loud. If it comes in and seems to take over the mix, either it's too loud, or it needs to be EQed.

Electric bass: Does the level provide enough of a solid low-end foundation to support the mix and keep it from sounding thin and top-heavy? Still, the bass shouldn't overwhelm other instruments with low- to mid-frequency components. Also important, can you hear the individual notes' pitches? If they're more or less indistinguishable, try bringing up the low-mids and perhaps taming the lows. (Blurry pitch may also be a sign that the instrument itself is inferior.) Finally, does the bass blend well with the kick drum? Ideally, they should mesh together somewhat to provide a unified sense of foundation and power, but you should still be able to distinguish their sounds from one another.

Clean electric guitar: Is it bright and crisp enough? Keep in mind this is often an ornamental, background instrument, so it usually doesn't need to be very loud. Are its high frequencies distracting from the vocals? If so, consider reducing its level and/or changing its pan position to give the vocals a little more space. If the guitar sounds thin and flat, like it isn't holding its own against the other sounds, consider fattening it up with an effect or doubling the performance on another track.

Acoustic guitar: Are the highs bright without being annoying and clangy? If the mix is sparse, is there enough body and *oomph* to keep the instrument from sounding tinny? A tinny electric guitar often works fine, but a tinny acoustic guitar usually doesn't sound like one—in a sparse arrangement, the body is an important characteristic of its sound. (Then again, if the body is muddy or woofy and is disproportionate to the top, it may be time to adjust the EQ.) In a busy arrangement, the body isn't necessary and can quickly muddy up the mix, so you can clean up the sound by removing some low mids.

Distorted rhythm guitar: This is often mixed at a bold, aggressive level. If you'd like the instrument to sound aggressive (which is usually the case), does it achieve that function in the mix, or is it wimpy? Perhaps the problem is in its bottom end: Does the guitar have enough heavy bottom to complement the bass and kick drum, without having so much that it competes with these instruments for the lowest frequencies? Or, do its high-frequency components detract from the low end in a buzzy, annoying way? Check the pan positions—do the crunch guitar tracks interfere with the vocals? If so, try panning them apart from the vocals so they can be mixed sufficiently up front.

Lead guitar: If there's a guitar solo, is it roughly on the same level as the lead vocal? Often, both sounds provide the same function: a melodic, up-front performance. So, when the lead vocal ends, it should sound like it's "handing off" to the lead guitar. The lead guitar shouldn't sound like it's saying, "Step aside!" when it comes in, 6dB hotter than the vocal. Then again, the solo is probably the song's focal point for that stretch, so it shouldn't sound timid or weak, either. (If guitar is your passion, my guess is that you *never* mix your solos too low!)

Piano, organ & other keyboards: Can you hear the notes sufficiently without the instruments overpowering everything else? Keyboards are often an important part

What's Wrong With This %@#&! Mix?

Occasionally, a mix simply goes bad. Everything seems to be going fine, and then you make some adjustments, then some more—and all of a sudden everything sounds like total garbage, but you have no idea why. Everything you try to fix the problem only makes it worse, and you just want to throw out the whole thing and start over. Well, sometimes that's the best thing to do—you just have to start mixing a song again, from scratch.

If you've reached wit's end, mute everything and start over. Begin with the kick and snare, keeping in mind that the kick often needs to be louder than the snare at this point in order for the two to balance each other in the final mix. Bring in the hi-hat next; don't overdo it, as setting the hi-hat too loud is one thing that can make a whole mix sound mysteriously wrong. Next comes the bass; spend a little time massaging the EQ so it speaks clearly and blends well with the kick drum. Next, bring in the other rhythm instruments—keyboards and guitars. Finally, bring in the background vocals and the melodic lead instruments: lead vocals, lead guitar, etc. With any luck, your mix will have a smoother, more balanced sound than the one that was giving you so much frustration. With the major problems solved, you can get to work fine-tuning your mix into perfection.

of the low-mid to middle part of the frequency spectrum, so make sure they aren't being shortchanged in these areas. Do the keyboards fill out the spectrum's lower half, without sounding so thick that they're muddy?

Background vocals: Background vocals are just that—they usually sound best in the background. People often put them too forward in the mix, perhaps because BVs can be a mix's slickest-sounding component. But ask yourself: Are they *supporting* the lead vocal, or does it sound like the lead vocal is supporting them? Also, if there are harmonies, are they blended in the proper proportion? Higher harmonies pop out more than lower harmonies, so you may need to balance them apart by a decibel or two. Finally, are the BVs sufficiently crisp, or are they muddying each other up? BVs don't need a lot of low mids; as long as they don't sound irritatingly tinny, you can let the lead vocals fill in the lower end.

Lead vocals: Finally we come to this all-important ingredient. If applicable, can you hear all of the words? If not, you may need to work a little harder tweaking the level, or process them with a limiter plug-in (see page 195). Is the top end crisp, without hissing and spitting like a pan of frying bacon? If the highs sound dull, you may need to boost them, which in turn may necessitate a de-esser plug-in to tame sibilance. Is there enough "body" to the vocal to give the performance warmth? Listening at several different volumes and on different listening systems, scrutinize the way the lead vocal sits in the mix. Is the level at a comfortable place, appropriate for how you want the lead vocal to function in the song? If you're having trouble setting the lead vocal's level, it's probably under-compressed; you may be able to correct for this with a plug-in. Take your time setting the lead-vocal level, as it can make or break a song. When a track is sufficiently compressed and/or limited, an overall level change of 0.3dB should be enough to audibly alter the "feel" of the vocal in the mix. When your ears get really dialed in, you may find yourself going back to remix a song days later just to change the lead-vocal level by that small an amount.

Digitally "Riding The Faders"

If you've ever watched a professional mixing engineer working at a console, you probably noticed that the faders rarely remain stuck at their levels as the song runs. A good mixing engineer makes constant adjustments—kind of like the way you constantly adjust the steering wheel as you drive down even a straight road. This is called "riding the faders." Learning how to do this well in real time can take years—but fortunately, in the digital studio, we can automate these actions. So, in the digital world, "riding the faders" is really all about learning to draw level changes that improve the mix, both artistically and technically. Fig. 1 shows a vocal track with "fader-riding" level changes drawn in. But good fader-riding can involve all of the tracks, as well as the overall level of the mix. Here are some reasons for spending a little time putting these subtleties into your automation:

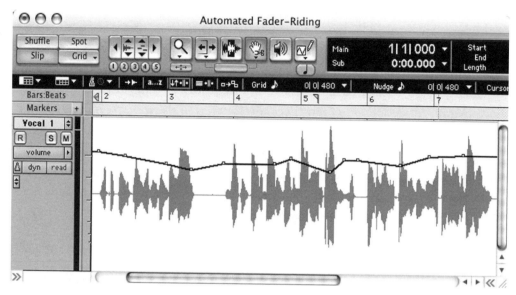

Fig. 1 You can get very specific with automated "fader-riding" if you spend a little time editing levels.

Smoothing overall levels. If a song starts out quietly—perhaps with no drums—then it may be a good idea to boost the mix's overall (master) level at the beginning, and then bring down the virtual console's master fader(s) when the louder instruments (such as drums) come in. It's important for a song to begin with strength and presence; otherwise the listener's first impression may be that the song is wimpy and weak—even if it could crush cars once the acoustic-guitar intro is over. Later in the song, if some of the louder instruments drop out and the overall level goes down, consider bringing the master level back up again. But understand that doing so may compromise the drama created by the sudden change in dynamics. Again, it's a tradeoff.

Sometimes one part of a song is just louder than the others due to the arrangement, not necessarily because you *want* it to be louder. If your song's bridge always causes your meters to peak out during mixdown, don't let the level in the bridge dictate the mix level of the song overall. Simply draw in a volume change, heading into that bridge, that brings down the master level by 1dB, or whatever amount prevents the meters from hitting the red; then ramp the level back to normal heading out of the bridge. If this causes the levels in the bridge to be similar to the levels in the rest of the song, you've done your job well.

Working the emotion. If a vocal or instrumental track reaches an emotional peak during the course of a song, you may be able to enhance its impact by creating a subtle dynamic arc that follows the emotional arc. But like most other aesthetic decisions, don't overdo it—if the listener can sense that you're milking the performance with overly dramatic level changes, the effect can go from artistic and stirring to ham-handed and embarrassing. Just 1dB might be all it takes to create a subtle, but not really noticeable, effect.

Bringing out obscured phrases. Sometimes certain things just aren't as audible as you'd like, requiring some automation help. Maybe a vocal goes into a lower register, or some instruments or background vocals come in right at the moment of the song's key lyric phrase. You can bring out these things with a bit of level automation.

Exploding entrances. A mix can sound more bold if you "explode" entrances slightly: When a new part comes in, start it 1dB or even 2dB louder, and then have it settle into its optimal level after just a couple of seconds. Done properly, this can create a subtle but exciting effect where new instruments seem to be saying, "Listen here!" whenever they enter. Without this treatment, the listener's ear may kind of wander around the mix, unsure of what deserves focus and attention.

Enhancing drum dynamics. Sampled drums can seem lifeless, or unforgiving and relentless, if you don't give their overall dynamics some attention. Don't be afraid to bring up the drum levels as the song's energy increases, and bring them down as the energy subsides. Real drummers respond to a song's energy by varying their dynamics—try to get this element into your sampled drums as well.

Mixing Internally vs. Externally

When it comes time to actually mix a song down, there are two ways to do it: internally, meaning the computer makes digital calculations and writes a new audio file to your hard drive (my recording program calls this function "bounce to disk"), or externally, meaning the music leaves your computer as audio, and you record that mixed audio back into the recording program as if you were laying down a new stereo instrument. Internal mixing is the way to go if you don't use a mixing board and you do all of your processing and MIDI with plug-ins and virtual instruments. If you use external effects and hardware MIDI instruments, you pretty much have to mix externally, unless you print all of your effects and MIDI sounds beforehand. But most people are somewhere between these extremes—for instance, they use plug-ins for effects, but they have a hardware sampler and a synth. Personal preference also comes into the equation; I for one like to hear what I'm mixing as it's being mixed, partly because if I hear something I don't like, I can stop the mixdown then and there. Of course, converting your files to audio and then back to digital is a step some recordists would rather not make unless necessary. Use whichever method appeals to you and is appropriate for your particular studio setup.

Audio Options For Mixdown Files

If you mix externally, your mixdown files will appear on your hard drive with the same audio settings as the rest of the song's audio files. If you're recording at 48kHz sampling frequency and 24 bits (see page 32), your mixdown files will have those specs as well. But you cannot burn files like these directly to an audio CD; audio files destined for the CD player need to be in a particular format (which I'll get to in a moment). Most people make this conversion in the next stage, mastering, discussed below.

If you mix internally, your program will probably ask you to specify the settings you want in the mixdown file. Assuming you'll be mastering the song, choose the same settings as the rest of the song's audio. If you aren't mastering and just want to make a rough-mix CD, specify the outputted file to be stereo interleaved, 44.1kHz, and 16 bits. The file can then be burned directly to an audio CD.

Mastering: The Essential Finishing Touch

see page 231

It's amazing how many home recordists are still unaware of the importance of *mastering*. Mastering is the process of making slight EQ adjustments to an entire mix, optimizing dynamics for maximum impact, and when you're assembling a CD of songs, making adjustments so your mixes are more uniform and balanced from one song to the next. Professional mastering engineers get paid handsomely to massage projects for major labels. Once upon a time, when everything was analog, nobody else could do what they do—if you made a record, you had to take it to a mastering facility before it could get pressed onto a vinyl LP. With the digital revolution and the invention of the CD burner, though, now we can master our own projects at home—or at least we can try. Pro mastering engineers still get big bucks for their golden ears and arsenal of super-expensive gear, but we home recordists can do a few mastering operations ourselves to improve our projects.

In the home studio, mastering is done right inside the recording program with a plug-in or a set of plug-ins. Several companies offer good-quality software "mastering suites" for this purpose, which are bundles of mastering plug-ins that might include an EQ, a compressor, and a limiter. You start mastering by importing the mixdown audio file into the recording program. If you mixed the song externally, the file will already be there in its own stereo track, so all you need to do is solo that track (which will mute all of the raw tracks). Next, apply a mastering plug-in or mastering suite to that track. Now all you need to do is adjust the mastering settings, and you're good to go.

Mind Your Digital Signal Chain

When you're mastering, make sure the various digital processes happen to your mix in the proper order. The mix should encounter the EQ first, followed by compression/limiting, and finally, a global level cut, if there is one. If the EQ comes *after* the dynamics plug-ins and there's an EQ boost of any kind, the mix will likely go over 0dB, resulting in digital clipping. Finally, don't confuse this digital signal chain with the order that you follow when you're doing a mastering job: set up your compression/limiting first, then add EQ, and last, configure the global level cut (if necessary) and any other level changes, including fade-ins and fade-outs.

Do mastering work when your ears are fresh—not after a long day of recording or mixing. Mastering shouldn't be an afterthought; it's an important step, and if you do a lousy job, you could very well make your song sound worse than if it had never been mastered at all.

Mastering for levels. A raw, unmastered mix will not be able to compete with commercially recorded music that has gone through the mastering process. The unmastered mix will sound small and wimpy in comparison, because the mastered mix's dynamic range has been optimized to make the music sound bigger and louder. As I mentioned back in Chapter 2, louder almost always sounds better—and because of this phenomenon, mastering engineers try to get mixes to sound as loud as possible without significantly compromising the sound. To do this, they put the mix through compressors and limiters; these units can bring the music very close to the 0dB top of digital's dynamic range—sometimes for the duration of the entire song (see Fig. 2). There's a tradeoff, though, as piling on too much compression and limiting can flatten out a song's natural dynamics and can make the song sound like it's pushing too hard or even coming apart. Part of the skill of mastering involves knowing how much of this processing is too much.

The basic idea is that you want the mastering plug-in(s) to boost the level of the song, while bringing down peaks in level that would otherwise blast through that 0dB digital ceiling. The way you do this depends, of course, on the plug-ins you're using. For years I used a basic plug-in with one slider that could increase the level in 0.5dB increments, while automatically taming the peaks. I usually found myself boosting songs by about 4dB, with okay results. But if a song has a quiet nature, such as a solo

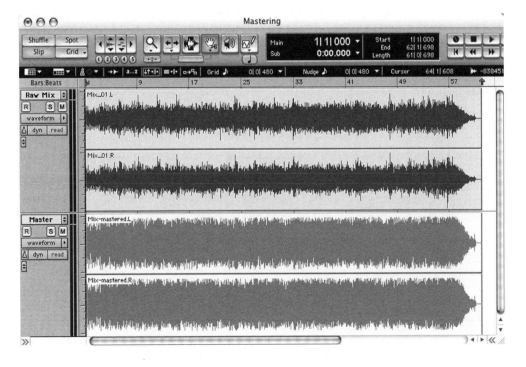

Fig. 2 You can usually tell whether a song has been mastered just by looking at its waveforms, zoomed out. At top, the two channels of an unmastered song reach maximum levels only occasionally. At bottom, the same segment after mastering. Notice how the overall level is higher, making the song sound bigger and louder.

acoustic guitar and vocal arrangement, you may need just 1dB or 2dB of gain, or even none at all. On the other hand, if you mixed the song at a low level for one reason or another, you may need to pump it up by 7dB or 8dB to bring it to the front where it needs to be.

When I'm mastering, I usually just employ trial and error—I try some settings and listen, constantly bypassing the plug-in I'm tweaking to hear exactly what it's doing to the sound. I've found that as you increase the settings, there seems to be a point where you start to add too much of a good thing and the song starts to sound bad. When I know I've gone too far, I back off a bit or try something else.

Mastering for EQ. Unless you are very good at mixing and/or you're lucky, your mixdown will not be as balanced across the entire frequency spectrum as it could be. Unfortunately, that's not an easy thing to judge, so here's another chance to bring in some professional help—in the form of a professionally mastered song. Do this stage *after* you've given the song a boost in level, as the boost can have a big effect on your mix's frequency balance. And don't be afraid to go back and tweak your level settings after you've made EQ adjustments.

Find a commercially released song that's similar to yours in overall dynamics and instrumentation. Ideally, actually import its audio into your song file, so you can put it alongside your mix and easily "A/B" (compare) them. Of course, don't put any mastering or other plug-ins on the commercial song (it's already been mastered), and make sure both songs are playing at the same virtual-console fader level (which will probably be 0dB). Now, toggle back and forth from your song to the other one. How do the highs compare? How about the lows? Do you perceive "holes" or other flaws in your song's frequency balance—perhaps the low mids sound empty, or the high mids are obnoxious? Do you now wish you had time to remix the song? We've all been there—but a few gentle EQ boosts and cuts at this point can do wonders to make your song more on a par with the commercial recording.

Inevitably, if you mix ten songs over a period of time, they won't all have the same balance of frequency components from one song to the next. Some will be brighter than others, some will have a boomier low end, and some will have more midrange presence. A big part of mastering a CD project involves achieving an overall consistent sound among the songs. So, if a compilation is your goal, wait until you've mixed all of the songs to start mastering them, or go back and remaster them when you're finished. Be sure to burn test CDs with the songs in the proper order, so you can hear how they compare and move from one song to the next.

Nixing the subsonics. Mastering engineers often apply an extreme cut of very low frequencies—for example, –12dB below 30Hz—to ensure that any subsonic frequencies that got onto the recording somehow don't mess up the mastering job. Lows carry a lot of energy; if these subsonics are in your mix, you won't be able to hear them, but they will show up on meters. As a result, you'll have to master the song at a lower level, and the song will have a lower apparent volume than the meters suggest—all because

---

"Fake Mastering"

So how do you master a song if you don't have fancy mastering-suite software? Well, there are a couple of things you can do to "fake" the mastering process. Start by mixing your song at the highest possible level. If there are portions of the song—from entire sections to brief moments—that are louder than the rest, find ways to bring these down so that the whole song can come up by a similar amount. After you've mixed the song, import it and get to work drawing in level automation that keeps the loud parts of the song close to 0dB. Make sure a drop in level (to tame a peak) lasts only as long as it needs to, quickly returning to its original level; otherwise the level change could be audible. Doing all of this can be very tedious, but the more

fine-tuning you do, the more "mastered" your song will sound. You might be tempted to slap on a general-purpose compressor plug-in instead, but that's probably not a good idea. A compressor not made for mastering could easily make your song sound worse, not better.

After you've spent some time smoothing out levels, add a multi-band EQ that will work on a stereo track, and follow the steps in Mastering For EQ. But understand that if you boost *anything* at this point, your fine-tuned levels will probably now go past 0dB. So you can either cut frequencies only, or do another round of automation-tweaking after you've made EQ adjustments.

In addition to being labor-intensive, this kind of "mastering" won't do what a proper mastering suite will do. It may not even come close. But it's better than nothing.

---

of something you can't even hear. So, if you're able, pull these frequencies out with an EQ plug-in or the EQ portion of the mastering suite.

A final cut. Mastering typically includes a very small level cut across the song's duration (perhaps –0.1dB). The reason is that some professional CD-burning software will balk if it detects that your mastered mix hit and stayed at exactly 0dB—even for just an instant—as this is a sign that the song tried to go over the 0dB ceiling and digitally clipped, even if it's harmlessly inaudible. But you'll never hear a –0.1dB cut, either, so it's not a bad idea to perform this cut (it may be built right into your mastering suite). Make sure this cut comes last, *after* the EQ and gain stages in the computer's digital signal chain.

Final touches. Mastering is a good time to add fade-ins and fade-outs. Just draw a ramp on the mix track's volume-automation window. And sometimes, for aesthetic reasons, you need a song to sound quieter than its neighboring songs on the CD. The mastering step is the time to make this happen: Just add an overall level cut of a few decibels at the end of the digital signal chain.

. . . And It's A Wrap

When you're happy with your mastering settings, select the block of audio representing the song in the recording program, and choose the appropriate Export function—probably under the File menu. Make sure that all level changes, EQ, and plug-ins are taken into account (check the documentation), and export the song as a single stereo-interleaved .aiff file, at the CD-standard 44.1kHz sampling rate and 16 bits of resolution. That's it! Burn the song to CD, and you're done.

Burning A Compilation CD

It's easy to make a compilation—any CD-burning program will allow you to compile and order audio tracks to be included on the disc, and you'll probably be able to specify the pauses between songs as well. But if you want to build segues between songs that exist as individual files, or insert track numbers in the middle of long pieces of audio, that's a little more complicated. You'll need a special program, specific for burning audio CDs. Like just about everything else, these come in the form of inexpensive consumer programs, and expensive industrial programs.

If your compilation is destined to be pressed at an actual CD-duplication plant, make sure your program burns the master CD with "Red Book standard" specifications, as this is the kind of encoding the duplicator requires.

Analog Recording

This Appendix is specifically for those recording on analog tape systems, expanding on concepts and techniques discussed in the main part of the book. Some of the concepts also apply to linear digital formats such as ADAT, as well as standalone digital recorders—any system in which automation options are limited.

Planning Ahead For Tape

You'll get a lot more mileage from your analog studio if you plan your course of action *before* you start recording a song. This isn't always possible; sometimes a song starts as a spontaneous idea, and you just want to start putting your ideas down without getting out graph paper and making a flow chart. And that's absolutely what you should do in this case. Nothing can squelch a creative idea faster than having to interrupt inspiration and draw up a plan. But if you *do* know exactly what a song will need—say, if you've already roughed out a quick sketch version, and now you want to polish the tune—sit down and plan it out. Sure, you can throw a song together and hope for the best; this is how most people do it. But in Guerrilla Home Recording, where your goal is to get a pro sound, such forethought pays big dividends.

A key tool for session-planning is the *track strip*. A variation of the track sheet familiar in pro studios, a track strip shows the tracks you have available, with your intended course of action progressing from left to right. On a track strip you plan the order each instrument will go down in, on which tracks, also indicating steps like bounces and sound-on-sound passes. Fig. 1 shows an example of a track strip for a complex session on analog 8-track. A track strip allows you to see into the future and prevent conflicts and other problems, before they arise. You may learn that your intended arrangement won't be possible if you don't have a friend play shaker while you play acoustic guitar, for instance, and you'll learn this before you need to compromise some other aspect of your recording in order to realize your vision for the song.

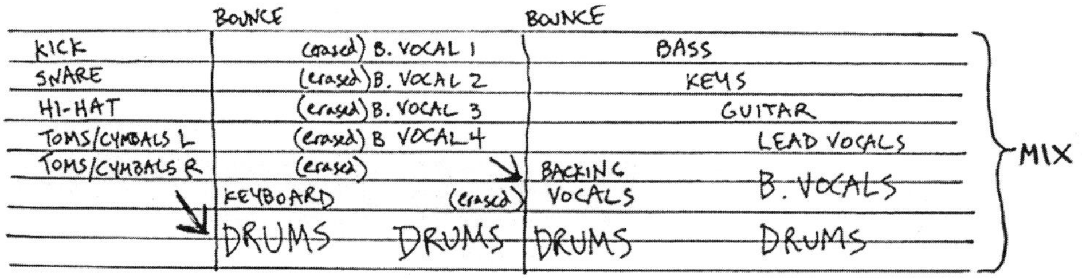

Fig. 1 A track strip can
help in planning a com-
plex course of action.

	BOUNCE		BOUNCE		
KICK	(erased) B. VOCAL 1		BASS		
SNARE	(erased) B. VOCAL 2		KEYS		
HI-HAT	(erased) B. VOCAL 3		GUITAR		
TOMS/CYMBALS L	(erased) B VOCAL 4		LEAD VOCALS		MIX
TOMS/CYMBALS R	(erased)		BACKING VOCALS	B. VOCALS	
	KEYBOARD (erased)				
	DRUMS DRUMS		DRUMS	DRUMS	

Documenting Your Mix

You've probably experienced getting the "perfect" mix of a song, only days later deciding that something needs to be louder or quieter. So maybe you went back and banged out another mix. Often this is easy enough—but if the mix is complex, with lots of mixer-fader moves and effect changes, you may decide to just live with the less-than-perfect mix rather than try to improve upon it.

Digital recordists typically don't have this problem, as they're able to automate most aspects of the mix; remixing something, even months later, can be as simple as opening a file, making a few tweaks, and bouncing the adjusted mix to disk. As an analog recordist, though, you can help your cause by thoroughly documenting all aspects of the mix immediately after you do it, while it's still fresh in your mind. Write down all the fader and EQ settings, including all special moves to be made during the course of the song (see Fig. 2). Include which recorded tracks or track routings are associated with your board's channels, and anything unusual about other routings, such as effect-send assignments. Don't forget to note all effect-send and return levels, as well as the master-fader output levels, and write down (or store) all of your effect parameters. It's also a great idea to photograph the board from above, with every control at its top-of-the-song position; label the channels as necessary with masking tape and a black marker. You might even want to make a video of the mixdown. Who knows—if you come up with a song like Beck's breakthrough hit, "Loser" (which he recorded on analog 8-track), your footage might end up on a VH-1 special someday!

Sound-On-Sound

Sound-on-sound is one of the oldest techniques for getting more tracks onto an analog recording. It refers to recording a track, and then playing back that track while mixing in a new sound source, and recording the blend of the original track and the new sound. You may have gotten your first taste of "multitrack" recording this way: Perhaps you recorded an acoustic guitar and vocal on a cassette deck, and then added a harmony vocal and perhaps another guitar part as you transferred the sound onto another cassette deck. This can be done again and again to build up the "tracks"—but of course, there are serious disadvantages. In addition to the various performances being forever inseparable (you can no longer adjust their balance once they're mixed together), the sound of the original performances deteriorates with each pass. You can

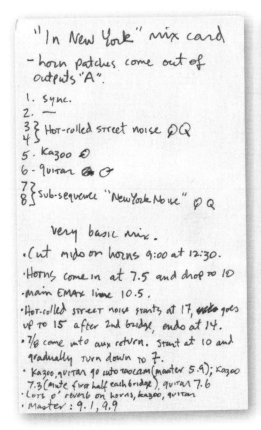

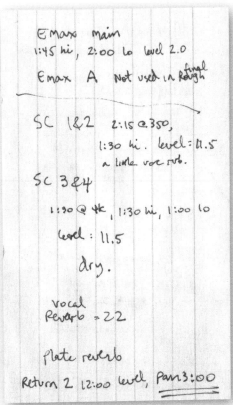

Fig. 2 An index card may be all you need to document how you mixed a particular song.

get away with a certain amount of sonic deterioration; if you and a few friends are trying to create the sound of a couple dozen people partying for the background of a song, sound-on-sound is a great way to go. But you wouldn't want to build an important track (such as a layered lead vocal) this way. It would probably just sound bad.

"**Real sound-on-sound.**" Back in my cassette 4-track days, I actually used a technique that was a more literal form of sound-on-sound: I would lay down a track, and then I would *literally* lay down a little piece of masking tape over the 4-track deck's erase head. With the erase head disabled, I could lay new performances of the same part on the same track, building it up in layers. How did it sound? Not great; with each pass, the record head messed with the already-recorded tracks somewhat. It wasn't a very good technique, but I got some interesting effects nonetheless, and it was easy to do. (Note: Ask first before trying this out on your dad's vintage Studer 24-track!)

Analog Bouncing

Bouncing is an indispensable technique with analog recording, because of the fixed number of tracks. On an 8-track, it's possible to bounce seven tracks to one mono, or six tracks to two stereo (see Fig. 3). But as with sound-on-sound, there are disadvantages. First, on an analog machine the sound will always degrade a bit when you play it

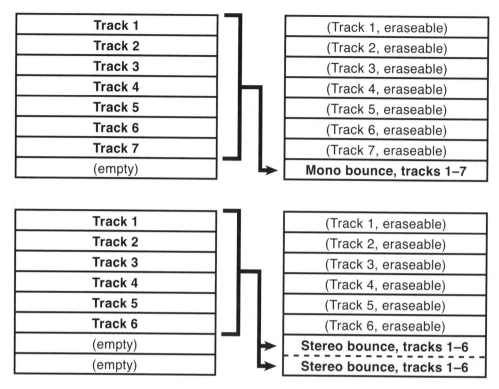

Fig. 3 Bouncing seven tracks to one mono (top), or six tracks to stereo (bottom).

back and re-record it. (The sound degrades on digital systems, too, but not as much.) Second, on an analog machine, sometimes you get unexpected howling, electronic feedback when you're trying to bounce tracks. What's going on here? Typically, this happens when one of the tape tracks you're bouncing *to* is physically adjacent to one of the tracks you're bouncing *from*. To the tape machine's record head, the source and destination tracks are just too close for comfort.

There are a couple of workarounds. The best solution is to leave a "guard track" between your source tracks and your bounce tracks, and always bounce to a track or tracks on the physical edge of the tape (i.e., tracks 1 and 2 or 7 and 8 on an 8-track), not in the middle (tracks 3 through 6). So, if you plan to bounce drums to tracks 7 and 8, try to leave track 6 empty and record your drums only to tracks 1 through 5. Obviously on a 4-track this is impractical, and even on an 8-track it may be difficult.

If you need one more track to bounce, put the instrument that will end up being the quietest—maybe the hi-hat in sampled drums—on the border track (track 6 in the above example). Since you'll record this raw track at full volume for the sake of good gain-staging (see page 43), you'll need to turn down the track during the bounce—and that will make the track much less likely to feed back.

When you're bouncing to stereo, you can also elude feedback by having the instrument on the border track panned to the opposite side of its neighboring bounce track. For example, if you're reserving track 7 for the left channel of the bounced drums, and you normally pan your sampled hi-hat to the right, put the hi-hat on track 6. That way, you'll be pumping very little of track 6's signal onto track 7 (most of the hi-hat will go to the right channel, on track 8), reducing the chance of feedback.

Obviously, bouncing works better on 8-track formats and higher, because if you're recording on 4-track, you can only bounce three tracks to one mono track, or two mono tracks to two tracks in stereo (both with the risk of track feedback). But you can stretch the technique further by . . .

Combining Bouncing With Sound-On-Sound

If you're bouncing your drums to stereo and you anticipate a track shortage later on, take the opportunity to lay another sound (such as a bass line) into the drum mix while you're bouncing. One advantage here is you'll get to hear what the bass and drums sound like together, before you've finalized the bounce blend. If you do a bounce and realize (on playback) that the bass is obscuring the kick drum, you can turn up or EQ the kick's sound, and bounce again while laying down another bass-line take. Or, perhaps you want to blend in a sound that doesn't need to be synced to the music, like a long sound effect or party noise. Cue up that sound and let it run into the mixer while you're doing the bounce. For maximum efficiency, add in a bass line while the drums are bouncing *and* the sound effect is playing. The result: two tracks containing a good stereo drum mix (maybe with reverb on the snare), a bass line, and sound effects—with all of the other tracks now available for more sounds.

Using A Drum Machine As A MIDI Recorder

If your MIDI gear is limited to a drum machine and a keyboard—and you have no way of recording MIDI—you may be able to stretch things by getting your drum machine to play a very simple keyboard part. Here's how: In the drum machine's menu, see if you can assign a MIDI note and channel to each of the drum-machine sounds you won't be using. Turn down (or mute) the levels for those sounds in the drum machine, and assign those sounds to one specific MIDI channel, such as channel 16. (Make sure none of the drum sounds you are using are set to that channel.) Finally, connect the drum machine's MIDI out jack to the keyboard's MIDI in (see Fig. 4), and set the keyboard to receive MIDI channel 16 only. Now, by adding "silent" drum sounds on particular beats, you can build MIDI-keyboard notes right into the drum pattern; maybe you could have it play a simple bass line or arpeggiated part. Start the drum machine, and both it and the keyboard should play, in perfect sync. You can now record the drums and the keyboard to two tracks in stereo—no bouncing or sound-on-sound required. And of course, you can always blend in a performed part, maybe rhythm guitar, and maybe even a sound effect, during the bounce.

As you might imagine, when things get this complicated, you can easily run out of mixing-board channels. So, how do you get it done? Any way you can, that's how! See if there are additional inputs on your board, such as sub in jacks or an effect return, that you aren't using. Look for *anything* among your gear that's capable of blending

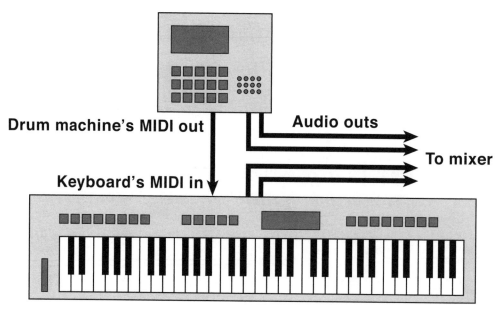

Fig. 4 Using a drum machine to "play" a simple keyboard part.

Drum machine's MIDI out

Audio outs

To mixer

Keyboard's MIDI in

two sounds, and see if you can take advantage of it. As a last resort, you could try mixing signals with simple Y adapters—although that gets dicey, as you can't just merge audio signals like hot and cold water at the faucet.

Virtual Tracks

Sometimes, the best way to record a drum machine, sampler, or keyboard sound is to not record it at all. By that, I mean the sounds don't go down onto your multitrack; they're produced by the sources themselves every time the multitrack tape plays. In order to make this happen, you need something that will produce and read a *sync tone*. A sync tone is an audio sound that you record, onto one track in mono, which contains information about timing and can synchronize your MIDI gear and any audio that you subsequently put onto the multitrack. This tone tells your MIDI gear when to start running, and how fast to run. (More about sync tones in a bit.) The MIDI sounds are said to exist on "virtual tracks," meaning they play alongside and in sync with the recorded audio, even though they aren't themselves recorded. Fig. 5 shows how a drum machine, capable of producing and reading its own sync tone, can be "slaved to tape" in the simplest virtual-tracks setup. (Note: Don't confuse this original definition of virtual tracks with another one commonly applied to stand-alone digital recorders. A digital recorder may allow you to play back only eight tracks at a time but may have dozens more "virtual tracks," or alternate takes, available on disk to swap out. This kind of virtual tracking is a powerful feature—but so is the original definition of slaving MIDI gear to a recorded sync tone.)

Although you can "record" just a drum machine pattern as a virtual track, you can't experience the true power of virtual tracks unless you have some way to record complex MIDI information, like those from keyboards. There are a couple of ways to

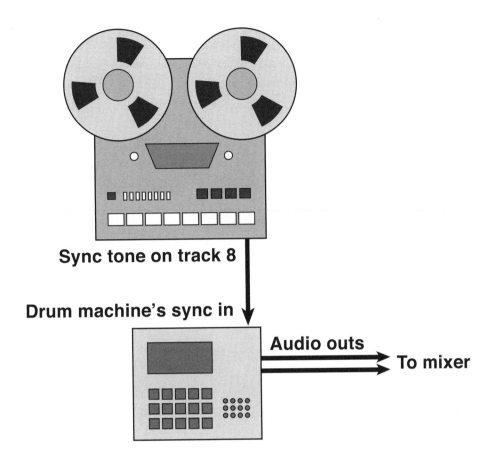

Fig. 5 Using a sync tone to drive a drum machine as a "virtual track."

Sync tone on track 8

Drum machine's sync in

Audio outs

To mixer

do this. Shortly after digital drum machines came out in the early '80s, the first *MIDI sequencers* appeared; these devices worked (and looked) similar to drum machines but could store a lot more MIDI information. MIDI sequencers have been made obsolete by digital recording programs, so you can probably find one for dirt cheap.

Perhaps a better alternative, though, is to use a computer and a MIDI recording program. That's right—you *can* use a computer to record, even if you aren't actually recording audio onto it. I used this setup for years—I had an analog 8-track recorder, and I ran it in sync with virtual MIDI tracks on my computer. The program could store and play back many independent MIDI parts, displaying the notes onscreen in different colors, similar to the way modern digital recording programs do. Unlike full-on digital audio recording, though, MIDI recording requires almost no processing power (my old program, Opcode Vision, worked great even on a circa-1988 Mac Plus!)—so as long as your computer is powerful enough simply to run the program, you'll be fine. Plus, it's a great way to get your feet wet with recording on a computer, as you can edit the MIDI parts onscreen, just as with an audio recording program.

To get the most out of virtual tracks, you'll need a piece of gear called a synchronizer to produce and read sync tones; synchronization functions are often included in higher-end MIDI interfaces. (These can be pricy, but I used a no-frills sync box that cost only $100 new.) Once you've recorded a sync tone onto the multitrack, you play it back, and the synchronizer interprets the tone and communicates with the other devices via MIDI. The synchronizer tells your MIDI-recording program when to start, and the computer sends multiple channels of MIDI (one per instrument or sound) back to the sync box/MIDI interface, which gets this MIDI where it needs to go. (See Fig. 6.) So, what you've got is analog tape and MIDI sounds running together, in perfect lockstep—with only one track on tape representing all of the MIDI sounds *combined*, and with none of the downsides of bouncing and sound-on-sound. It should be clear how this can be powerful for the Guerrilla recordist!

Virtual tracks also give you the option of changing your drum pattern, drum mix, and MIDI-keyboard sounds (and even their individual notes) right up until mixdown. The audio of the drums and other MIDI gear is first-generation fresh when the mix finally goes to tape or disk. Is it live or is it Memorex? Well, at least until you mix down to stereo, the drums and keyboards are actually live, each time you roll tape. You've gotta love that.

Sync tone basics. All the gory details of sync tones are beyond the scope of this book, but by far the most useful and modern type is *SMPTE timecode*. (SMPTE, pronounced "simp-tee," stands for the Society of Motion Picture & Television Engineers.) SMPTE timecode is the industry-standard sync tone; it carries imbedded information about time, in the units of hours, minutes, seconds, and frames (as in

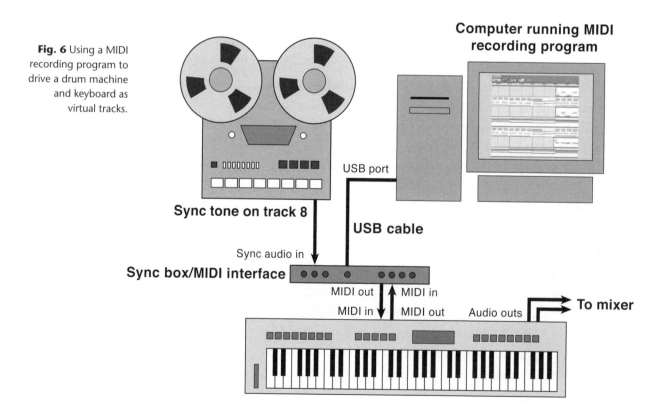

Fig. 6 Using a MIDI recording program to drive a drum machine and keyboard as virtual tracks.

video and film). You'll need a sync box that reads and writes SMPTE. You "stripe" the tape with timecode before you start recording anything. In fact, it's a good practice to stripe an entire reel of tape from beginning to end the first time you use it; that way you don't have to perform this task for each song. Then, in your MIDI song file on the computer (sometimes called a MIDI sequence), you specify the exact time—in timecode units—when the song is to begin. When the sync box "hears" this time, by way of the audio-recorded timecode, it tells the program, "Go!" The program then runs at exactly the right speed, based on the timecode units coming off the tape, the song's specified tempo, and its starting point. The tape can even start in the middle of a song; as long as the timecode is after the starting point, the program will "chase" and synchronize with the tape. When you stop the tape, the program stops. It's thrilling the first time you experience this, especially if you've been held captive by only four or eight audio tracks for a while.

For those really behind the technological curve, there are other types of sync tones that can be produced and read directly through "sync" jacks on old drum machines and sequencers. The tone goes out of the sync jack and straight to tape, and on playback, it's right back to the jack again—no synchronizer required. The best of these formats is called Smart FSK (Frequency Shift Keying). Unlike SMPTE timecode, Smart FSK conveys units of beats and sub-beats, along with measure numbers. The downside to Smart FSK is that once you decide on a song's tempo and length and you lay down the sync tone, you're locked in. With SMPTE timecode, you can do things like extend the song or change meters, even after audio tracks are down. On the plus side, if you have one of these old drum machines or sequencers, you can enjoy the benefits of virtual tracks right now, without buying any more gear.

SMPTE from the devil. As with bouncing, it helps to put your sync tone on an edge track, with an unused "guard track" between it and those tracks used for actual audio. Otherwise, the sync tone can bleed onto the next track—and believe me, there's nothing musical about an audible sync tone. Also, audio signals on adjacent tracks can bleed over and mess with the sync tone, particularly if they have a lot of sharp attacks. If a guard track isn't feasible, at least use the track for an audio signal that will be at low level in the mixdown (to help prevent sync tone from bleeding over), and don't record the border track's audio at too high a level—record it at only a moderate level to reduce the chance of the signal contaminating the sync tone.

Noise Reduction For Tape Systems

If you're recording to analog tape, my guess is you're using a ¼" or ½" reel-to-reel system. If you happen to be using a cassette 4-track, all I can say is you are a true Guerrilla recordist, and best of luck! Actually, you can get a decent, reasonably quiet sound on a cassette 4-track if you're careful. Bruce Springsteen recorded his classic 1982 album *Nebraska* on one, and Ween made its 1991 breakthrough CD, *Pure Guava*, on one as well. But cassette 4-tracks are all but extinct now, long since replaced (in the analog world) by reel-to-reel machines. A ½" 8-track, such as the trusty old Tascam 38, can sound fantastic—even better than digital, some believe. But all tape systems are noisy, so you can greatly clean up your sound by adding noise reduction to your setup.

Using a consumer-level noise-reduction scheme, such as Dolby B or C, is arguably better than using no noise reduction at all—but these adversely affect sound enough that you should probably avoid them. The dbx system is a much better option for the home recordist; it's very quiet and sounds surprisingly transparent. The best option of all is to have a noise-reduction system that's optimized for the multitrack machine you're using. For example, dbx made the DX-4D system specifically for the Tascam 38, and the two systems working together sound amazing. **Important:** If you use noise reduction, particularly dbx, be sure to defeat (turn off) the system on any track carrying a sync tone, both on recording the tone and playing it back. Noise reduction can make a sync tone unreliable or useless, and of course, the sync tone doesn't need to be noise-reduced.

Punching In & Out Manually

Some analog multitracks have a scheme for automating punch-in and punch-out points, based on the tape location as shown in the counter display. This might be fine if you don't need more than a few takes to get your punch right; past that, though, the counter will drift and the machine may start to punch in later or (worse) earlier than you want. In that case—or if you just don't trust your counter display—you'll want to punch in the old-fashioned way: with a footswitch.

This takes a little practice, but it's easy once you get the hang of it. Typically, you need to hit that switch on a weird offbeat or a fraction of a beat before the moment where you want the punch to happen. Make sure you don't hit the switch right on the beat, as if you were tapping your foot to the tempo; if you do, you may miss your ideal punch-in point and/or cut off the attack of the first new note you record. Work on hitting that switch just before the downbeat; there should be a tiny time lag between hitting the switch and playing the first note, and of course, hitting the switch should not cause you to play the note late. Again, this just takes practice. But even if you do everything right, you still may not get a good punch—particularly if a note on tape is still sounding, or if you punch in at the moment of a note's attack.

Punching out on an analog system is a whole different question. Because analog tape needs to pass over the erase head before it passes over the record head, there will be a slight gap of erased (but not re-recorded) audio after the point where you punched out. This analog-specific phenomenon means you can seamlessly punch out *only* if the part you're recording has a rest right after the punch-out point. Also, you need to punch out early enough during this rest so you don't erase any portion of the existing track that you want to keep. On a reel-to-reel machine, the rest might need to last only one-tenth of a second; on a cassette deck you might need up to a half a second. I always thought punching out was too tricky to do on an analog system, so I rarely did it. If I was laying down a track and made a mistake, I'd stop the tape, punch in before the error, and try to finish the track, rather than finish a take that I knew would have to be punched into (and out of) later.

Compositing A Performance With Tape

On an analog system, the first steps in creating a composite track (see page 190) are the same as on digital: You simply record a series of takes of the same part, each on a different track. Then, you listen to the takes and determine which phrases are good enough to make it onto your comp. The last step is where it gets tricky: You bounce the composited performance onto an open track, which means you need to manually ensure that the proper take of each phrase—and nothing else—gets bounced.

There are a couple of ways to do this. The easier method is to work your mixing board's mute switches—start out with all of the performance tracks muted, un-mute a track when it's time for a phrase on that track to make it to the comp, and mute it again when the phrase is over. The downside is that if your board makes any electronic click or other noise when you mute a channel (it shouldn't, but the switch's parts may be dirty), that noise will likely make it onto your comp. You also run the risk of suddenly chopping off the beginning or end of a phrase if you don't hit that switch at the exact moment. So, you can work the faders instead. This adds its own challenges, though—you have to get the fader to the right level before the phrase starts. (I used to press pieces of modeling clay onto the face of the board to stop the fader's travel and prevent myself from overshooting the mark, which worked pretty well.) Obviously, this is a lot easier when there are pauses between the vocal phrases; otherwise, you have to make quick, skillful cross-fades. The upside to comping with faders is you have an opportunity to "print" slight level adjustments to the performance, to bring out quieter phrases and bring down ones that are too loud, which will simplify the mixing process.

Unless your comping moves are simple, the best way to comp a performance manually—at least without tearing out your hair by the roots—is to have a chart showing which phrases from their respective tracks need to make it onto your comp. The "Take Report Card" (see page 190) is a good way to do this.

If you're comping a lead vocal, this is a great time to give the vocal another compression stage. If you're compressing with an insert sub-chain (see page 52), you'll probably have to plug it into an insert jack on your board's outputs, if your board has output inserts. If it doesn't, you can use an effect send, or rewire the signal chain so the compressor goes between the board's output and the multitrack. Alternatively, if you don't plan to use the compressor during mixdown, you can insert it into the comped vocal channel at that time.

Flying In Bounced Tracks With A Second Recorder

This is a powerful (if laborious) technique for those working with analog tape, or any linear system for that matter—anyone with a limited number of available tracks.

Before I owned a sampler, I'd often want to build up a complex backing-vocal part on my 8-track tape deck, but with only eight total tracks, I'd run out quickly—and short of numerous, layered bounces, there was no way to get the part down and into the mix. My solution was to get the drums and keyboards together as virtual tracks first, and then I'd record the background vocals as the first audio tracks. That way, I'd have six full tracks to work with (eight minus two for the sync tone and guard track). Then I'd mix down *only* the background vocals to two channels in stereo, recording them onto a DAT machine. Finally, after erasing the six original tracks, I'd run the DAT and record the vocals in stereo back onto the 8-track. The tricky part was getting the bounced part synchronized with the drums and keyboards. It was basically trial and error, although after a while I got pretty good at knowing exactly when to press "play" on the DAT machine. (In terms of timing, background vocals are somewhat forgiving. You'd probably drive yourself crazy trying to fly in something like a percussion part this way.)

A side benefit to flying in tracks is that you can duplicate them in various parts of the song. If all three choruses have the same background-vocal part, for instance, just fly your BVs into each of the three choruses, one at a time. Of course, this won't work if there are tempo changes from one chorus to the next.

Flying In Bounced Tracks With A Sampler

If you have a sampler with plenty of memory, you can use it to fly in tracks. Compared to an analog tape or DAT machine, it's much easier to control a sampler's timing—and if you can trigger the sampler with a MIDI-recorded sequence, you can get the timing both exact and perfectly repeatable. In that case, you can fly in pretty much anything, no matter how precise the timing needs to be. And if you're strapped for tracks, maybe you don't need to fly them back to the recorder after all—you can keep them on the sampler as virtual tracks, triggered by the MIDI recording program. (For extra credit, figure out how you could trigger a BV part on a sampler using only a drum machine.) Also, for the track-challenged, why devote two tracks to just the flown-in part? Blend in something else—like bass or guitar—while the sampler is flying the part in. Be sure to save the flown-in part to disc; that way, if you later need to redo the live-played instrument or adjust the blend, you can just load the part back into the sampler and go at it again.

Mixing In Sections

If you're working on a linear (tape) format, it can help to mix a song in sections rather than in one piece—especially if your mix is complicated. After all, if you need to move five faders and three pan knobs all to new settings just as the chorus ends and the guitar solo starts, you're going to have trouble—you'll have to compromise just to make your mixdown physically feasible, let alone exactly the way you want it. That's not the case if you mix in sections, though: You can get the verse mix just right, stop the tape, set up the board for the guitar solo, and then mix that section. When you're finished, you splice together the pieces of tape, or edit them together digitally. On one of the last songs I mixed on my old all-analog system, I ended up splicing together over 15 pieces of tape. It meant having to do some extra work, but the result—a wild, schizophrenic chop job of a mix—simply would not have been possible otherwise.

Keep in mind that if any prominent sound exists on both sides of a splice point (such as a held vocal note), you'll need to mix it similarly on each side of the splice; otherwise you'll be able to hear the edit. This is especially true if you'll be splicing tape. (If you're mixing to a digital medium, you may be able to smooth over the splice by adding a digital crossfade.)

How to splice analog tape. This requires practice, so do a few dry run-throughs on rough mixes before you start cutting up your perfect mixes. Use only splicing tape made for that purpose, and use a proper splicing block; these are inexpensive, save a lot of hassle, and make your splices more precise. Carefully rock the reels of your mixdown tape machine to find easy-to-locate transient moments (such as the downbeat at the beginning of a new section), mark the point on the back of the tape with a white splicing pencil, and cut *just* before that point. The transient will help disguise any imperfections in your splice. Once you've spliced the previous section together with the current section, fast-forward and rewind the splice back and forth a few times; this will loosen up and flatten the splice joint, making it play more seamlessly.

Mastering An Analog Mix

Even if you're a fanatic for analog gear, you'll need to digitize your mixes at some point to get them onto a CD or the Internet. So, it makes sense to do your mastering after you've digitized the mix. If you don't have a computer with a good soundcard and sound-processing software (and if you're reading this Appendix, I'm guessing you don't), it probably doesn't make much sense to upgrade just for mastering purposes. Ask around to find out if someone you know has a digital recording system, preferably with a collection of plug-ins (ideally, ones made for mastering), and see if they'd be willing to help you finish your project. Mastering is a good way to get your feet wet with digital recording and sound processing.

Alternatively, if you really want to milk the "analog vibe," you could take your analog mixes to a mastering facility with analog mastering gear, and digitize the music at the very last step. Understand that this will cost you, though.

Twenty Songs In One Day:
Immersion Music Method

As you get better at recording, you may notice an evil trend: It starts to take longer and longer for you to get anything done. Especially among perfectionists, the desire to get sounds as well as performances exactly right—coupled with the fear of failure that many creative people secretly harbor—means that eventually it can take three months to record a song rather than three days or even three hours. After a while, this saps a lot of the fun out of making music; rather than being a form of play, writing and recording becomes increasingly tedious, and those intoxicating moments of spontaneous joy and discovery become fewer and further between.

This disease has a cure, though, called Immersion Music Method. IMM's co-inventor, Nicholas Dobson, and I wrote a book about it called *The Frustrated Songwriter's Handbook* [Backbeat Books]. The basic idea is that you set aside a chunk of time (preferably a whole day) to do nothing but create music, and during that time, you write and record as many songs as you possibly can. The goal is to record 20 original songs in one day—and while that may sound impossible, it definitely can be done. In practice, the method typically results in three to eight songs.

The first time I did an IMM session, almost immediately I realized that I had forced myself into a very different creative mode. When the clock is ticking down, there is no time to waste—to redo a flawed take, to fuss over a sound, or even to think about what to do next. There is also no time for writer's block: Not having an idea is simply never an option. No matter what you recorded last or how you are feeling, you have to pick up an instrument, start recording, and *just play*. It's a given (a requirement, really) that some of these songs will be failures, but that's okay. The point is that you just plow ahead—and with some luck, at the end, you'll find a few gems among the rubble.

And guess what? You almost always do. By the end of my first session, I had finished ten songs, and I was amazed at what I had accomplished. I had no idea I was capable of that kind of output; it was easily the most creative day of my life. Best of all, the IMM mindset of simply plowing ahead, without pondering and self-editing, resulted in music that was very "me": Liberated from nagging internal voices of negativity, my musical personality was free to flow forth at its most authentic, to explore complete, playful abandon, and to run wild.

Since I got involved with Immersion Music Method, I've noticed that a similar mindset exists in other disciplines. When I tutored writing in college, "freewriting"— essentially a 15-minute exercise in immersion writing—was a way to loosen up nervous writers who lacked confidence. I've visited improvisational comedy workshops where people learned to cut loose and be free to make fools of themselves in front of others. Even business consultants who teach brainstorming techniques aim for similar goals. One thing ties all of these endeavors together. In each case, participants learn to open up, go out on a limb, and most important, *celebrate failure*. If failure is okay and has no negative consequences, particularly if you and your fellow participants can laugh at them together, your potential to create freely—and ultimately, to create something of value—becomes that much greater.

If you feel constrained by your own high self-expectations, or you just feel stuck in a rut, give this method a try. I think you'll find it a valuable, even life-changing, experience. Almost as a side benefit, you'll learn how to get things done faster in the studio and to put together a reasonable-sounding production in just a few minutes. And the next time you read about how Joe Famous Rock Star has been holed up in some rented mansion for a month without coming up with any new songs, you'll think, Jeez—just get over yourself and *start making some music!*

For more on Immersion Music Method, check out *The Frustrated Songwriter's Handbook*, or go to the website of the Immersion Composition Society at www.ics-hub.org.

Re-Production:
A Guerrilla Home Recording Exercise

Since Guerrilla Home Recording aims to get a professional sound, it makes sense for us to study actual professional recordings to improve our craft. The best way to do that is to try to reproduce, as closely as you can, a professional recording that you admire. In other words, make a sound-for-sound (even note-for-note) cover recording. This may seem like a silly idea; after all, why would anyone be interested in hearing your karaoke-like clone of someone else's song? Well, that's not the point—maybe they *shouldn't* hear it. This kind of recording is just for you; it's a production exercise, not necessarily a great work of art. That's not to say you can't have some fun and put your own touches on the song—you can change the words or insert a guitar solo or a new instrumental bridge if you want. But the real goal of "re-production," as I call it, is to listen to each sound and challenge yourself to reproduce it exactly, by any means possible.

Years ago, I took a shot at re-producing one of my favorite recordings, Donald Fagen's "New Frontier." The end of the tune features a tasty harmonica solo—and since I can't play harmonica, nor do I know anyone who does, I had to come up with a way to approximate the sound. Simply trying to get my old Ensoniq Mirage sampler to approximate the part would have been hopeless; there were just too many performance nuances. I ended up rigging together one of the craziest signal chains I've ever done. I started with a MIDI recording of the notes I wanted the harmonica to play, which drove a harmonica sample on the Mirage. I thought I might be able to approximate the performance nuances by using a "talk-box" concept, but I didn't have a talk box. (A talk box is a guitar effect that pumps an amplified sound into a tube, which you place in your mouth; mouthing vowels and consonants then causes your mouth to emit vocal-like guitar sounds, which you capture with a microphone.) My solution: I ran the Mirage signal into a reel-to-reel tape deck that had a particularly powerful headphone amplifier, got an adapter, and plugged a pair of Walkman-style headphones onto the jack. I then wrapped one of the earpieces with plastic wrap, secured the wrap with a rubber band, and placed this contraption in my mouth. When I played the MIDI recording, the harmonica line started coming out of my mouth, and I was able to mimic the original's nuances, capturing the sound with a compressed and gated microphone. It certainly wasn't a real harmonica performance, but it didn't sound half bad.

Re-production yields plenty of challenges like this, but nothing is more effective for teaching yourself how to record good sounds. You quickly learn what your pile of cheap studio gear—along with a large helping of creativity and ingenuity—is really capable of. If something is a little off from the original, try to figure out why, and then try to get it closer. Perhaps even more beneficial than improving your studio ear, this kind of exercise is great for your *musical* ear. Sussing out the subtle harmonies of "New Frontier" was tough, but I wrestled with the original for hours, going back over the keyboard and vocal parts again and again. And that exercise, along with many similar experiences since, has made it easier for me to deconstruct chords, progressions, vocal arrangements, you name it.

Even if nobody ever hears your re-productions—and you might not want anyone to—aiming for a pro sound in this way is incredibly rewarding. And it makes sense why: you won't know what pro sound really is until you actually study pro sounds closely.

Using Your Studio For Multimedia Projects

You might think your home studio is for recording music and nothing else. But music is just a form of audio, and if you know how to record music well, you know how to record *all* audio well. The knowledge you've acquired (as well as your gear) can greatly improve the quality of any audiovisual project you're working on—from a comedy video to a corporate presentation. Applying all of the concepts you've learned, including gain-staging, compression and expansion, etc., can make your multimedia projects much more professional than those made by people who don't know as much about audio and treat it almost as an afterthought.

For one thing, whenever possible, don't rely on recording audio with a built-in mic on a video camera, a computer's mic input, etc. Instead, actually record your audio using your studio gear (or at least a smaller version of your studio), exactly as if you were working on a song. This may mean you need to either videotape your multimedia project in your studio, or take a minimal audio setup to the video-shoot location—for example, by bringing a laptop and an audio interface.

Here's what to do: You'll record some audio on the video camera, using the built-in mic, but only as a reference. Put up a good condenser mic just out of the video frame, run the signal through a compressor/expander/EQ sub-chain if you have one (adjusting the settings for the lower audio levels of speech), and set up to digitally record. If the project is destined for DVD, record at 48kHz, which is the sampling frequency on DVDs. (That way the audio won't need to be converted later.) When you're ready to shoot, do just what they do on the set of a film: Start recording both audio and video, and then do a "slate"—you know, the striped clapper thing that they hold in front of the camera just before someone yells, "Action!" Since you probably don't have a real slate, just clap your hands. This will provide a synchronization reference among the video, the audio on the videotape, and the audio going to hard drive.

When you're ready to edit your project, import the raw video into your video-editing program, and then import your "good" audio underneath it. You should be able to use the same hard-drive file that your audio program wrote as the camera was rolling. Find the "slate" in the audio: Show the waveform, and look for a peak near

Fig. 1 Creating a simple "slate" allows you to easily synchronize your audio and video. The point at which you clap your hands (top) will have a corresponding peak in the camera audio track (below). Import your studio-recorded audio into the video editor, and adjust its start point so the clap sound occurs on the same video frame (bottom).

the beginning—that's what you want. Then, in the video track, find the frame where your hands clapped together. Finally, line up the "slates." (See Fig. 1.) Play the video, with both versions of the audio going, to hear if the audio tracks are synchronized. What you want to hear ideally is a phased or flanged sound between the audio tracks; that indicates they're almost perfectly in sync. If you're hearing an echo or slapback, try moving the "good" audio track ahead or back by a frame until the echo goes away. Your raw video and audio are now synchronized. If you want, you can scroll to the end of the take and make sure everything is still synced up. (As long as both audio and video were captured digitally, there's no reason why it wouldn't be.) Finally, mute the camera audio track, and export a movie file of the video with only the "good" audio. This is the video file you'll edit—not the raw one.

When you're done editing your video, you can put your studio chops to work again. Export an .aiff audio file from the edited video, and import this file back into your recording program. (Use settings that don't require the file to be converted.) Almost certainly, your recording program is more powerful for working with audio than your video program is. So, here's your chance not only to expertly blend in other audio sources, such as music and sound effects, but also to enhance the audio. The vocal needs to be more intelligible? Try processing the entire file with a limiter plug-in (see page 195). EQ it if necessary. Add fade-ins and fade-outs, and even effects. When you're done, export the audio mix as a single stereo file, and reimport it back into the video program. As long as the new audio file starts on the first video frame, they should still be synchronized. Mute the (previous) audio track on the video once more, and export both the edited video and the mixed, polished audio as a self-contained, finished movie.

Other multimedia artists may treat audio as a necessary annoyance—but in your projects, the audio can be every bit as artistic and slick as the video. Believe me, it makes a huge difference.

Acknowledgments

I would like to thank Mike Edison at Hal Leonard for asking me to do an expanded and updated edition of *Guerrilla Home Recording*, something I've wanted to do almost since the first edition came out. Thanks also to Mike Lawson for seeing the project through, Barbara Milbourn for giving the manuscript a laser-like read-down, Yvonne Perry for a final proofread, and Stephen Ramirez for a fantastic layout. This book never would have happened without Richard Johnston, who originally bought the idea for Backbeat. The editors of *Bass Player* magazine, past and present, have taught me a ton over the years (and gave me a shot at a career fresh out of college). Thanks to Dave and Jennifer Goldwag, and to Steven Clark, Nicholas Dobson, Michael Mellender, and everyone else involved in the Immersion Composition Society (www.ics-hub.org). Bunny Knutson was a tremendous help with the section on recording live drums. Gino Robair, the technical editor of the first edition, did a lot to get this book in shape, and I remembered his advice as I revised the manuscript. Finally, thank you to all the readers of *Guerrilla Home Recording*—keep your ears open and your listening skills growing. Even if your music never makes it to satellite radio, just know that as long as you get pleasure from making and listening to your own creations, the time and effort is well worth it.

—KC

About The Author

Karl Coryat is the co-author of *The Frustrated Songwriter's Handbook*, the guide to letting go and unlocking your inner prolific songwriter, which has become a cult favorite among musicians obsessed with creating. Karl was also an editor at *Bass Player* magazine for 14 years, where he was the staff recording guru and wrote a series of columns on recording and technology. Under the names Eddie Current, the Progeny of Sodomy Featuring Lumpy Fatt, and several other obscure monikers, he has been creating eclectic music since the mid 1980s—first on cassette 4-track, then analog 8-track, and currently Pro Tools. He is a founding member of the Immersion Composition Society's Wig Lodge (www.wiglodge.com), and he has also worked in the studio with the late Kevin Gilbert (Giraffe, Toy Matinee), Eric Valentine (Smash Mouth), Dan Vickrey (Counting Crows), and others. Karl is currently a consulting editor for *Bass Player* as well as a freelance writer, motion graphics artist, and subversive comedian.

Index